From Guilt
to Glory
VOLUME I

From Guilt to Glory

VOLUME I

Hope for the Helpless

RAY C. STEDMAN

MULTNOMAH · PRESS

Portland, Oregon 97266

Unless otherwise identified, Scripture quotations are from the Holy Bible: New International Version, copyright 1978 by the International Bible Society. Used by permission of Zondervan Bible Publishers.

Scripture quotations marked RSV are from the Revised Standard Version of the Bible, copyright 1946, 1952, © 1971, 1973, Division of Christian Education, National Council of the Churches of Christ in the USA. Used by permission.

Scripture quotations marked KJV are from the King James Version.

Quotations from C. S. Lewis's *Mere Christianity* are copyright © 1943, 1945, 1952 by Macmillan Publishing Co., Inc., New York.

Cover design by Phil Malyon and Judy Quinn
Photograph by Russ Keller

FROM GUILT TO GLORY
Volume One
© 1978 by Ray C. Stedman
Published by Multnomah Press
Portland, Oregon 97266

Published in cooperation with Discovery Foundation
Palo Alto, California

Printed in the United States of America

Library of Congress Cataloging-in-Publication Data

Stedman, Ray C.
  From guilt to glory.

  Contents: v. 1. Hope for the helpless.
  I. Bible. N.T. Romans—Sermons.   2. Sermons,
America.   I. Title.
BS2665.4.S73   1985   227'.1077   85-29657
ISBN 0-88070-123-4 (v. 1)

85 86 87 88 89 90 – 10 9 8 7 6 5 4 3 2 1

CONTENTS

PREFACE

Paul's letter to the Romans is a description of the power of God let loose amid the ruin of man. It declares the good news, the gospel of Jesus Christ. God has found a way, through the death and resurrection of Jesus, to justify the ungodly. That includes us all, because we are all ungodly. Romans teaches us that God sees and understands all that is in our hearts. No one can therefore count upon his own righteousness in the presence of God. As Paul tells us, "There is none righteous, no, not one." There is no sweet little old lady, no strong virile man, no boy or girl who has lived a clean moral life, who is able to stand in the presence of the demands of the law and the love of God. We are ungodly to start with.

If we understand that, then we can be justified. To be justified means to be given the gift of righteousness, the gift of God's loving acceptance. That is where true life begins. As long as we remain self-righteous, we don't have a chance. If we recognize our ungodliness, we qualify.

In this book we will look at only the first eight chapters of Romans. In bite-sized sections we will follow Paul's masterful logic as he explains the process God takes us through to reach an extraordinary goal: to make us like God's Son, while somehow also making us more uniquely ourselves. This process involves our entire being. Paul explains to us what we have in Christ so that we will be able actively to participate in God's plan for us. We are not being acted upon by some blind force. Rather, our Lord is prodding us awake to make us realize the almost incredible potential of our lives, both now and in eternity.

1
INTRODUCTION TO LIFE

(Romans 1:1-17)

The letter to the Romans is unquestionably the greatest and widest in scope of all of Paul's letters. It is intense and penetrating, and is one New Testament book with which every Christian ought to be thoroughly familiar. If you cannot think through the book of Romans without a Bible before you, then I urge you to make that your goal. Master the book—be so well acquainted with it that you can outline it and think of its great themes without referring to your Bible. This will require careful reading, study, and working it through in detail.

Romans is probably the most powerful human document ever written. During this country's bicentennial celebration the Freedom Train traveled around the nation displaying great documents from American history, such as an original copy of the Constitution and Thomas Jefferson's copy of the Declaration of Independence. We rightly value these great documents of human liberty. In many ways, our freedom rests upon them and we Americans honor and respect them. But even they cannot hold a candle to the impact the epistle to the Romans has had upon human history.

To this letter we owe the conversion of some of the greatest church leaders of all time. St. Augustine, whose shadow has loomed large over the church since the fifth century, was converted by reading but a few verses of the thirteenth chapter. The sixteenth verse of the first chapter spoke volumes to Luther's heart as he thought and meditated on the great phrase, "The righteous will live by faith." The effect on Luther ushered in the Protestant Reformation, the greatest awakening our world had seen since the days of the apostles.

John Bunyan, studying Romans in the Bedford jail, was so caught up by the themes of this great letter that he wrote *Pilgrim's Progress*, which since the 1600s has taught countless people how a Christian relates to the world. John Wesley, listening one day as Luther's preface to his commentary on Romans was being read, found his own heart "strangely warmed"; and out of that came the great evangelical awakening of the eighteenth century. In our own day, Karl Barth's studies in Romans have shaken the theological world. We may not always agree with everything Barth has written, but one thing is clear: His arguments on the book of Romans were devastating to liberal theology.

Romans was written about A.D. 56-58, when Paul was in the Greek city of Corinth on his third missionary journey. As you read this letter, you can catch glimpses of conditions in Corinth. Located at a crossroads of trade, it was one of the most wicked cities in the Roman Empire. Much of that atmosphere is reflected in Paul's words.

Romans was written only about thirty years after the crucifixion and resurrection of the Lord Jesus. The memory of these events was still sharply etched in the minds of Christians all over the empire. This letter was sent to teach and instruct them, to remind them of the meaning of these events that so startled and amazed men in that first century.

Bull's-Eye

The first seventeen verses of Romans are introductory. Here are the great themes of this epistle, which Paul returns to again and again as he boldly details concepts that have dramatically altered men's lives. Besides their literary order, these themes also have a logical order—a progression that forms a kind of target, as shown on page 13. The bull's-eye, the heart of the target, is the major theme: Jesus is Lord. We see this theme in the first seven verses of the introduction.

> *Paul, a servant of Christ Jesus, called to be an apostle and set apart for the gospel of God—the gospel he promised beforehand through his prophets in the Holy Scriptures regarding his Son, who as to his human nature was a descendant of David, and who through the Spirit of holiness was declared with power to be the Son of God by his resurrection from the dead: Jesus Christ our Lord. Through him and for his*

name's sake, we received grace and apostleship to call people from among all the Gentiles to the obedience that comes from faith. And you also are among those who are called to belong to Jesus Christ.

To all in Rome who are loved by God and called to be saints:

Grace and peace to you from God our Father and from the Lord Jesus Christ (Romans 1:1-7).

At the heart of Paul's argument is the central figure, Jesus Christ our Lord. The lordship of Christ is the theme of Romans, as it is the theme of all Paul's writings and all the New Testament. Our union with Christ as Lord is the central truth God wants us to see, as Paul himself wrote in the letter to the Colossians: "Christ in you, the hope of glory" (Colossians 1:27). That is the great salvation theme from which all others flow. Some commentators and Bible teachers identify certain central elements that come from this truth. Some may emphasize justification by faith, or sanctification—that is, solving the problems of sin. But these themes all stem from the great, central theme: union with Christ. That is why the *person* of the Lord Jesus is always central in the apostle's thinking, just as he is central in God's program for mankind everywhere. We are not simply followers of a philosophy, or even of a philosopher, but of a *savior,* a *redeemer,* a *person*—and he must be first in all things.

From this central point Paul builds a logical progression of concentric circles, like a target. The *gospel* of our Lord Jesus Christ is the next theme flowing out from the person of Jesus himself. Next, since the gospel is brought to us through the apostle, Paul

speaks of himself as the apostle to the Gentiles,
through whom the gospel is spread. Next comes
those who receive that gospel—the Roman Christians to whom this letter was written, as well as ourselves, the twentieth-century recipients of the letter.
Then, as the final outthrust of this movement, the
gospel reaches out to all nations—to Jew and Gentile
alike. We will see this logical order as we go through
the introductory paragraph of the letter.

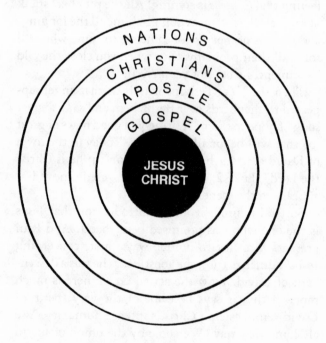

The Promised One

Paul first points out that the gospel was predicted
long before Jesus came; God foretold it all in the Old
Testament. The gospel was "promised beforehand
through his prophets in the Holy Scriptures." One of
the most important things we can learn about our

faith is that it comes to us through the anticipation and prediction of centuries of teaching and preaching. Recall Jesus walking with the two men on the road to Emmaus, and how "beginning with Moses and all the prophets" he taught them the things concerning himself. Jesus saw himself clearly in the Old Testament. We too can see him there, in great messianic passages that point unerringly to Jesus.

To read the Old Testament is to be gripped by the feeling that *Someone* is coming! All the prophets speak of him, all the sacrifices point to him, all the longings and dreams of men are of someone to come who will solve all their problems. But when you close the Old Testament, he has not yet arrived.

Then the New Testament tells us that angels appeared to shepherds near Bethlehem and sang a great song of hope to them: "I bring you good news of great joy that will be for all the people. Today in the town of David a Savior has been born to you; he is Christ the Lord" (Luke 2:10-11). The Promised One at last appears on the scene.

So Paul reminds us in his introduction that Jesus is the one who was promised beforehand. And Paul presents him in two unique ways: first, concerning Jesus' human nature, the apostle says he was a descendant of David. Now the actual Greek here is much more earthy; it says he came of the very sperm of David, emphasizing Christ's intense humanity. We all come that way. We come by the union of sperm and ovum in the miracle of conception. Jesus came in the same way, through the sperm of David. Thus his humanity is emphasized and underscored. But second, linked with that, is his deity; Christ "through the Spirit of holiness was declared with power to be the Son of God." That phrase, "the Son of God," unmistakably describes the deity of our Lord. He was

God. Paul emphasizes this several times throughout his letter. But he also stresses that in the uniqueness of his personality Jesus combined all that was human and all that was divine.

And yet, as we will learn later, Christ voluntarily laid aside the exercise of his deity. He did not come to act as God, but as a man filled with God. This is hopeful and helpful to us. If we are called on to act like God we might as well give up right now. We won't make it. But we are called on to be men and women possessed by God. This is the level on which Christ lived, and on which we too can live. This is the heart of the gospel. God has made it possible for us to live as Jesus lived and to follow his example. Paul will develop these thoughts much more thoroughly in this epistle.

There were three things, Paul says, that marked the deity of Jesus. First, "power." This refers to the miracles, the displays of remarkable power Christ exhibited among men. These were a sign that he was a man of God, a man fully indwelt and possessed by God.

Second, "the Spirit of holiness." I have always been concerned about how we so often misunderstand holiness. We don't like the word *holy*. It is something bad—good, but bad. We don't like to be called holy ourselves, and when we call someone a "holy Joe" it isn't a compliment. And yet it is a great word! Perhaps its meaning can be recaptured if we use a similar term that comes from the same root, the word *whole*. Paul is saying that when Jesus came, he was a whole person. He demonstrated whole humanity— humanity as it was intended to be.

We too are called to be whole persons. The glory of the good news is that God's goal is to make us whole, so that we are capable, able to cope, ready to walk through the pressures and turmoils and tragedies of this world and handle them as whole persons—*holy* persons. This wholeness is what Jesus fully demonstrated.

The third great authenticating mark of Jesus' deity is "his resurrection from the dead." On this our faith ultimately rests. We can have confidence that God has told us the truth by the unshakable fact that he raised Jesus from the dead. No one can remove that fact from the annals of history. It happened, and our faith rests on it.

Whenever anyone persists in trying to shake your faith, ask him about the resurrection. It cannot be explained away. It is the undeniable fact through which God has broken into history, and Paul rests his whole story upon it. This too will be explored further in his letter.

The way these opening verses are worded also tells us much about the Roman Christians. And what Paul says about them also applies to us. In verses 6 and 7 he says:

> *And you also are among those who are called to belong to Jesus Christ. To all in Rome who are loved by God and called to be saints: Grace and peace to you from God our Father and from the Lord Jesus Christ.*

First, Paul says the Roman Christians (the "saints") are "called." We are not self-made saints, we are not manmade saints; we are "called" saints. God called us. Every one of us can tell a different story of how it happened—how God's voice was heard, how we felt the drawing and pulling of God's Spirit in our life. This is true of every Christian, and it reveals a remarkable thing: God sought us! We really did not seek him. We thought we did, but he sought us. This is why Jesus said to his disciples, "All that the Father gives me *will come to me*, and whoever comes to me I will never drive away" (John 6:37, italics mine). And thus we came—called by God, sought by God.

The remarkable thing about this calling is underscored by Paul: "We are loved by God." Paul always starts his letters on the basis of God's love for us. He may have to scold the saints he is writing to, he may have to correct them, he may have to speak sharply to some of them; but he always starts by reminding them they are loved by God. Paul understands that this is the fundamental relationship we have with God. *He loves us*. We don't deserve his love, but nevertheless we have it because of Jesus. We ought to remind ourselves of that every day, as I am sure these Roman Christians did.

The grace and peace God gives his saints are proof of his love. The word *grace* stands for all the empowerment and enrichment God can give—all that he daily pours into our lives. We do not earn grace, but it is given us in view of our daily needs. All those moments when strength and courage flow into our lives, when God's Word comforts and heals us—this is God's grace. And the result is peace, rest! Grace and peace are our inheritance. They ought to characterize Christians everywhere, all the time, so that the world sees the difference in our lives.

Startling Faith

Paul points out a second characteristic of the Roman Christians in verse 8.

> *First, I thank my God through Jesus Christ for all of you, because your faith is being reported all over the world.*

Notice that the *faith* of the Roman Christians is being talked about, not the number of buses they operate, or the size or cost of the organ, or the size or cost of the building in which they meet. It was their faith that startled the Roman world. These were vital believers, and Paul gives a clue as to why this was true in the next verses:

> *God, whom I serve with my whole heart in preaching the gospel of his Son, is my witness how constantly I remember you in my prayers at all times; and I pray that now at last by God's will the way may be opened for me to come to you (1:9-10).*

Their faith was reported all over the world because the apostle and other Christians were praying for them. Paul had never been to Rome, and while he had met some of these people elsewhere, he had never known many of them. But he prayed for them "constantly . . . at all times"! That is why this church flourished. If there is one thing we need more than anything else today, it is to recover again this sense of concern and prayer for one another. It would make all the difference in the world if we began to uphold each other regularly in prayer.

The third characteristic mentioned about the Roman saints is this: They were strengthened by gifts.

> *I long to see you so that I may impart to you some spiritual gift to make you strong—that is, that you and I may be mutually encouraged by each other's faith (1:11-12).*

The exercise of spiritual gifts is what makes a congregation strong. When Paul says, "I want to impart to you some spiritual gift," he does not mean he has all the gifts in a bag which he carries around like an ecclesiastical Santa Claus, doling them out to people. "Impart" really means "share with you." Only the Holy Spirit can give spiritual gifts, and Paul wants to share with the Roman believers the gifts God has given him. He wants to minister to them, as they are expected to minister to him with the spiritual gifts they have. Thus they will all be mutually strengthened by one another's faith. This is how God wants a church to function—the saints ministering to each other, building up one another by their faith, and exercising the gifts God has given them.

Set Apart

Going back to the logical outline of this epistle, remember that Jesus as Lord is at the center, with the gospel next to that. Then comes Paul himself as the apostle through whom the Gentiles were being reached. What does Paul say about himself? In verse 1, he says he was "called to be an apostle and set apart for the gospel of God." Paul is a called apostle. God did the calling, and he did this—as we learn in Galatians—before Paul was born.

This is the wonder of the God we serve. He does not have to wait until we appear in human history to call us, but does so long before we are conceived, long before our family tree ever begins to take shape. Then he sets us apart. This is the process of eternal history, and this is what happened to Paul. All the events of his younger life—his training under Gamaliel, his ascendancy among the Pharisees, even his antipathy toward the gospel—all these were part of God's process of setting him apart to be an apostle. And when the time came, God pulled the trapdoor and Paul fell through. He was caught. This is what happens to us all; this is the way God works in our lives.

What is an apostle? Paul tells us in verse 5. Through Christ "and for his name's sake," he says, "we received grace and apostleship to call people from among all the Gentiles to the obedience that comes from faith." An apostle is a man sent to call people out. As Paul himself tells us in verse 14, "I am obligated both to Greeks and non-Greeks, both to the wise and the foolish." Paul sensed a deep imperative to tell all people the gospel because he knew they desperately needed it. If you alone had a remedy for cancer, would you be quiet about it, or would you feel compelled to share the secret with others? This is what Paul says urged him on—this constant consciousness that he had the secret of release which all people desperately needed.

As an apostle, he ventured out to take them this secret. He begins to tell how in verse 9: He says he served God "with my whole heart in preaching the gospel of his Son." Here is a wholehearted, single-minded man with his spirit fully engaged in his work. He tells us more in verse 15, where he speaks of being "so eager to preach the gospel also to you who are at Rome" after mentioning his obligation to all the world's people. If Paul is going to reach the nations, why does he preach the gospel to the Christians at Rome? It is because *through Christians* the nations will hear the gospel. The changes God brings in the lives of his people will cause others to take note. This is how true evangelism occurs, and Paul says this is why he wants to preach the gospel to those at Rome. And by "the gospel," Paul does not mean simply explaining how to become a Christian. These Romans were already Christians. Rather, the gospel includes all the great facts about humanity and about God that God wants to impart to us—facts that will enable us to be whole persons.

That brings us to the message itself. This is what Paul says of the gospel in verses 16 and 17.

> *I am not ashamed of the gospel, because it is the power of God for the salvation of everyone who believes: first for the Jew, then for the Gentile. For in the gospel a righteousness from God is revealed, a righteousness that is by faith from first to last, just as it is written: "The righteous will live by faith."*

This quotation from Habakkuk ("The righteous will live by faith") is the Scripture that gripped Martin Luther's heart. Paul says this is the great fact he is expounding in the gospel. He says he is not ashamed of it—which is a way of saying he is proud of it. He can't wait to get to Rome that he might fully declare it.

Powerless Romans

Especially to the Romans is Paul unashamed of the gospel; for the gospel is "the power of God," and the Romans appreciated power, just as Americans do. The Romans prided themselves on their power. Their military might could conquer any nation standing in their path. They could build tremendous roads and cities, and they had some of the greatest lawmakers in history. They had the power to create great literature and art. But Paul knew the Romans were powerless when it came to changing hearts. They were powerless to eliminate slavery—half of the empire's population were slaves. They couldn't eliminate violence and corruption—the Roman world was full of it, and the suicide rate was extremely high. They were powerless to change the stubborn, hostile, hateful hearts of men and women. The Romans could do nothing about any of that. That is why Paul was so proud of the gospel: it is the power of God to do the very things that men cannot do. We never need to apologize for the gospel. It is absolutely without rival.

Some years ago I received a letter from Dr. Richard Halverson, chaplain of the United States Senate. He wrote to tell me of the book *Born Again* by Charles Colson, one of the men who went to prison in the Watergate scandal. This book tells how Colson became a Christian. Halverson said the story was so remarkable it could be compared only with the conversion of the apostle Paul. Colson's experience was so drastic and different that people still have trouble accepting it. But there is no question he is a changed man. Anyone who has heard him speak or followed his life since those dark days after Watergate knows his conversion was genuine.

Now what got hold of Colson's heart and changed him like that? The gospel of the blessed God—the good news about Jesus Christ. It is the power of God for salvation!

Second, Paul is not ashamed of the gospel because in it "a righteousness from God is revealed." *Righteousness* is an old word that we don't understand very well. I would like to substitute for it a modern term, "worth." Full acceptance, or worth, before God is given to us in the gospel. We cannot earn it and we certainly do not deserve it, but it is given to us. God really accepts us because of the gospel, because of the good news of the work of Jesus Christ on our behalf. It is something that you or I or anyone can have. It is complete, perfect, needing nothing from us to supplement it.

The last thing Paul says is that this righteousness is received by faith. We can never earn it, but we can have it by faith anytime we need it—and that is good news! Our worth before God is not something we receive once at the beginning of our Christian lives. It is something we have continually and are to remind ourselves of every time we feel despairing or defeated. God has loved and restored us, and we have perfect value in his sight. He already accepts us and loves us as much as he possibly can; nothing more can be added to it. This is the righteousness revealed in the gospel; by faith it is available to all who believe, no matter what their background or training.

So these are the great themes of Romans. Centering upon the Lord, the gospel Paul preaches is the power of God to release men from their vicious cycle of sin and to establish them as whole people, filled by God and able to appropriate by faith their true worth before God. I hope these themes will have their effect upon our hearts as they did upon many in the first century church.

2
THE TRAGIC
SENSE OF LIFE

(Romans 1:18-23)

Paul's introduction to Romans concludes with the tremendous declaration, "I am not ashamed of the gospel, because it is the power of God for the salvation of everyone who believes; first for the Jew, then for the Gentile. For in the gospel a righteousness from God is revealed, a righteousness that is by faith from first to last" (1:16-17). By that statement Paul sets in focus the great theme of this letter—the power of God to heal our hurts and free us from the bondage of evil.

Beginning with verse 18, however, a more somber note is sounded. This section introduces the most extensive, careful, and logical analysis of the human dilemma ever penned. Extending through chapter 3, verse 20, it is introduced thus:

> *The wrath of God is being revealed from heaven against all the godlessness and wickedness of men who suppress the truth by their wickedness, since what may be known about God is plain to them, because God has made it plain to them. For since the creation of the world God's invisible qualities— his eternal power and divine nature— have been clearly seen, being understood from what has been made, so that men are without excuse (1:18-20).*

In the preceding verses Paul spoke of the Son of God—the key and the heart of the gospel. He declared that the power of God is released among men as they believe the gospel; he declared that the righteousness of God is granted to us by faith—a gift which we cannot earn or deserve, but which is ours nevertheless. Yet now Paul speaks of the wrath of God. It is the first negative note in this letter, but it is necessary because it introduces a passage that tells us why we need the gospel. We need it precisely because men everywhere suffer the wrath of God.

Judgment and Lightning

What do you think of when you see the words *the wrath of God?* Most think of it as something yet to come, something that follows death—the judgment of God. It is true that hell and all that may follow are an expression of the wrath of God. But that is not what it means at this point. Others think of the wrath of God as thunder, lightning, and judgment, fire and brimstone, and the sudden destruction and catastrophes that may come upon obviously guilty sinners. Indeed these are examples of God's wrath.

But the wrath of God isn't only something yet to come; it is present *now*. As the text says, it is "being revealed from heaven." It does not pour down from the skies upon us. The phrase means it is everywhere present. It comes from invisible forces at work in our lives; therefore it is inescapable. Everyone is confronted with and suffers from the wrath of God, without exception. His wrath is everywhere present, and it shows itself in the invisible resistance of God to the evil of men.

In 1962 I visited Mexico City with a group of businessmen. We were invited to hold witnessing sessions in the homes of businessmen and wealthy leaders of Mexico. To properly orient us to the country's unique culture, we had a session in a downtown hotel in Mexico City. In a beautiful and elegant address, Dr. Baenz-Camargo, a local Christian and a very wise university professor, captured for us the heart of Mexican life. He said we should understand five traits of the Mexican people. The first is that they have a sense of the dramatic; they love eloquence and oratory. With that comes a love of beauty and pageantry. Third, and stemming from these first two characteristics, is a deeply embedded sense of inferiority—the Mexicans feel they are a small nation and an inferior people, desperately trying to catch up with the rest of the world. That sense of inferiority produces the fourth mark of Mexican society, a resistance to authority. Rebelliousness and revolution are close to the surface in Mexico. All these traits find their ultimate expression in a kind of fatalism, which is the fifth characteristic, a strong belief in the role of chance and a lack of a sense of personal responsibility.

As Dr. Baenz-Camargo discussed the first characteristic, the awareness of the dramatic, he used the phrase "the tragic sense of life." I have not forgotten

that phrase because I find that it applies not only to
the Mexican people, but to people everywhere. We
are continually confronted with this tragic sense of
life. It describes the wrath of God which Paul is talking about.

Why is it that tragedy is so close to life's surface?
Even in our moments of joy and gladness we experience it. We have all felt this bittersweet side to life
when, in the midst of the warmth and joy of the home
circle, there comes an underlying sense of fear, of the
probability of the whole thing suddenly turning into
tragedy and sorrow. Why at Christmas time, for instance, when men are traditionally more glad and
joyful and mellow (perhaps) than at any other time of
year, does someone commit suicide? Anyone who has
borne loneliness throughout the year knows that it
can be deeply etched in bitter symbols upon our
hearts at Christmas. Sorrow and grief seem to be
more foreboding then than at any other time. Why?
It is because of the wrath of God. God's resistance
against human evil is creating a sense of tragedy and
darkness that we must all live with.

Moses expresses this perfectly in Psalm 90.

> For all our days pass away under thy wrath,
>   our years come to an end like a sigh.
> The years of our life are threescore and ten,
>   or even by reason of strength fourscore;
> yet their span is but toil and trouble;
>   they are soon gone, and we fly away (9-10
> RSV).

The shortness of life, the brevity of it, the sorrow
of it, the tragedy of it—all this is part of what Paul
captures in his words, "The wrath of God is being revealed from heaven." No one escapes God's wrath; it

is revealed, and we have to face it. It tinges with sorrow all our brightest days.

The rest of verse 18 reveals that God's wrath is drawn forth by "the godlessness and wickedness of men who suppress the truth by their wickedness." Life's tragic aspect is caused by the attitudes and subsequent actions of men; first godlessness, then wickedness. The order is never reversed. It is the godless attitude that produces the wicked actions, and this is why the wrath of God is being revealed constantly from heaven against man.

The Secular Attitude

What is godlessness? It is not necessarily atheism, the belief that God does not exist. Godlessness is *acting* as though he doesn't exist. It is disregarding God, never taking any account of him, not expecting him to be active. This attitude is still widespread today, and it is what the apostle speaks of here.

Godlessness makes men unrighteous, wicked, selfish, and spiteful. Why do we hurt each other? Because we disregard God. This is Paul's analysis—and he says these hurtful and selfish acts suppress the truth. That is just the problem! In a world where truth from God is breaking out all around, men are busy covering it up, hiding it, suppressing it, keeping it from being prominent in their thinking. Against this, the wrath of God burns. The reason so many lives have turned tragic is that the world is deprived of the truth necessary for life and freedom and godliness. The truth is being hidden and suppressed by men.

Verses 19 and 20 tell the kind of truth that is suppressed:

> *. . . since what may be known about God is plain*
> *to them, because God has made it plain to them.*
> *For since the creation of the world God's invisible*
> *qualities—his eternal power and divine nature—*
> *have been clearly seen, being understood from what*
> *has been made, so that men are without excuse.*

The truth men labor to suppress is the greatness of God, that he is the God of eternal power and majesty. Job 9 eloquently expounds this truth that the world hides:

> *His wisdom is profound, his power is vast.*
>   *Who has resisted him and come out unscathed?*
> *He moves mountains without their knowing it*
>   *and overturns them in his anger.*
> *He shakes the earth from its place*
>   *and makes its pillars tremble.*
> *He speaks to the sun and it does not shine;*
>   *he seals off the light of the stars.*
> *He alone stretches out the heavens*
>   *and treads on the waves of the sea.*
> *He is the Maker of the Bear and Orion,*
>   *the Pleiades and the constellations of the south.*
> *He performs wonders that cannot be numbered (4-*
> *10).*

How great God is! And yet men seem loath to mention him in public, or to act as though he had anything to do with their affairs. Isn't that strange? An unknown poet put it this way in "The Humanist":

> *He exists because he was created.*
> *He's here because he was placed here.*
> *He's well and comfortable*
>   *because divine power keeps him so.*
> *He dines at God's table.*

He's sheltered by the roof God gave him.
He's clothed by God's bounty.
He lives by breathing God's air
  which keeps him strong and vocal
  to go about persuading people that whether
    God is or not,
  only man matters.

There are times when men cannot evade the fact of God. But when those times come, when they simply must speak of God, they often resort to euphemism. They call God something else. They may call him "nature," for example. Nature, they'll say, is responsible for the way we are.

This, of course, is because "nature" is what we are. Nature is the sum total of all the phenomena of the natural world. But to say that the sum total of the phenomena of the natural world produces the phenomena of the natural world is nonsense, though everywhere this is the way men talk. Or they may call God "fate" or "karma" or "destiny." Those are simply other ways to avoid recognizing God at work in human affairs.

Yet one of the ironies of life is that God, who sits in the heavens, has arranged it so that men can't even rip off a round oath without mentioning his name. You never hear people swear, "By nature, I'm going to do this." You never hear them say, "Fate damn you!" Though they will not acknowledge him in any other way, God sees to it that men recognize his presence when they must be most emphatic.

Revelation in the Stars

How has God made plain the truth about himself? Scripture says God has revealed it. Truth isn't a vague, invisible, difficult thing to comprehend; it is clearly seen. God himself has ensured that. How? Paul says in Romans 1:20 that it is "understood from what has been made"—that is, from everything around us—and that it has been evident "since the creation of the world." It is present everywhere, and always has been, for everyone to see. No one is left out—all can read God's revelation if they want to.

One night my daughter Laurie and I were out walking at Forest Home in the mountains of Southern California. It was one of those beautiful evenings when the stars were out in all their glory—we were above the smog. We walked through the darkness and looked up at the stars and felt the sense of awe that comes upon the human spirit on occasions like that. I pointed out the Milky Way and explained to Laurie that it was part of the galaxy to which our world belongs, and that millions of galaxies like this were whirling on in their determined courses—never late, always on time, strange and mostly unexplorable by man. I pointed out the Big Dipper, the North Star, the Pleiades. We talked about the universe.

Then I jokingly said, "But remember, dear, all this happened just by chance; all these things came together by accident." And she began to laugh. How ridiculous that anyone should say this imposing display of beauty and light and order all happened by chance! Laurie sensed the total nonsense of that claim. For how can we say that watches are built by intelligence and wisdom and skill—but that stars shine and hearts beat and babies grow and roses smell simply by chance. It's ridiculous!

This argument from design and order has never been refuted. Those who disregard God cannot avoid or explain away the evidence because the truth about

God breaks out everywhere around us. Elizabeth Barrett Browning wrote,

> *Earth's crammed with heaven,*
>   *and every common bush aflame with God.*
> *But only those who see take off their shoes;*
>   *the rest sit round it and pluck blackberries.*

Thus, as Paul says, "men are without excuse." No one who really wants to find God need miss him. But what about someone who has never heard the gospel? One of the great verses confronting this problem is Hebrews 11:6—"And without faith it is impossible to please God, because anyone who comes to him must believe that he exists and that he rewards those who earnestly seek him." Just two things are necessary for such a person.

First, he must believe that God is there. Everything in his life is telling him that. Everything about himself is shouting at him, shrieking at him, that God has planned all these things. The easiest thing in the universe to believe is that God is there. You must work hard at convincing yourself that he's not there, and it seems only the highly educated are able to do it. The rest, who simply see facts and believe them, readily accept that God is there.

Second, he must diligently seek God. The Scriptures promise that if we seek after God he will give further light on himself, and this light will eventually lead to the knowledge of Jesus Christ—for without the Son, no man can come to the Father. There is no other name under heaven given among men whereby we must be saved. And knowledge about Jesus starts with where you are and with the revelation in nature and in yourself about the majesty and power and greatness of God.

To Suppress the Truth

In verses 21 through 23, the apostle details *how* men suppress the truth about God.

> *For although they knew God, they neither glorified him as God nor gave thanks to him, but their thinking became futile and their foolish hearts were darkened. Although they claimed to be wise, they became fools and exchanged the glory of the immortal God for images made to look like mortal man and birds and animals and reptiles.*

Three steps are traced here, all having distinct effects upon the race. First, men neither glorify God nor give thanks to him. They ignore him. There is an obvious conspiracy of silence about God. That is why children are not allowed to sing Christmas carols in many of our public schools. That is why there is great resistance to having the Bible read on almost any public occasion. No one wants to admit there's a God.

The effects are immediate. Paul says two things appear when this attitude prevails: the people's thinking becomes futile; and their hearts become darkened. Futile thinking means that clever ideas and procedures and programs will fall apart and come to nothing. In my own lifetime I have lived through the New Deal, the Fair Deal, the New Society, Peace with Honor, and the Great Recovery. All of them have failed dismally! They all started with brilliant promises, with glowing words of hope and expectation. And each one came to the same futile end.

When hearts are darkened, human needs which ought to evoke pity and response are ignored. People lose compassion and awareness of the struggles of others. Perhaps you've seen newspaper accounts of people in desperate need, calling out for help, while passersby ignore them because they don't want to get involved. This is a sign of a darkened heart, and it is the result of ignoring God.

The second device men use to suppress the truth is the claim to be wise. They imitate God. They claim the ability to know everything and to handle anything. Paul describes the result in one brief, blunt, pungent phrase: *"they became fools"!* Just read the intellectual magazines of our day and see how clever the secular writers are. They are masters at taking some simple discovery and making it sound impressive and profound, as though it were on par with the creation of the universe as recorded by Moses. They claim to be wise, but they become fools, and their inventions cause greater problems than the ones they solve.

Of Men and Snakes

The third device men use to suppress the truth is to exchange God's immortal glory "for images made to look like mortal man and birds and animals and reptiles." Notice the descending order. When idolatry begins, it begins first with men making images of men. Then it degenerates to likenesses of birds, animals, and finally reptiles. Man is at one end and a snake at the other!

I believe it's no accident how we tend to name our cars. We once named them after men: Lincoln, Ford, Chrysler, Dodge, DeSoto, Edsel. Since then, birds and animals have become more popular as names: Thunderbird, Firebird, Impala, Cougar, Mustang, Pinto, Jaguar, Rabbit, Panther, and even a Greyhound bus! Reptiles may be in fashion next: We already have a car called the Cobra, and we may soon have the Python, the Viper, and (a larger, slower model) the Crocodile!

Just like the statues in ancient times, today's world is filled with images that are either worshiped themselves or are symbols of ideas that men worship.

But these images invalidate God; they debase him by substituting something for God that makes him seem less than what he is. This is what idolatry always does, making it a destructive force in human affairs.

But do people today really worship images and bow down before idols? Why else do we have rock stars and athletic heroes? What are movies and television shows, but images attracting our devotion? We worship forces like sex, ambition, and greed. We worship beauty, youth, adventure, leisure, life. We worship military power—planes, guns, bombs, tanks. All these are our gods, aren't they? We have exchanged the glory of the undying God—in all his majesty and greatness—for mere images.

Comparing our own society and the first-century world Paul is analyzing, we find them exactly the same: idolatrous. We are right where they were. And the effect upon us is profound and terrible.

The amazing thing in Romans is that this accounting of God's wrath in chapter one is shown to be wholly and fully met by the righteousness of God. God's righteousness cancels his wrath. Wouldn't you think, therefore, that men everywhere would be eager to discover this marvelous gift? All our pain and heartache and darkness, the death, the depression, the despair—all come from God's wrath, and are the products of ignoring God, trying to replace God, and invalidating God in our lives. Wouldn't you think men everywhere would rush to accept the good news of how to escape God's wrath, and enjoy the righteousness that heals our hurts, corrects our errors, and gives a sense of peace and joy and forgiveness to the heart?

Yet the wonder of our times, and the hallmark of our twisted, demoralized, distorted world, is that we cling to our hurts and refuse the healing of God.

3
THE DEEPENING DARKNESS

(Romans 1:24-32)

Just how much progress have we made in the last twenty centuries? Anyone reading Romans 1 recognizes that today's moral climate is no different from that in the first century when Paul lived. The apostle mentions two characteristics of the civilization he lived in, and they also describe our society today. The first characteristic is *godlessness* ; the second, *wickedness*.

Godlessness is disrespect of God, and it results in wickedness—injury and hurt to others. The epistle to the Romans is built on the thesis that in every generation there is godlessness, resulting in wickedness.

The apostle has traced the source of godlessness. He begins with God's self-disclosure in nature; God has spoken to this world and has shown himself in the natural scene. Nature includes mankind, for we are all part of nature. God has made himself knowable in every age and place. The truth about God pours out from every direction, if only we have eyes to see. But men respond to this truth, the apostle says, with an unspoken agreement to suppress it. You may have seen the rather remarkable television presentation called *The Ascent of Man*. Here was a clear example of man's attempt to trace all that has happened to mankind without a single reference to God.

When Men Lose God

In verses 24 through 32 of Romans 1, the apostle reveals the effect of this godlessness—wickedness inevitably follows. When men lose God, they lose themselves. They do not understand what is happening and are not able to diagnose the sicknesses and problems that break out in society.

In *The Great Divorce*, C. S. Lewis said hell is made up of people who live an infinite distance from each other. That alienation is the result of the loss of God in their lives.

Wickedness at Work

Paul says wickedness follows a three-step process. The process is identified in this passage by the thrice-repeated phrase "God gave them over," a phrase that explains what is going on in our culture.

The first reference is in verse 24:

> *Therefore God gave them over in the sinful desires of their hearts to sexual impurity for the degrading of their bodies with one another.*

The first mark of wickedness in a godless society is widespread sexual immorality—the degrading, or dishonoring, of the body. Note that the sentence begins with the word "Therefore." This immorality is a result of the idolatry into which men fall. Idolatry is common in our day, although we do not worship idols and images so much as concepts and ideas. But such idolatry leads to widespread sexual immorality.

Many read "God gave them over" as though it said God "gives up" on people because of the evil they do. They believe God washes his hands of such people because they are so filthy. But this certainly is not what the account says. When men run after other gods and refuse the testimony of their own hearts and of nature around them, when they do not glorify or thank the true God, God removes his restraints—"giving them over"—so that what was done in secret is allowed to break out into the open and be widely accepted. This is the sign of the wrath of God. The first mark of wickedness in a civilization is that sexual immorality (which has always been present) becomes widely accepted.

This means God allows men and women to experience the full effects of their attempts to satisfy their hungers, cravings, and desires apart from him. He allows people to discover they do not have the answer. God removes the societal restraints so that immorality comes to the surface. He thereby forces us to suffer the full effect of what we do. God makes us harvest the crop we insisted on sowing, however much we now want to abandon our field. God says we cannot keep on sowing wild oats without reaping the evil results. We must live with them. This is what Paul calls, "the wrath of God at work among us."

The Supreme Vice?

You may ask, "Why is it that sex always seems to be singled out in God's judgment? Why is sexual immorality the first sign of a disintegrating civilization?"

There is a good reason. Many Christians have wrongly concluded that sexual sins are the worst kinds of sin. But that is not true. Sexual sins are not the worst kind. C. S. Lewis saw this clearly, and in *Mere Christianity* he says,

> *If anyone thinks that Christians regard unchastity as the supreme vice, he is quite wrong. The sins of the flesh are bad, but they are the least bad of all sins. All the worst pleasures are purely spiritual: the pleasure of putting other people in the wrong, of bossing and patronizing and spoiling sport, and backbiting; the pleasures of power, of hatred. For there are two things inside me, competing with the human self which I must try to become. They are the Animal self, and the Diabolical self. The Diabolical self is the worse of the two. That is why a cold, self-righteous prig who goes regularly to church may be far nearer to hell than a prostitute. But, of course, it's better to be neither.* (from "Sexual Morality" in Book III, *Christian Behavior*)

This passage in Romans confirms Lewis' words. Wickedness begins with sexual impurity and then proceeds to sexual perversion. But the final outcome, in the climax of the chapter, is not sexual sin but the sins of the spirit. Widespread animosity and heartlessness—these are the worst sins.

But God allows perverted sexual practices to become publicly acceptable to show us what is going on in our spiritual lives. It may sound curious, but sex is linked with worship. A serious reading of the Scriptures will make this clear. Sex is man's longing after worship. It is a desire to possess another body and to be possessed by another. It is a deep-seated craving inherent in every human being. We have all heard the statement, "Women give sex in order to get love; men give love in order to get sex." Superficially this is true. But what both are really after is not sex at all; they are after worship. They really want to worship and to be worshiped. They want a sense of total fulfillment, a oneness, an identity. And this is what they think they are getting when they indulge in illicit sex.

The Scriptures tell us that only God can give this fulfillment. Only God can satisfy our deep sense of longing for complete identity and unity with another person. This is what we call worship. When we worship, we long to be possessed of God, and to possess him fully. Thus the highest possible description of the relationship between a believer and God is found in the words of Jesus in John 15, "You in me, and I in you." When men think they will find this fulfillment in sex, in effect God says to them, "Look, it won't work. But you won't believe me until you try it out." So he removes the restraints and allows immoral sexual practices to become widely accepted, knowing that men indulging in these things will finally find themselves just as dissatisfied, empty, and hopeless as they were when they started. Only thus will they learn that sex is not the way to find fulfillment. This is true even in marriage. We find complete fulfillment only in a relationship with God.

Shameful Lusts

This brings us to the second mark of a godless and wicked society, found in verses 25-27:

> *They exchanged the truth of God for a lie, and worshiped and served created things rather than the Creator—who is forever praised, Amen. Because of this, God gave them over to shameful lusts. Even their women exchanged natural relations for unnatural ones. In the same way the men also abandoned natural relations with women and were inflamed with lust for one another. Men committed indecent acts with other men, and received in themselves the due penalty for their perversion.*

Homosexuality is the second sign of a godless and wicked society. Paul says shameful lusts arise from inside, desires that are part of the soul of man. The apostle thus describes the rise of widespread psychological confusion. Notice the irony. This is God's silent way of forcing men to demonstrate their sin so they can see what is going on in their lives. Paul says that because they have exchanged truth for a lie and exchanged the Creator for created things, God allows them to exchange natural functions for unnatural functions—to use a man for a woman, and a woman for a man.

When restraints are removed, homosexuality becomes widely accepted. It was a common practice in Paul's world of the first century. The great philosophers, for the most part, extolled and practiced it. Socrates and other great thinkers of ancient Greece had been homosexuals, as were fourteen of the first fifteen Roman emperors, some of them openly and blatantly.

Once again the restraints are being removed, and these things are thrusting themselves into public acceptance. The truly awful thing about the rise of homosexuality today is that homosexuals widely believe the lie that their condition is biological and cannot be helped. They are encouraged to adjust to it. Even churches are falling into this trap and consenting to this deceit. One newspaper article reports the inclusion of a homosexual church into the local council of churches. It is hard to believe that pastors stood up and said they could not judge whether homosexuality was good or evil.

Yet I was also encouraged by a paper sent to me by a Christian who is an ex-homosexual. It was written by other Christians like him who had been delivered from homosexuality by the power and grace of the gospel of the Lord Jesus. To help those still enmeshed in this vice, they published a forthright plea to those trapped in homosexuality not to believe the lie that it is a biological condition and that they cannot help themselves. This widely believed lie holds its victims in a fatal grip. As long as homosexuals believe it, there *is* no help for them. But if they understand that homosexuality is a sin like other sins, that it can be forgiven, and that they can be delivered and freed from its power by the might and grace of Jesus Christ, then there is tremendous hope in the midst of their darkness.

Paul speaks also of a "due penalty" for this perversion. Anyone who has spent time with homosexuals knows what this penalty is. It is a loss of one's sense of identity, an uncertainty as to one's role and place. We see this to a considerable degree in the women's liberation movement, as well as in androgynous dress styles and in the unisex emphasis in education. Its ultimate expression is a sex change operation that mutilates the sex organs. The sexual confusion that results from all this is an attempt to mar and defeat God's precise plan in making us male and female.

Desire to Exploit

The third and final mark of a godless and wicked culture is given in verses 28-32.

> *Furthermore, since they did not think it worthwhile to retain the knowledge of God, he gave them over to a depraved mind, to do what ought not to be done. They have become filled with every kind of wickedness, evil, greed and depravity. They are full of envy, murder, strife, deceit and malice. They are gossips, slanderers, God-haters, insolent, arrogant, and boastful; they invent ways of doing evil; they disobey their parents; they are senseless, faithless, heartless, ruthless.*

This is a terrible list of sins, and they are marks of a civilization nearing collapse. They reflect a contemptuous and arrogant disregard for others—in a word, a desire to *exploit* other people. The term "depraved mind" literally means an unacceptable mind, a mind that cannot be lived with, a mind that refuses to fit into any kind of civilization or culture or society. A depraved mind destroys, rends, and fragments everything it touches. And its public hostility is marked by increasing cruelty and violence.

Probably the most vivid picture of this in our day is given in Aleksandr Solzhenitsyn's *The Gulag Archipelago*, in which an entire culture is characterized by this terrible, senseless cruelty. But we in the Western world are not escaping. Every day our newspapers report senseless vandalism, along with vicious and unprovoked attacks upon innocent and often helpless people. The rise in child abuse is a symptom of this. It culminates, as Paul makes very clear in verse 32, in an attitude of callous disregard:

> *Although they know God's righteous decree that*
> *those who do such things deserve death, they not*
> *only continue to do these very things but also ap-*
> *prove of those who practice them.*

Sneering at the fact that harm comes from their wickedness, they try to spread it more widely. They invade the field of education; they dominate the media; they seek legal status for their evil ways and defy all attempts at control. This is what is going on today. The deepening darkness that Paul traces in his own day is spreading in our day as well.

But it is also clear that God does not turn his back on man. This passage is not a record of people whom God despises and therefore turns aside from with contempt. The Bible never views man as an object of contempt, or as a worm. Rather, God's concern for humanity underscores these words. He is at work to bring men to their senses, to awaken a drugged and dying civilization and show how desperately it needs deliverance—which can come only as a gift of right-eousness from God's hands.

You may ask, "Why does God give a civilization over to this kind of thing?" He does it because it is only when darkness prevails, and despair and vio-lence are widespread, that men welcome the light. Remember Isaiah's prediction:

> *The people walking in darkness*
> *have seen a great light;*
> *on those living in the land of the shadow of death*
> *a light has dawned (Isaiah 9:2).*

In the first century, mankind was sunken in the darkness of despair. Idolatry had spread through the whole world; men had turned from the true God, whom they could have known. Hopelessness and misery lay like a heavy blanket upon the earth.

In that hour, in the darkness of the night, over the skies of Bethlehem the angels broke through and a great light of hope shone forth. From that hope all light streams. The angels told of the coming of the Lord Jesus, of the availability of God's gift of righteousness.

Against the growing darkness of our own time we need to make this message as clear as possible—by our testimony, by our lives, by the joy and peace of our hearts. God has found a way to break through human weakness, arrogance, despair, and sinfulness to give us peace, joy, and gladness once again. Just as Jesus was born in Bethlehem so long ago, so he can be born in your heart now. This is the good news of the gospel. In this decaying world we can see again the glory of this truth as it delivers people from their sins. "Thou shalt call his name JESUS, for he shall save his people from their sins" (Matthew 1:21 KJV).

4
SINFUL
MORALITY

(Romans 2:1-11)

Many people think they do not belong in the picture of degraded society Paul has been describing. I am sure there were thousands in Paul's day—and millions today—who do not see themselves in Romans 1. "That isn't talking about us," they say. "We're not like that. It may describe others, but it does not describe us."

Whenever you read this first chapter of Romans, that division immediately becomes evident: "others" and "us." The "others" are obviously gross, wicked people; "we" are not. Many would say, "We're law-abiding, home-loving, clean-living, decent people." Many have been church members most of their lives.

Others perhaps do not go to church at all, but nevertheless pride themselves on their moral standards, their ethical values, and their clean, law-abiding lives. They believe the world is in its present condition because of the wickedness of gangsters, radicals, revolutionaries, prostitutes, pimps, and the perverts of our day; but they see themselves as the salt of the earth.

It is on these people that the apostle turns his spotlight in chapter 2. We will see his argument developed in three separate steps. The first is given in verse 1.

> *You, therefore, have no excuse, you who pass judgment on someone else, for at whatever point you judge the other, you are condemning yourself, because you who pass judgment do the same things.*

Here the subject is those who pass judgment on others. If anyone reading this book does not belong in that category, you can go on to the next section. But to those who have, at one time or another, passed judgment on someone else, I want you to notice that the apostle makes two points about such people.

First, he indicates that they know the difference between right and wrong; otherwise they would not presume to judge. They have a clear standard. They know that one thing is wrong and another right. They are clearly aware, therefore, that wrong actions merit the judgment and wrath of God.

Guilty Judges

Paul's second point is devastating. He says these people are guilty because they do the same things themselves. The judges are as guilty as the ones they have in the dock.

As a practiced, self-righteous hypocrite, I am always surprised at this statement. "What do you mean?" I want to say, "How could this be?"

Such a response brings to mind our Lord's account of his return, when he will separate all people into two bands, the sheep and the goats. He will make judgment according to how they have treated one another. He will say to the sheep, "When I was thirsty you gave me drink, when I was hungry you fed me, when I was naked you clothed me, when I was in prison you visited me." To the goats he will say, "When I was thirsty you did not give me drink, when I was hungry you did not feed me, when I was naked you did not clothe me, and when I was sick or in prison you did not visit me." Both groups are taken by surprise and say, "When did this happen? When did we see you thirsty or hungry or naked? We don't remember that!" This feeling of surprise shows how little men understand themselves, and why we all need a passage such as this. *We are all guilty*, even though we are not consciously aware of it.

Blind Spots

If my own attitudes are typical, then I see three ways in which we try to deny our guilt for doing the same things we condemn in others.

First, we are congenitally blind toward many of our own faults. We are just not aware of them. We do not see that we do the same wrong things others do. I don't see it, and neither do you see it in yourself; and yet others see it in us. We all have these blind spots.

One of the greatest lies of our age is the idea that we understand ourselves. We often argue, "Don't you think I know myself?" The answer is no. We are blind to much of our lives. There may be very hurtful and sinful areas of which we are unaware. "A man's deeds are right in his own eyes," the Old Testament says.

I once stayed with a pastor and his delightful family. The oldest son was about sixteen, and—not unusual for someone his age—very concerned about the faults of his twelve-year-old brother. One day he came in all upset and said, "Who does he think he is? Why, he acts as though he's as good as the rest of us!" What a typical example of the attitude we all have— only this boy was honest enough to admit it.

I often tell someone, "Relax! Take it easy!" Only afterward do I hear my own voice and realize that I myself am neither relaxed nor taking it easy. Have you ever lectured your children on the sin of procrastination and then completed your income tax return barely on time, if at all? How blind we are! We just do not see many of our own faults, and thus we can indeed be guilty, as the verse says, of doing the very things we accuse others of doing.

A second way we deny guilt is to conveniently forget our own wrong. We may have been aware of our sin at the time, but somehow we assume God will forget it, so we need not acknowledge it in any way. As the sin fades from our memory, we think it fades from his as well.

Let's consider our thought life, for example. Much of this passage in Romans must be understood in light of our Lord's teaching in the Sermon on the Mount. Jesus says that God, who looks at the heart, sees what is going on inside and judges on that basis; he doesn't judge as men judge, according to appearances. In the Sermon on the Mount we learn that if we hold a feeling of hatred against someone, if we are bitter and resentful and filled with malice, then before God we are as guilty of murder as if we had taken a knife and plunged it into that person's breast. If we find ourselves lusting for the body of another, if we play with this idea over and over in our mind, and treat ourselves to a fantasy of sex, we have committed fornication or adultery. If we are filled with pride, yet put on the appearance of being humble and considerate, we are guilty of the worst of sins, for pride of heart destroys humanity.

We think these things will go unnoticed, but God sees them in our hearts. He sees everything we have conveniently forgotten. When we demean people, or speak with spite and sharpness and deliberately try to hurt them, he sees it. He sees it when we are unfair in our business, and when we are arrogant toward someone we think is on a lower social level. When we are stubborn and uncooperative in trying to work out a tense situation, he sees that too. All these things God notices. We, who condemn these things in others, are guilty of the same things. Isn't it remarkable that when others mistreat us we think it is horrible, demanding immediate correction? But when we mistreat others we say, "You're making so much out of a little thing! Why, it's so trivial and insignificant!"

The third way we try to evade our guilt is by cleverly renaming things. Other people lie and cheat; we simply stretch the truth. Others betray; we are simply protecting our rights. Others steal; we borrow. Others have prejudices; we have convictions. We cry, "Those people ought to be stoned!" Jesus says, "He that is without sin among you, let him cast the first stone." We are all guilty of the same things we accuse others of doing.

Only One Standard

In verses 2-4 Paul develops the second step of his argument by asking two questions. Here is the first:

*Now we know that God's judgment against those
who do such things is based on truth. So when you,
a mere man, pass judgment on them and yet do the
same things, do you think you will escape God's
judgment?*

What a ridiculous ground of hope! How tenuous
to hope that God—who sees all men openly and inti-
mately, who sees not only what is on the outside but
also what is on the inside—will pronounce judgment
on others but not on us. People will say, "How can a
just and loving God permit the injustice and vileness
that takes place in this world? How can he allow a
tyrant like Hitler or Stalin to arise and murder millions of innocent people? How can he allow these
godless regimes to come into power and crush
people, usurp their rights, put thousands in prison,
and spread destruction and sorrow across the land?
Why does he allow these things to go on year after
year? Why doesn't God judge these men?"

The question we ought to ask is, "Why didn't he
judge me yesterday, when I said that sharp, caustic
word that plunged like an arrow into a loved one's
heart and hurt her badly? Why didn't he shrivel my
hand when I took a pencil and cheated on my income
tax? Why didn't he strike me dumb when I gossiped
on the phone this morning, sharing a tidbit that
made someone look bad in someone else's eyes? Why
didn't God judge that?" The God of truth and justice
sees all of this; so how, Paul asks, do we think we can
escape the judgment of God?

Then Paul asks the second question, the other horn
of the dilemma.

*Or do you show contempt for the riches of his kind-
ness, tolerance and patience, not realizing that
God's kindness leads you toward repentance?*
(2:4)

First Paul asked, "Why are you acting this way—constantly judging others so critically, yet never seeming to judge yourself? Surely you don't think you're going to escape! If you know God judges according to truth, you must be included in that judgment as well." But now he says in verse 4, "If you know you can't escape his judgment, then you must be treating with disdain the opportunities God gives you to repent."

Why are you alive? Why are you being allowed to experience life today, with all its opportunities to correct wrong attitudes and behavior? It is because God's goodness, tolerance, and patience are giving you a chance to change, a chance to acknowledge your sins and be forgiven. A faithful God, judging the innermost part of our lives, gives us these opportunities. He knows we are blind. He knows we often struggle to recognize what is wrong in our lives. So he gives us these opportunities to repent and change, moments of truth that are extremely important.

In Romans 2:5-11, the apostle presents the last step of his argument and describes what lies ahead for those who refuse to face the true condition of their lives.

> But because of your stubbornness and your unrepentant heart, you are storing up wrath against yourself for the day of God's wrath, when his righteous judgment will be revealed. God "will give to each person according to what he has done." To those who by persistence in doing good seek glory, honor, and immortality, he will give eternal life. But for those who are self-seeking and who reject the truth and follow evil, there will be wrath and anger. There will be trouble and distress for every human being who does evil: first for the Jew, then for the Gentile; but glory, honor and peace for everyone

who does good: first for the Jew, then for the Gentile. For God does not show favoritism.

I am amazed to see in my own heart how often I expect God to show favoritism. Even as a Christian, I expect him to overlook areas of my life without my having to acknowledge them. I hope he'll forget them without revealing to me what they are really like. Yet the Scriptures tell us that God constantly allows us moments when we can see ourselves clearly—and what valuable times these are!

Treasures of Wrath

Here in Romans 2, Paul says that when we refuse to judge the sinful areas of our lives that God allows us to see, we are storing up wrath for ourselves. In the King James version the word is "treasures." We are laying up treasures—but the treasure is wrath! This is the same word Jesus employed when he said, "Lay up treasures for yourselves in heaven." We are constantly making deposits in a bank account which we must one day collect. In his wrath, God allows us to deteriorate. We become less than what we wanted to be, and it is because we are receiving back the deposit of wrath we have laid up for ourselves.

C. S. Lewis has described this eloquently in *Mere Christianity.*

> *People often think of Christian morality as a kind of bargain in which God says, "If you keep a lot of rules I'll reward you, and if you don't I'll do the other thing." I do not think that is the best way of looking at it. I would much rather say that every time you make a choice you are turning the central part of you, the part of you that chooses, into something a little different from what it was before. And taking your life as a whole, with all your in-*

numerable choices, all your life long you are slowly turning this central thing either into a heavenly creature or into a hellish creature: either into a creature that is in harmony with God, and one with other creatures, and with itself, or else into one that is in a state of war and hatred with God, and with its fellow-creatures, and with itself. To be the one kind of creature is heaven: that is, it is joy and peace and knowledge and power. To be the other means madness, horror, idiocy, rage, impotence, and eternal loneliness. Each of us at each moment is progressing to the one state or the other. (from "Morality and Psychoanalysis" in Book III, Christian Behavior)

God is a righteous God. He judges men and assesses wrath against those who do wrong. No matter how the outward life may appear, he sees the inward heart and judges on that basis. Righteous judgment is waiting; and yet it comes (in part) throughout all of life, because we experience the wrath of God even now. But a day is coming when it will be fully manifested.

The question Paul brings out here is this: What do you really want out of life? What are you seeking? Do you "by persistence in doing good seek glory, honor and immortality"? That is, do you want God's life, do you want to be his kind of a person, do you want to honor him and be of value to him? If that is what you really want above everything else, then you will find it. God will give you eternal life. In the context of the whole Scripture, this means you will find your way to Jesus Christ, for he *is* life eternal. You will find him as your Redeemer and Lord and Savior. You will grow increasingly like him as you judge these evil areas of life, and honestly confess them rather than assuming God will pass over them.

What do you really want? Is it pleasure, fame, wealth, power, and prominence? Do you want to be the center of things and have everyone thinking of you and looking at you and serving you? If so, then according to this passage, for you and "for every human being who does evil" the reward "will be trouble and distress."

Consistent with Love

Now if all this sounds harsh and unloving, you have not read the passage in its context. For the picture given is of a God who loves us so much that he tells us the truth—and that is true love. He loves humanity and wants to restore it. Having fallen into the trap of self-deceit, we hear him tell us the only way out.

God's love helps us see that there is only one way to deal with sin: Admit it is there, and recognize that God has already dealt with it in Christ. On this basis, God offers us full and free forgiveness. There is no other way.

Other voices lead us to rationalize our faults and accept them as something other than ugly sins before God. But anyone who listens to these voices will discover ultimately that he has stored up a treasure house of wrath. That is why God tells us the truth now.

In great love and at tremendous cost, God has provided a way out. It is that we surrender self. We must give up self-seeking and living for ourselves and begin to live for the God who made us. By the power of the Lord who forgives us and restores us and makes us his own, we will have heaven instead of hell.

This principle of giving up self must run all through life, from top to bottom, as C. S. Lewis urges (again, in *Mere Christianity*):

*Give up yourself, and you will find your real self.
Lose your life and you will save it. Submit to
death, death of your ambitions and favorite wishes
every day and death of your whole body in the end:
submit with every fiber of your being, and you will
find eternal life. Keep back nothing. Nothing that
you have not given away will ever be really yours.
Nothing in you that has not died will ever be raised
from the dead. Look for yourself, and you will find
in the long run only hatred, loneliness, despair,
rage, ruin, and decay. But look for Christ and you
will find Him, and with Him everything else
thrown in. (from "The New Men" in Book IV,
Beyond Personality)*

This is the gospel at which Romans 2:1-11 is aiming. There is no hope, none whatsoever, except in a
day-by-day yielding to the plan and the program of
God as we find it in Jesus Christ our Lord.

Perhaps you are now seeing yourself in a new light.
You see your need to stop justifying and excusing
yourself, and you know you need God's forgiveness
just as much as if you were a cold-blooded murderer.
We all do.

Or perhaps as a Christian you are realizing how
often you condemn and criticize other people,
thereby blocking the flow of God's life within you,
and keeping back the joy and peace he wants you to
enjoy.

If so, then above all else take seriously God's way
of escape. Admit your sins freely. Receive the forgiveness of God on the basis of the work of Jesus
Christ in his death on the cross, and take hold of his
resurrection life now available to us.

That is our only hope.

5
ACCORDING TO LIGHT

(Romans 2:12-29)

Men and women everywhere desperately need the gospel. In the gospel, God found a way to condemn our sin and to destroy it without destroying us. No man can do that. When we want to correct evildoers, we have to punish them by imprisoning them. Sometimes, to protect society, we have to take their lives. But God does not do that. Jesus, the center and heart of the gospel, *changes* people. He can change our most fundamental urges from self-centeredness and selfishness to loving concern for others, so that our behavior is altered. In the gospel God makes divine power available to us. God has promised to us and provided for us an ultimate destiny that is beyond our wildest dreams. And yet, amazingly, many people resist it and stubbornly hold out against it.

So far in Romans Paul has described the obviously wicked man (who defies God) and the self-righteously moral man (who deludes himself). Now we come to the last two types of people who resist the truth. The first is the unenlightened pagan. Here we will deal with the question of what to do about people who have not heard the gospel. What about those who live where the Bible is unknown, or those who belong to a different religion ignorant of the facts surrounding the life, death, and resurrection of Jesus Christ? In this passage Paul will show their problem is that they defile their consciences. The last type is the religious devotee who seeks deliverance from the judgment of God by religious practices, rituals, performances, and knowledge of the truth. His problem is that though he knows the truth, in his actions he denies that truth.

By Their Own Standards

These two types of people are introduced by a statement of the universal lostness of mankind:

> *All who sin apart from the law will also perish apart from the law, and all who sin under the law will be judged by the law. For it is not those who hear the law who are righteous in God's sight, but it is those who obey the law who will be declared righteous (2:12-13).*

This is probably the strongest statement Paul makes, and it answers the question non-Christians ask Christians more often than any other—"What about the people who have never heard of Jesus Christ?" Usually they are thinking of naked savages in jungles. They seldom think of the savages in the concrete jungles of our cities, but both are in the same condition. Paul's answer is that they will be judged by their own standards. God judges men, not according to what they do not know, but according to what they do know.

So far in Romans, Paul has made three great statements about the basis of judgment. In Romans 2:2 he says that God's judgment is according to truth—it is realistic. He deals only with what is actually there. God does not falsely accuse anyone, but he judges according to the truth. Then in Romans 2:6 he says God judges according to works. Now that is interesting, because it shows God is patient. God—who does see what is going on in our inner lives and who could judge immediately on that basis— nevertheless waits patiently until our inner attitude begins to work itself out in some deed, speech, or attitude. Therefore, God allows men to be their own judge, to see for themselves that what is coming out reveals what is inside.

In Romans 2:12-13 Paul says the judgment of God is according to light. God is not going to summon all mankind and declare that they are going to be judged on the basis of the Ten Commandments. Rather, he will say to each one, "What did you think was right and wrong?" And then, "Did you do the right, and not the wrong?" By that standard, of course, everyone fails. Paul makes that clear. He says, "All who sin apart from the law will also perish apart from the law." The fact that such people never heard the Ten Commandments (or anything else in the Bible) does not mean God will accept them. They will perish, not because they did not hear, but because they did not do what they knew was right.

Now Paul goes on to take up the case of the unenlightened pagan:

*(Indeed, when Gentiles, who do not have the law,
do by nature things required by the law, they are a
law for themselves, even though they do not have
the law, since they show that the requirements of
the law are written on their hearts, their consciences also bearing witness, and their thoughts
now accusing, now even defending them.) This
will take place on the day when God will judge
men's secrets through Jesus Christ, as my gospel declares (2:14-16).*

Verses 14 and 15 are in parentheses so as not to distract too much from the main flow of Paul's argument, which is that a day is coming when God will
judge the secrets of men everywhere and all that is
hidden will be revealed. Jesus himself spoke of that
day: "What you have said in the dark will be heard in
the daylight, and what you have whispered in the ear
in the inner rooms will be proclaimed from the
housetops" (Luke 12:3). There were some in Paul's
day who said that because the Jews had the law and
knew God's truth, they would not be condemned in
that final judgment. But Paul is saying, "Look, if
your knowledge of truth is what saves you, then
everyone will be saved, even the savages and the pagans, for they show they have a law, too. They know
a great deal about the law; it is written on their
hearts, and their consciences act as judges within
them, just as they do within those of us in the more
civilized world." On that basis, you see, everyone
would be saved. But God does not judge that way.

Written on Hearts

Now here we get a glimpse of what goes on in the
primitive world. Men and women who have never
heard anything about the Bible or Jesus Christ or

Moses or the Ten Commandments are nevertheless judged because they have truth written in their hearts. They know what is right and wrong—they show it in their lives.

An amazing book called *Peace Child* tells the remarkable story of missionaries who went to New Guinea to live among an isolated people so degraded, so sunken in immorality, that they actually admired treachery. They highly regarded any man who could win someone's love and trust, and then betray and murder him. Such a man was held up as an admirable person to follow. When the missionaries first came to these people they despaired of ever reaching them, for there seemed to be no ground of appeal to a people who had so reversed the moral standards of life.

As they lived among them and became better acquainted with their culture, however, the missionaries discovered that this moral reversal was not quite universal. In one particular practice—the exchange of a "peace child"—the people observed a high moral standard. If a tribe handed over one of its children to another tribe, the tribe receiving the child was then bound to honor its agreements and treaties with the first tribe. If they did not, they would lose face and be regarded as despicable. At this point the missionaries were able to introduce the gospel: They pointed out that God has given us a peace child in Jesus Christ, and therefore all tribes are bound to honor God. It is a remarkable story, showing clearly how God prepared the way for the gospel's entrance into this culture.

The Romans of Paul's day were living according to conscience; and yet the conscience, as Paul points out here, never brings a settled peace. People say, "Let your conscience be your guide," but that is a recipe

for unhappiness. If your conscience is all you have,
you are certain to alternate between fleeting peace
and fear.

An interesting article in *Christianity Today* by
Rachel Saint, sister of one of the five men cruelly
murdered by the Auca Indians in Ecuador in 1956,
describes the way the Aucas lived before the gospel
came:

> *The Aucas have been thoroughly acquainted with
> demons and devil worship for many generations.
> The result of this is a religion of terror. The witch
> doctor is the central authority, and he controls the
> tribe. Any death is supposed to be caused by the
> witch doctor. Then that death has to be avenged
> and the feuding starts. They are afraid that they
> might be speared at night in their own houses.
> Everyone is a potential enemy. If a father loses a
> son, he feels he must kill his daughter. If the group
> loses a marriageable girl, a grandmother is killed.
> Why should a worthless old woman live if a mar-
> riageable girl has died? This kind of thinking per-
> meates their culture.*

Thoughts like this appear not only in the jungles
of South America, but wherever people are governed
only by the law of conscience. Yet even under their
own law they will perish, just as certainly as do those
who are judged by God's law; for they do not obey
their own consciences.

Religious Braggarts

Paul goes on to take up the case of the religious
devotee of his day, the Jew. Today we need only substitute the title "church member" to apply it to ourselves. We American church members are in the
same condition as the Jew of Paul's day. We have a

great body of truth in which we delight, and we feel proud of our knowledge and our understanding of it. But unfortunately we often think our knowledge in itself will deliver us in the sight of God.

This is how Paul handles such thinking:

> *Now you, if you call yourself a Jew; if you rely on the law and brag about your relationship to God; if you know his will and approve of what is superior because you are instructed by the law; if you are convinced that you are a guide for the blind, a light for those who are in the dark, an instructor of the foolish, a teacher of infants, because you have in the law the embodiment of knowledge and truth— you, then, who teach others, do you not teach yourself? You who preach against stealing, do you steal? You who say that people should not commit adultery, do you commit adultery? You who abhor idols, do you rob temples? You who brag about the law, do you dishonor God by breaking the law? As it is written: "God's name is blasphemed among the Gentiles because of you" (2:17-24).*

Paul lists here the five great advantages which the Jews of his day had and on which they relied for their position before God. First, they rejoiced in having the law. Many people in our churches today rely greatly on the fact that the Bible is available to them. Many take pride in owning a specific version: "I'm a King James Christian," or "We're liberated! We have the NIV." Such bragging is exactly what the Jews were doing in Paul's day. They gloried in having the Torah.

Second, they boasted about their relationship to God. The Jew made it clear he had an inside track with the Almighty. You hear people talking the same way today: "God and I were talking the other day. . . ." We make it clear we have a special standing with the "Good Lord," and brag about it.

Third, the Jews knew the will of God. They had the Scriptures, they had the Ten Commandments and the knowledge of what God wanted. Many today boast about their knowledge of the Word of God, and they rest upon that fact.

Fourth, these Jews approved of what was superior—they rejected certain attitudes and actions and chose only what was regarded as morally preferable. Many, many church members do this. They take pride in saying they do not do certain things. I am amazed at how many people think God is going to be impressed by the things they do not do. "We don't dance, we don't drink, we don't go to the movies, we don't play cards, we don't drink coffee," and on and on.

Finally, the Jews were instructed in the law. Many could quote great passages of Scripture, and they took pride in that.

Now, there is nothing wrong with any of these advantages except that the Jews—and many of us today—depend on them for righteousness. We think we have a special standing with God because of them; and so did the Jews. In fact, Paul goes on to list four privileges which the Jews considered theirs because of these advantages.

First, they felt they were guides to the blind. Today we have people who are always ready to correct those around them, to set straight those unfortunates who have not yet learned anything.

Second, the Jews thought they were a light to those in the dark. Every now and then we run into people who are quite ready to dazzle us with their knowledge of the Scriptures. They know all about the antichrist, they know when Christ is coming again, they know all the elective decrees of God, they are thoroughly acquainted with the supralapsarian position of Adam before the fall, and so on. They take great pride in this knowledge.

Third, the Jews felt they were instructors of the foolish. A lady once came up to me after a service and told me a long, painful story of how she had injured her wrist in an auto accident. The doctor who took care of her in the emergency room happened to let a couple of curse words slip while working on her. She lectured him at great length about how she was a Christian, how she wouldn't listen to this kind of language, and how terrible it was that he took the name of God in vain. This attitude is typical of many who feel they are instructors of the foolish because they know the Scriptures.

The fourth privilege of the Jews was that they were teachers of children. I am amazed at how many want to teach Sunday School classes for the wrong reason. Now there is a right reason, but many want to teach simply to satisfy their own egos.

Paul's judgment of such people is, "You are guilty yourself." Paul finds in the Jew what he had condemned earlier in the moral Gentile. "You are outwardly righteous and correct, but inwardly you are doing the wrong thing." They were envious, proud, covetous, lustful, bitter, dangerous people.

Jews were notorious in the Roman Empire for being over-sharp in business deals. That is why Paul says, "You who preach against stealing, do you steal?" They were not above a little hanky-panky with the slave girls they had to deal with. Paul says, "You who say that people should not commit adultery, do you commit adultery?" They were ready to profit from trade with pagan temples. He says, "You who abhor idols, do you rob temples?" They bragged about the law, but Paul says, "God's name is blasphemed among the Gentiles because of you."

This was the ultimate judgment upon the Jews. Blasphemy was to them the worst of sins. Yet Paul says, "Though you claim to have so much and be so knowledgeable, yet what you have done is to blaspheme God. People have been turned away from God because of you." I do not think I have to detail how true that is of American Christianity. Not only in this country, but around the world, Christians have caused people to turn from God because of our attitudes and the way we approach people. Yet the people who keep close records of how many they win to Christ never seem to keep records of how many they drive away!

Resting on a Symbol

Now Paul singles out and seizes upon the supreme symbol of Jewish separatism—circumcision.

> *Circumcision has value if you observe the law, but if you break the law, you have become as though you had not been circumcised. If those who are not circumcised keep the law's requirements, will they not be regarded as though they were circumcised? The one who is not circumcised physically and yet obeys the law will condemn you who, even though you have the written code and circumcision, are a lawbreaker (2:25-27).*

The Jews, of course, prided themselves (and still do today) on the rite of circumcision, the symbol that they were God's people. You only need to substitute baptism, confirmation, or church membership to apply that to twentieth-century Protestant and Catholic Americans. So many Americans rest upon these things as the sign that they belong to God. Paul says this is useless and worthless unless something has happened in the heart.

Paul's conclusion about the religious man comes in verses 28 and 29.

> *A man is not a Jew if he is only one outwardly, nor is circumcision merely outward and physical. No, a man is a Jew if he is one inwardly; and circumcision is circumcision of the heart, by the Spirit, not by the written code. Such a man's praise is not from men, but from God.*

This last phrase is a play on words. The Hebrew word for *praise* is like the word *Judah,* from which we get the word *Jew.* Paul says the true Jew isn't praised by men but by God; and clarifies what constitutes a true Jew in God's sight.

Now this is one of the most hotly debated questions in Israel today. The Israelis are constantly trying to decide what is the basis of Jewry. What makes a Jew? Is it religion? Is it observing the Old Testament law? Keeping a kosher kitchen? Many Jews are atheists and have no use for the Old Testament. Yet they claim to be Jews because their ancestors, as far back as they know, were Jews. Is that the basis on which to claim Jewishness? There are black Jews who petitioned for a long time to belong to Israel, and some have recently been admitted. But other Jews say you have to be white to be a Jew. What makes a Jew?

Paul says nothing outward makes you a Jew. One becomes a true Jew when his heart is changed. As with Abraham and Jacob, you become a Jew when you believe in Y'shua Hamaschiach, Jesus the Messiah. The Jews for Jesus organization tells people this today. What makes you a Jew is not the culture from which you come, the ritual through which you have gone, the circumstances of your life or ancestry or history—but the fact that you have come to know the Lord Jesus Christ. This makes you a Jew. Paul wrote in Galatians 3:29, "If you belong to Christ, then you are Abraham's seed, and heirs according to the promise."

Paul's conclusion to Romans 2 is that man without Christ is hopelessly lost. He defies God, deludes himself, defiles his conscience, and denies what he himself teaches; thus he is absolutely, hopelessly lost until he comes to know the Lord Jesus and lives on the basis of that relationship. This is what makes a Christian. It isn't a question of whether you are baptized, galvanized, sanforized, or pasteurized. The question is, Do you have faith in the Lord Jesus Christ? And have you received the gift of righteousness which God gives to those who do not deserve it and cannot earn it, but receive it by his love and grace? We will see what additional problems this raises with the Jews in the next section of Romans.

6
TOTAL SHORTFALL

(Romans 3:1-20)

As we go through Romans, notice how logically and powerfully the apostle Paul develops his subject. Evidently he possessed a vivid imagination which he used skillfully to illustrate and illuminate what he wanted to say. I never fail to be delighted at how the mind of the apostle Paul works as he sets this truth out for us.

The first twenty verses of chapter 3 divide easily into two parts. The first eight verses are an imaginary dialogue the apostle holds with the Jews. The second part, verses 9 to 20, is his powerful description of mankind's condition before God.

The dialogue with the Jews grows out of the closing verses of chapter 2, in which Paul says the only thing that makes a man a Jew is faith in the Messiah. At this point Paul's vivid imagination comes into play; he sees an imaginary rabbi standing up and arguing with him. Perhaps this actually happened many times in the course of Paul's travels throughout the Roman Empire, speaking as he did in many synagogues and encountering many a knowledgeable rabbi.

Paul imagines three arguments from this Jewish objector. In our own culture, you can place any religionist in this Jew's place—a Mormon, a Christian Scientist, a Hindu, a Buddhist, a Muslim, a Baptist, a Presbyterian, a Catholic. Anyone who counts on religion will offer the same kind of argument.

The Supreme Advantage

Paul first imagines the rabbi saying, "Now, hold it! Wait a minute! These things that you say don't count are the very things God himself has given to us. Circumcision came from God and he required it of the Jews. God gave the law to the Jews, and called them his chosen people. So Paul, you're setting aside what God has established. If these things don't count, what advantage is there in being a Jew?" This question and Paul's answer are phrased in the first two verses of chapter 3.

> *What advantage, then, is there in being a Jew, or what value is there in circumcision? Much in every way! First of all, they have been entrusted with the very words of God.*

When Paul says "first of all" he does not mean first in a long list of advantages, though he did see many advantages in being a Jew. What Paul means by "first" is *supremely*, *chiefly*. The great glory in being a Jew in Paul's day was that the Jews had the law. They possessed the written Word of God. Paul says this is a tremendous advantage. Already he has shown that everyone is under law; nobody is without a moral standard. The conscience lays hold of the law written in people's hearts to tell them whether they are doing right or wrong. Light is given to everyone. No one lives in darkness.

But though everyone has light, the Jews had an additional degree. They were given the written Word on stone, permanently preserved. Thus they had knowledge of God's mind and will and character that other people didn't have. They had a greater opportunity to know and obey God than anyone else in that day. But they failed to make use of this tremendous advantage, and it did them no good at all. They were no better off than if they had never known the law because they did not put it to its intended use.

To Hunt for Needles

Imagine an island in darkness, filled with people. There is only one way to escape the island—a narrow bridge over a deep chasm—but the darkness is so great that only a few find their way across. Everyone on the island has been given a little penlight, but it dimly illuminates only a small space around them, barely enough to reveal even the most obvious obstacles in their path.

One group of islanders, however, is given a powerful searchlight that can shine thousands of yards into the darkness. They can use it not only to find their own way across the bridge, but also to show everyone else the way. Yet instead they spend their time using this powerful searchlight to look for needles in a haystack.

This, in essence, was what the Jews were doing. The rabbis were arguing constantly over infinitesimal theological differences. Jesus called this "straining at a gnat, but swallowing a camel." They argued over how many steps constituted a violation of the Sabbath and whether spitting on a rock is permissible on the Sabbath, or whether spitting on mud is a violation. One would be right, and the other wrong. This is what they used the law for. Though the Jews had a tremendous advantage in having the law, Paul says they failed to use it properly.

Now the imaginary rabbi comes back with a second objection:

> *What if some did not have faith? Will their lack of faith nullify God's faithfulness? Not at all! Let God be true, and every man a liar. As it is written: "So that you may be proved right in your words, and prevail in your judging"* (3:3-4).

The rabbi asks, "Paul, are you suggesting that if some Jews did not believe"—the rabbi is ready to admit this possibility—"then God would forget his promises to all the Jews? Are you saying that just because some of us don't measure up to what God required in the law, everyone in Israel has lost the promise God gave them? You seem to suggest that God isn't interested in the very rituals he himself instituted. Are you saying that all these things mean nothing to God? Are you saying God is so upset by the disbelief of just a few Jews that he has canceled all Israel's prerogatives?"

Paul's answer—"Not at all!"—uses the strongest negative words in the Greek language: literally, "May it never be!" or as translated in some versions, "God forbid!" To say otherwise would suggest God has failed, that he gave a promise and then did not keep it just because a few people failed to measure up. So God would be at fault. We always tend to blame God for what goes wrong in our lives, for our inability to fulfill what God demands, but Paul says, "Never let this be! Let God be true, and every man a liar." God keeps his Word no matter how men fail.

Let God Be True

Paul then quotes from Psalm 51, the second half of verse 4. When David repented of the twin sins of murder and adultery, he wrote this beautiful psalm, in which he confesses his sins to God:

> *Against thee, thee only, have I sinned, and done that which is evil in thy sight, so that thou art justified in thy sentence and blameless in thy judgment (Psalm 51:4 RSV).*

David had tried to hide his sins, refusing to admit them to God or to anyone else. He went on acting as though he were righteous, letting people think he was still the godly king of Israel. Then God sent Nathan the prophet, who speared him with his long, bony finger, and said, "Thou art the man!" David's sins were exposed; he admitted and confessed them to God. He said, "It is not you who are to blame, God; I did it." So Paul says, "Let God be true and every man a liar"—even if all Jews fail in their belief, God will still fulfill his promise.

How can God do this? God has said that some will believe. But if everyone fails to believe, how can he keep his word? Paul says, "That's your problem, not God's." When the Pharisees boasted to John the Baptist that they were children of Abraham," John said, "Don't you understand that God can raise up children of Abraham from these stones?" (see Luke 3:8). If men fail, God has unlimited resources to fulfill his promise. So there is no objection at this point. God will still fulfill his promises to the Jews (and all religionists) despite the failure of some; but that promise is based on faith, not ritual.

A third objection from the rabbi is raised in verse 5, and Paul responds in verse 6.

> *But if our unrighteousness brings out God's righteousness more clearly, what shall we say? That God is unjust in bringing his wrath on us? (I am using a human argument.) Certainly not! If that were so, how could God judge the world?*

As Paul says, this is a common argument. You still hear it today. People say, "If what we're doing makes God look good because it gives him a chance to show his love and forgiveness, how can he condemn us? We've made him look good. We've given him a chance to reveal himself, and that's what he wants. So he can't condemn us for our sins. In fact, let's sin more and make him look all the better!" They say, "If God is glorified by human sin and failure, as the Scriptures say, then let's sin all the more."

Locked into Evil

Paul's answer is to carry this argument to its logical conclusion. If everyone lived on this basis, no one could be judged and God would be removed as judge of all the world. It would demean God. God would be no better than the worst of men. He could not act as a judge if he actually arranged things so that sin would glorify himself. If God cannot judge, he is demeaned; if he does not judge, the entire world is locked into perpetual evil. There would be no way of arresting the awful force of human evil in this world. This is, therefore, a ridiculous argument.

The fact is, sin *never* glorifies God. Sin always has

evil results; it does not produce good. As the Scriptures say, "The one who sows to please his sinful nature, from that nature will reap destruction; the one who sows to please the Spirit, from the Spirit will reap eternal life" (Galatians 6:8). This is an ordained law of God which no one can break.

Paul strengthens his argument with a personal illustration in verses 7 and 8.

> *Someone might argue, "If my falsehood enhances God's truthfulness and so increases his glory, why am I still condemned as a sinner?" Why not say— as we are being slanderously reported as saying and as some claim that we say—"Let us do evil that good may result"? Their condemnation is deserved.*

The NIV text adds the words, "Someone might argue," but they do not belong here. Paul is saying that he includes himself in the circle of condemnation. He speaks of "*my* falsehood." If you look back in Romans you can see how he has narrowed this circle. In chapter 1 he talks about what "they" are like— "They are without excuse." Chapter 2 comes down to "You, O man, who judge another, you are without excuse." Then in chapter 3 it is "our unrighteousness," and finally, "my falsehood." I love this because it means that Paul does not consider himself, even as a believer, beyond the possibility of sin. He is just as capable of falsehood as anyone else. And his falsehood is subject to the condemnation of God just as anyone else's is. Paul does not hold himself up as better than others.

Paul continues, "Let's go on to say the logical thing: Let's do evil that good may come." What a ridiculous argument, he concludes. Why, that removes all difference between good and evil. This is what people are saying today. "There's no such thing as good or evil. Whatever you like is good; whatever you don't like, that's evil. The difference between good and evil is only in your mind." You see how up-to-date this argument is? Paul says it is ridiculous. The logical conclusion to such thinking is moral chaos and anarchy. No one could judge anything. We would simply plunge into an abyss of immorality in which anyone could do anything, and none would dare raise a hand in opposition. This would produce moral chaos. So, Paul says, condemning this kind of reasoning is well deserved.

In verses 9 through 20, Paul introduces and answers another question:

> *What shall we conclude then? Are we any better? Not at all! We have already made the charge that Jews and Gentiles alike are all under sin (3:9).*

I think it would be better to change the phrase "Are we any better?" to "Do we have any standing at all?" For this is what Paul is really saying. He has looked over all mankind and says, "Is there any ground by which a man or woman can please God apart from faith in Christ? Is there any way you can try to be good and make it?" His answer: None at all. No one can make it on those terms.

Already he has demonstrated the universal condition of both Jews and Gentiles. He has shown that blatantly wicked people end up defying God; therefore they cannot make it. The morally self-righteous, who pride themselves on their good conduct and clean living, simply delude themselves. So they cannot make it. Unenlightened pagans in all the jungles of the world defile their own consciences, and they don't make it because they don't live up to their own standards. The religious zealots deny in deeds what they teach in words, and so they cannot make it. They are all deficient.

Scripture Summary

Now comes the final touch in which Paul gathers up what the Scriptures say on this subject. We are living in a day when what men say is considered the final word. The Scriptures may be looked at, but are not taken as authoritative. The apostles, however, never treated Scripture this way. They listened to what men said, but when it came to final authority, they said, "What Scripture says is it!"

Paul compiles Scriptures from the Psalms, the Proverbs, and Isaiah to show that what he has described, God had already said. The content of the Scriptures he uses divides into three clear parts: first, the character of man as God sees it; then the conduct of man in both speech and action; and finally, the cause of all this.

Here is man's true character:

> *As it is written: "There is no one righteous,*
> *not even one; . . . " (3:10).*

Isn't that astounding? Surely the total depravity of the human heart is revealed by this statement. Think of all the nice people you know. They may not be Christians, but they are nice people—good neighbors, gracious people who speak lovingly and do kind things. Looking at them, God says: "There's not one among them who is righteous, not even one." (We mentally add, "Except me." Right?)

> *. . . there is no one who understands. . . .*

Think of all the people today who search to understand the mystery of life. All over the world—in temples, in universities, in nature—people are asking,

Why are we like we are? And in all that vast array of searchers, God says there is not one who understands, not even one.

> . . . *no one who seeks God (3:11).*

What a claim that is! Here are all these religious people flocking to temples and churches and places of worship around the world, going through various motions and rituals. What are they looking for? We would say they are looking for God, but God disagrees. He says no one searches for God. They are looking for *a* god, not *the* God—the God of truth and justice who created all things.

> *All have turned away*
> *they have together become worthless;*
> *There is no one who does good,*
> *not even one (3:12).*

This could hardly be clearer. No one—not one single person—does good. Do you find that hard to accept? Then imagine someone invented a camera that records thoughts. Imagine that at a Sunday morning service the camera would be scanning, picking up everything on your mind: what you thought when you sat down, what you thought when the person next to you sat down, what you were thinking during the hymn, and what you were thinking during the prayer. At the same time, the camera would be recording the thoughts of everyone else around you. Then you hear an announcement that next Sunday, instead of the regular service, a screening of the film from that camera would be presented. I wonder how many would show up? But this is the stark revelation from Scripture of what God sees when he looks at the human race. There is no one who does good, not even one.

Then he details why. First, our speech:

> *Their throats are open graves;*
> *their tongues practice deceit.*
> *The poison of vipers is on their lips.*
> *Their mouths are full of cursing and bitterness*
> *(3:13-14).*

This passage covers the whole realm of human speech. It begins down in the throat, it comes to the tongue, then the lips, and then the whole mouth. From the inward to the outward parts it moves. Deep down, Paul says, God sees an open grave with a stinking, rotten corpse and a horrible stench. Coming up from there it reveals itself, ultimately, in vulgarity and bitterness.

Do you ever wonder why children love toilet talk? Or why adults like words with double meanings? You hear them on television all the time. What is down in the heart comes out in the speech—not only vulgarity, but hypocrisy. "Their tongues practice deceit." Those little white lies, the way we erect facades, the way we claim to feel one way when we actually feel another—we think all this deceit is harmless and unnoticed. But God sees it. "The poison of vipers is on their lips." This is a picture of the tongue used to slander, to plant poison in another person's heart: the putdown, the sharp, caustic words, the sarcasm that depersonalizes and cuts off another human being. This is what is inside, and God sees it with the realism of his holy eyes.

"Their mouths are full of cursing and bitterness." If you do not believe that, just step out on the street and hit the first fellow who comes by right on the mouth and see what comes out. It will be cursing and bitterness! Cursing is blaming God; that is profanity. Bitterness is reproaching God because of the way he has run your life. This is what we hear all the time, even from Christians. We hear complaints about their circumstances, where God has placed them, and what he is doing with their life—cursing and bitterness.

Look now at the deeds that follow.

> *Their feet are swift to shed blood;*
> *ruin and misery mark their ways. . . .*

Wherever man goes, ruin follows. Do we need documentation of that today? Why do cities develop ghettos and slums? Why do our beautiful mountains and streams become polluted? It is because of the heart of man.

> *. . . ruin and misery mark their ways,*
> *and the way of peace they do not know (3:15-17).*

I have often thought this would be an appropriate slogan for the United Nations! "The way of peace they do not know." The United Nations is helpless to stop the cruel wars that continue to flare up all over the world because "the way of peace they do not know."

The cause of this follows, in just one sentence:

> *There is no fear of God before their eyes (3:18).*

That brings us right back to chapter 1, verse 18: "The wrath of God is being revealed from heaven against all the godlessness and wickedness of men." When men reject God, they lose everything.

In these verses we have a clear vision of why God gave the law. But since the Jews were so convinced that their possession of the law gave them special privileges in God's sight, Paul now returns to that subject.

Now we know that whatever the law says, it says to those who are under the law, so that every mouth may be silenced and the whole world held accountable to God. Therefore no one will be declared righteous in his sight by observing the law; rather, through the law we become conscious of sin (3:19-20).

When we read this terrible description of the human race as God sees it, it is almost impossible for us to believe that God does not say, "Enough! Wipe them out!" If all he sees is wretchedness, evil, deceit, hypocrisy, vulgarity, profanity, slander—in every heart, every one without exception— our natural instinct is to conclude that God doesn't want us. But the amazing thing is that across this kind of verse he also writes, "God so loved the world that he gave his only begotten Son." God did not send the law to destroy us (and this is very important); he sent the law to keep us from false hope.

The Wrong Road

Nothing is worse than going down a road to an important destination thinking you are on the right track, only to discover the road leads to nothingness. You find you have been on the wrong track and it is too late to go back. That was what was happening to man. So God, in his lovingkindness, has given us the law to keep us from taking a false path. Though the law condemns us, it is that very condemnation that makes us willing to listen so that we find the right path.

Paul says the law does three things to us. First, it stops our mouth. We have nothing to say. You can always tell someone is close to becoming a Christian when he shuts up and stops arguing. Self-righteous people are always arguing, "But I . . . yes, but . . . I do this . . . and I do that." Yet when they see the true meaning of the law, their mouth is shut.

A friend of mine was given a traffic ticket one day. She was guilty of doing what she was charged with, but she felt there was some justification for it. She thought she would go to court and argue it before the judge. She imagined how she would come in and the judge would ask her if she was guilty. She would say, "Yes, but I want to explain why." She would then proceed to convince the judge and all the court that what she did could hardly be avoided and that she was justified in doing it. Her argument was ready.

But that isn't what happened. "When I came into that court," she said, "and stood up there all alone, and the judge was there on the bench, dressed in his robe, and he looked over his glasses at me and said, 'Guilty or not guilty?', all my arguments died. I just said, 'Guilty.'" Her mouth was stopped. This is the first thing the law does: It silences you, and you do not argue with God anymore.

Second, Paul says, "The whole world is held accountable to God." This makes us realize that death will not suddenly dissolve all things into everlasting darkness, forever forgotten. The whole world has to stand before God. Hebrews 9:27 puts it so starkly: "Man is destined to die once, and after that to face judgment."

Finally, the law clearly reveals what sin is. What does the law want of us? Jesus said all the law is summed up in one word: love. All the law asks us to do is to act in love. All these things stated in the law are simply loving ways of acting. When we face ourselves before the law we have to confess that many, many times we fail to love. We do not love. That is what the law wants us to see. Only then, when all else fails, are we ready to listen to what follows.

Now we are ready for verse 21: "But now a righteousness from God . . . has been made known." This is what Paul wants us to hear. Now we can learn to love—not by the law, but by the provision of the Son of God.

7
BUT NOW

(Romans 3:21-31)

In the opening words of Romans 3:21 you can almost hear a sigh of relief. Now, after God's appraisal of man's efforts to achieve some standing before him, come God's words of relief, God's total answer to man's total failure:

> *But now a righteousness from God, apart from law, has been made known, to which the Law and the Prophets testify (3:21).*

This is God's great "nevertheless" in the face of man's failure. In the subsequent paragraphs, the apostle develops this in his usual reasoned and logical style. For a little guide to this section, here is the way it breaks down: In verse 21 we have God's answer to man's failure; in verses 22-24 he tells us how this gift of righteousness is obtained; verses 25 and 26 tell us how and why it works; and in verses 27-31 he gives the results that follow.

Let us look again at the beginning of this passage that is one of the greatest declarations of the gospel:

> *But now a righteousness from God, apart from law, has been made known, to which the Law and the Prophets testify.*

This is what Paul elsewhere calls "the glorious gospel of the blessed God," the good news of a gift God gives us—the righteousness of God himself. We have already seen that this word *righteousness* is greatly misunderstood. Often it is associated with behavior. If people behave in a right way, we say they are behaving righteously. But in this part of Romans, righteousness does not directly touch on behavior. It does not refer to what you do, but to what you are. The gift Paul is talking about, the gift from God, is that of a righteous standing before him.

The real meaning underlying this word is found in the word *worth*. People everywhere are looking for a sense of worth. Psychologists tell us this sense of worth is the most essential element in human activity, and that without it you cannot function. Therefore, whether we know it or describe it in these terms, we are all looking for a sense of worth. But the gospel announces that it is *given* to us. What people strive all their lives to achieve is handed to us right at the beginning when we believe in Jesus Christ. According to the gospel, we can receive it but we cannot earn it. *That* is the good news. What a wonderful thing it is!

In reading an article on some of the movements of our day, I came across these words by Dr. Lewis Smedes, a professor at Fuller Theological Seminary:

> *Anyone who can see the needs of people today must recognize that the malaise of our time is an epidemic of self-doubt and self-depreciation. Those whose job it is to heal people's spiritual problems know that the overwhelming majority of people who seek help are people who are sick from abhorring themselves. A prevailing sense of being without worth is the pervasive sickness of our age.* (from the 1973 article "God's Noble Lad" in *The Reformed Journal*)

These words come from a man who spends a great deal of time with people seeking help for emotional problems and personality difficulties. Millions of people openly acknowledge they need such help, and come looking for it. Others never ask, but behind their smiles and confident airs are insecure hearts and a consciousness of deep self-doubt. This is the basic problem of mankind.

The gospel, therefore, deals with something tremendously significant. It does not have to do only with what happens when you die. This is one of the reasons why hundreds of churches today are half-empty; so many people do not know that self-worth is what the gospel is all about. Young people today are looking for a ground of worth. They want to be loved. All of us do.

But far, far deeper than the need to feel that some human being loves us is our need to know that God loves us, and that we are acceptable in his sight, that we have standing, value, and worth to him. Something about us—that bit of eternity planted in our hearts by God himself—bears witness that this is the ultimate issue. Somehow life can never be satisfying if this issue is not settled. Therefore this good news comes with powerful relevance today. What God is offering is a gift of righteousness—his own perfect righteousness that cannot be improved upon, a perfect value. By faith in Jesus Christ he gives us a sense of worth and acceptance. There could be no better news than that.

Paul adds two points to make this clear. First, this righteousness is apart from the law. That is, it is not something you earn through obedience; it is a gift. You cannot gain it by doing your best to please God, and anyone who approaches God on such terms has already failed. There is no way anyone can measure up to God's standards. The sweetest, dearest little old lady you know cannot make it on her own, because God knows her heart.

Known from of Old

Second, Paul says, this righteousness is witnessed by "the Law and the Prophets." This gift is not something entirely new in history, something only Jesus Christ brought to light. He did make it known, so that we understand it far more clearly, but it is found in the Old Testament as well as in the New. The saints who lived before the cross knew and experienced the wonder of this gift just as much as we do today, although they came to it by a different process.

The law bore testimony to this righteous gift of God by providing a series of sacrifices. The Jews knew in their hearts that they did not measure up to God's standards. The law itself provided a system of offerings and sacrifices that could be brought and offered on the altar. This system pictured the death of

Jesus; the whole sacrificial system of the Old Testament is a witness that One is coming, the Lamb of
God who takes away the sins of the world. They bear
witness to this righteous gift.

The Old Testament prophets also—such well-
known men as Abraham, Moses, David, Isaiah,
Jeremiah, and others—not only talked about this
gift, but experienced it themselves. In Psalm 32
David says, "Blessed is he whose transgressions are
forgiven, whose sins are covered . . . whose sin the
Lord does not count against him." David understood
that God found a way to give the gift of worth to
men, even before the cross occurred in history. This
gift is not new, Paul says; nevertheless, it is clearly
explained and made fully available to us in the cross
of Jesus.

In the next division Paul tells us how to obtain this
gift. Perhaps you are looking for this sense of worth,
this sense of value, of being loved and wanted by
God. How do you get it? Here is Paul's answer.

> *This righteousness from God comes through faith
> in Jesus Christ to all who believe. There is no dif-
> ference, for all have sinned and fall short of the
> glory of God, and are justified freely by his grace
> through the redemption that came by Christ Jesus
> (3:22-24).*

There is one way—expressed here in four different
aspects, but only one way—through faith in Jesus
Christ. Notice first how Paul's answer centers immediately on the person of the Savior; not only on his
work or his teaching, but on his person. It is by faith
in Christ himself that you come into this standing.
He is the Savior; it is not what he taught, not even
what he gives, but it is *he* who saves us. Therefore the

gift involves a relationship to a living person.

This is why John's Gospel does not say, "Believe in what Jesus did," but rather, "As many as received him, to them he gave power to become the sons of God." That means there must come a time when you open your life to Christ, when you ask him to be what he offers to be: your Lord.

Later in this epistle Paul will say, "If you confess with your mouth, 'Jesus is Lord,' and believe in your heart that God raised him from the dead, you will be saved [another term for this gift of righteousness]. For it is with your heart that you believe and are justified, and it is with your mouth that you confess and are saved" (10:9-10). In the Book of Revelation Jesus himself says, "Here I am! I stand at the door and knock. If anyone hears my voice and opens the door, I will come in and eat with him, and he with me" (Revelation 3:20). There is no other way. In all the religions of earth, we find no way to bring men into a sense of value and standing in God's sight, and of worth and love before him, except this way—by faith in Jesus Christ.

The Hand That Takes the Gift

Second, Paul stresses here that it is "all who believe" who are saved; righteousness is not automatically and universally applied. Many today teach that the death of Christ was so effective that whether people hear about it or not, they are already saved. They do not even need to know about it, for they are saved by the death of Jesus. But Paul is careful to explain that this is not true. You are saved when you *personally* believe. Faith, therefore, is the hand that takes this gift God offers. What good is a gift if you do not take it? Only then does it become your property.

The third element that describes how we obtain this gift is in the phrase, "Justified freely by his grace." Do you see what that says? It is God who does this. If you try to say there is anything man must do to be justified, you will destroy the gift, because it is all of God. We are justified, made righteous, declared of worth in God's sight, by his grace. If you add baptism to that, or church membership, or anything else, then you destroy the grace of God. It is God who freely and completely and wholly saves us. We do not contribute a thing. Have you ever sung the hymn, "Nothing in my hand I bring; simply to Thy cross I cling"? That is one beautiful way of expressing it.

The last word in this section is this: The gift comes "through the redemption that came by Christ Jesus." That is, Christ is the one who accomplished the work of redemption. Here we are brought face-to-face with the cross, with the death of Jesus. Many churches are given over to following the teachings of Jesus but hardly ever refer to his cross. If you find a "Christianity" that does not emphasize the cross, you are listening to "another gospel" which is not the true gospel. The real gospel is based only upon the redemption which Jesus accomplished in his cross.

Paul now gives a brief explanation of how and why this redemption works. "How" is found in the opening words of verse 25, and "why" in the verses that follow.

> God presented him as a sacrifice of atonement, through faith in his blood. He did this to demonstrate his justice, because in his forbearance he had left the sins committed beforehand unpunished—he did it to demonstrate his justice at the present time, so as to be just and the one who justifies the man who has faith in Jesus (3:25-26).

This is the heart of the gospel, and the ground of assurance. Many people, even though they become Christians, struggle with assurance. They do not rest upon the fact that these words are true, so they often struggle with doubts and uncertainty. They have a sneaking suspicion, deep inside, that perhaps, despite all these wonderful words, God is still not quite satisfied; if something should happen to them, they might be lost. Pay careful attention to Paul's argument here. He gives a full answer to that struggle.

First, he says that God has accomplished a propitiatory sacrifice. God presented Jesus as a "sacrifice of atonement" through faith in his blood. "Sacrifice of atonement" is translated "expiation" in some versions and "propitiation" in others. I know those words are theological terms, and may not make much sense; but it is important for us to understand their meaning, for herein lies the heart of the gospel.

To Release Love

Expiation satisfies justice; propitiation releases love. Both of these terms are involved in the death of Jesus, but expiation does not go quite as far as propitiation. Propitiation carries us clear through to the releasing of God's love toward us. That is why I think "propitiatory sacrifice" is a better translation than "expiation." Let me illustrate the difference.

In these days we often read of industrial accidents. Let us say that someone has been injured in the course of his work and has been partially paralyzed. His company is at fault, having neglected to provide safety equipment, thus creating the conditions that put this man in danger. So the company is held accountable for the man's injury and subsequent paralysis. Therefore the court awards this man a tremendous sum of money, to be paid by the company.

When the money is paid, the company has expiated its wrongdoings; it has satisfied the demands of justice. No longer does it have any responsibility toward this man; it has paid its costly debt. This is what expiation means.

But how does the man feel toward the company? He may yet be filled with resentment, bitterness, even hatred. He may spend the rest of his life abhorring that company's name, even though it has given him all the money he could possibly use. The debt has been expiated, but he has not been propitiated.

What Paul is saying here is that human sin has injured God, just as the employee was injured by the negligence of the company. Our sin has hurt and injured God, and justice demands that we be punished for that sin. In the death of Jesus this punishment was accomplished so that God's justice was satisfied. If you read this as expiation, that is all the cross means. In a way, it means that God was paid off, so that he no longer holds us to blame. But that is not all Paul is saying here. The word means also that God's love has been awakened toward us; he reaches out to love us, and grants us the feeling of worth, acceptance, and value in his sight. This is what propitiation means, and it is what the death of Jesus does. It satisfied God's justice, but it went further; it released his love, and now he is ready to pour out love upon us.

Paul shows us *why* this had to happen, beginning in the middle of verse 25: "He did this to demonstrate his justice, because in his forbearance he had left the sins committed beforehand unpunished." What is he talking about? He is referring to all the centuries when God apparently had done nothing about the wrongdoings of men. People are still questioning this today. They say, "Where is the God of

justice? How is it that a just God lets tyrants rise up
and murder millions of people? How can he let
people live in poverty and squalor and filth? He never
seems to do anything about oppressors. Where is the
justice of God?" These questions have been raised for
centuries; we even find them in the Psalms.

The last time in history that mankind got a clear
idea of God's holy justice was in the Flood. Responding to the wickedness of men toward other men, God
wiped out the whole human race except for eight
people. The Flood was a testimony to God's sense of
justice, but there has never been a demonstration of
it to that degree since. So these thoughts arise: "God
doesn't really care. It doesn't matter whether you do
wrong or not, God will let you get away with it. God
won't do anything to you." David writes, "Why do
the wicked flourish, and the righteous suffer? Where
is the God of justice?" God has been patiently re-
straining his hand in order that the human race may
continue, but people do not see that. Therefore the
justice of God seems compromised by his self-
restraint.

No Compromise

But the cross settles that. The cross says that God
remains just. All the stored-up punishment we
amply deserve is now poured out without restraint
upon the head of Jesus on the cross. God did not spare
his Son one iota of the wrath that we deserve. Though
Jesus was his beloved Son he did not lessen the
punishment a single degree. All of it was poured out
on him. That explains the cry of abandonment that
comes from the cross, "My God, my God, why hast
thou forsaken me?"

In the Garden of Gethsemane, Jesus faced the possibility of being shut away from all love, all beauty,

all truth, all warmth, all acceptance, the possibility of being forever denied all that makes life beautiful. There he faced an eternity of emptiness in the judgment of God, and this is what he experienced on the cross; it was all poured out on him.

Paul's argument is that God did this to demonstrate his justice—so as to be just, and yet free to extend love to us who deserve only his justice. This is the glory of the gospel. God's love has been freed to act toward us, and his justice satisfied, so that he is not compromised when he forgives sinners.

In the closing paragraph, Paul gives us the results of this forgiveness:

> *Where, then, is boasting? It is excluded. On what principle? On that of observing the law? No, but on that of faith. For we maintain that a man is justified by faith apart from observing the law. Is God the God of Jews only? Is he not the God of Gentiles too? Yes, of Gentiles too, since there is only one God, who will justify the circumcised by faith and the uncircumcised through that same faith. Do we, then, nullify the law by this faith? Not at all! Rather, we uphold the law (3:27-31).*

Paul raises and answers three simple questions to show the natural results of the acceptance God gives us in Jesus Christ. First, who can boast? No one, absolutely no one. How can we boast when everyone receives the gift of grace undeservedly? All ground for self-righteousness is wiped out. This is why the ugliest sin among Christians is self-righteousness. When we look down on people who are involved in homosexuality, or greed, or gambling, or whatever—when we begin to think we are better than they are—then we have denied what God has done

for us. All boasting is excluded. There are no grounds
for anyone to say, "Well, at least I didn't do this, or
this, or that." The only ground of acceptance is the
gift of grace.

Second, no one is excluded from grace, Jew or
Gentile. No special privilege or favor counts in God's
sight. He has no "most-favored nation"; all are alike
before him. Paul argues, "Is God the God of Jews
only? Then there must be two Gods—one for the
Jews and one for the Gentiles. But that cannot be;
there is only one God; God is one." Therefore he is
equally the God of the Gentiles and the God of the
Jews, because both must come on exactly the same
ground. This is the wonderful thing about the gospel. All mankind is leveled; no one can stand on any
other basis than the work of Jesus Christ on his behalf.

Paul's third question is, "Does this cancel out the
law or set it aside? Do we no longer need the law?"
His answer is no; the gospel fulfills the law. The
righteousness which the law demands is the very
righteousness given to us in Christ. So if we have it as
a gift we no longer need to fear the law—because the
demands of the law are met. But it is not something
we can take any credit for; indeed, whenever we act
in unrighteousness after this, the law comes in again
to do its work of showing us what is wrong. This is
all the law is good for: It shows us what is wrong, and
immediately all the hurt and injury accomplished by
our sin must be relieved by the grace and forgiveness
of God.

God's forgiveness is not something we receive only
once, but again and again. It is the basis on which we
live, constantly taking fresh forgiveness from the
hand of God. John's letter puts it this way: "If we

confess our sins, he is faithful and just, and will forgive our sins and cleanse us from all unrighteousness" (1 John 1:9 RSV). This is God's gift, and we need always to take it afresh from the hand of God.

When we find ourselves slipping into self-righteousness, when we find ourselves looking down our noses, when we find ourselves filled with pride and acting in arrogance, being critical, callused, caustic, and sarcastic toward one another, or feeling bitter and resentful—and we are still capable of all these things—our relationship to a holy God demands that we immediately acknowledge our sin. We can come back, and God's love is still there. He still accepts us and highly values us. We are his dearly loved children, and his love never changes.

This is what God's gift of righteousness means. It is wonderful news indeed, that we never need fear the condemnation of God. The God of ultimate holiness, the God who lives in holy light, whom we cannot begin to approach, has accepted us in the Beloved, and we stand on the same ground of worth that he himself does. We can remind ourselves, as I seek to do every day, of three things:

1. I am made in God's image; therefore I am able to act beyond the capacity of any animal on earth. I am not an animal; I am a man made in God's image.

2. I am possessed of God's Spirit. I am forgiven, I am freed, and I am filled.

3. I am part of God's plan. I am part of the working out of his purposes in the world today, and God will make everything I do fit into his plan.

Because these things are true, I can go on with purpose, with confidence, and with love. I can go on without guilt or fear or any sense of inadequacy. I have perfect freedom to concern myself with the

problems around me, and not be consumed by the
ones inside, which are all taken care of. That is truly
wonderful freedom!

8
THE FATHER
OF FAITH

(Romans 4:1-12)

In chapter 4 of Romans, Paul uses Abraham to illustrate a man who found the fantastic gift of righteousness, this gift of worth and acceptance and significance before God. Abraham is one of the great names of history. Few names are as well-known and honored throughout the world as Abraham's, which is revered by three faiths—Judaism, Islam, and Christianity. Here is a man who, by any reckoning, stands head and shoulders above most of humanity. Paul uses Abraham as an example especially for the Jewish readers of his letter.

In the first twelve verses of chapter 4 Paul discusses three important questions about Abraham: How was

Abraham made righteous? When was Abraham made righteous? And why was Abraham made righteous? Paul introduces the first question in verses 1- 3:

> *What then shall we say that Abraham, our forefather, discovered in this matter {that is, in regard to being acceptable before God}? If, in fact, Abraham was justified by works, he had something to boast about—but not before God. What does the Scripture say? "Abraham believed God, and it was credited to him as righteousness" (4:1-3).*

Paul says Abraham discovered two ways to gain a sense of worth. One, Paul suggests, is by works. Abraham was a man of good works. When God appeared to him and spoke to him, Abraham believed God, responded to his call, and set out on a march without a map. He trusted God to lead him to a land he had never seen, to take care of his family, and to lead them into a place that would fulfill the promises of God. So Abraham appears in Scripture as a man of great works.

Something to Boast About

But Paul says, "If in fact Abraham was justified (that is, made righteous) by works, he had something to boast about." Abraham discovered early in his life one way of gaining a sense of significance, importance, or self-respect: performance. If you can perform well you will be highly regarded and appreciated. You will have a feeling of self-respect, and you will be able to function on that basis. If Abraham was righteous because of works, he had something to boast about. If we can look at the record and show people what we have done and why we ought to be appreciated—it helps! We may not boast openly, but we all have subtle ways and clever tricks of getting it out into the open so people can see what we have done. We drop a hint, hoping that people will ask more about it. Somehow we manage things so that people will know we are significant. This is the way the world is today, and the way it was in Abraham's day.

"But," says Paul, "it doesn't work that way in God's eyes." God is never impressed by outward performance. God sees the heart. He knows the selfishness, the greed, the grasping, the self-centeredness, the ruthlessness behind our actions. He sees all the maneuvering and manipulating, the clever arranging that goes on in our lives and in our hearts.

For the purposes of God, then, that outwardly beautiful performance is utterly invalid, worthless. This is why the sense of righteousness resulting from our performance before men never lasts. It is but a temporary shot in the arm that we need to recover again and again, almost as though we were addicts. But it always lets us down in the hour of crisis. Only the righteousness that comes from God is lasting and will work—not only in time, but for eternity. This is what Abraham discovered: righteousness which comes from performance is worthless.

How did he discover this? Paul says, "What does the Scripture say?" He refers to the fifteenth chapter of Genesis, where God appeared to Abraham. He took him out one night and showed him the stars in the heavens. "Abraham, look up!" Abraham looked up into the stillness of that oriental night, with the stars blazing in all their glory. God said to him, "Even if you can number those stars, you cannot number your descendants. Their number will be far more than all the stars of heaven" (see Genesis 15:5). And, Paul says, "Abraham believed God, and it was reckoned to him as righteousness"—self worth, standing before God, acceptance, a sense of love and value in the sight of God was his, by faith!

Fill in the Blanks

When Scripture says "Abraham believed God," we have to be careful. These Old Testament accounts are highly condensed. They do not give us the details; we have to fill them in from elsewhere in Scripture, and often we need to use a bit of sanctified imagination, guided by what the passage gives us. From other passages we know that God did not just say, "Abraham, see the stars? So shall your seed be." But we learn that God explained to Abraham what he meant by "seed."

In the letter to the Galatians Paul tells us that God made it clear to Abraham that when God said, "so shall your seed be," he was talking about Jesus Christ, who would be the seed of Abraham. God evidently explained to Abraham that there was One coming who would fulfill all the promises and that Abraham would have a heavenly seed as well as the earthly seed of his physical descendants. With regard to his spiritual descendants God said his seed would be Jesus. It is through Jesus that all Abraham's heavenly seed would come.

When the Pharisees once said to Jesus, "Abraham is our father," he said to them, "Your father Abraham rejoiced at the thought of seeing my day: he saw it and was glad" (John 8:39,56). God evidently explained to Abraham—and Abraham understood by faith—that the seed of righteousness, Jesus the Lord, was coming. He would die on the cross to remove the penalty and guilt of man's sin and to settle the question of the justice of God. He would rise again from the dead as the living Lord to give his life to men and women everywhere, fulfilling the promise to Abraham. And Abraham believed God. He believed God's promise about the seed, and so he was justified, made righteous, given the gift of worth.

Interestingly enough, when James quotes this passage from Genesis 15 he says (in James 2:23), "Abraham believed God, and it was credited to him as righteousness," then he adds, "and he was called God's friend." That is acceptance, isn't it? Abraham became God's friend—not because he behaved so well, or because he was a godly man and obeyed God—but because he believed God's promise about the seed. Abraham is a beautiful example of what Paul is talking about here in Romans. Paul illustrates this in verses 4 and 5:

> *Now when a man works, his wages are not credited to him as a gift, but as an obligation. However, to the man who does not work but trusts God who justifies the wicked, his faith is credited {or reckoned} as righteousness (4:4-5).*

Here is an illustration taken from common life, and it is very up-to-date. There is a tantalizing regulation in the income tax law that awakens my cupidity every year. The rule says that if money is given to you as a gift, it is not taxable. I keep looking for ways that will make it appear to the IRS that all the money I receive from my various functions as a pastor is really a gift. But the IRS will never buy it. They insist that if you work then what you are given isn't a gift, but wages, and must be reported.

This is exactly the argument Paul uses. If you work for something, then what you get is never a gift, it is what you have earned. You have it as a result of your labor; it is an obligation that must be paid. Therefore

you can take credit for having earned it. But then
Paul draws a conclusion in verse 5: "However, to the
man who does not work but trusts God who justifies
the wicked, his faith is credited as righteousness." He
is reckoned righteous—not because he earned it, but
as a gift. Who is Paul talking about? From the context it is clearly Abraham. This could read: "However, to this man Abraham, who does not work, but
trusts God who justifies the wicked (the ungodly),
his faith is credited to him as righteousness—worth,
acceptance, standing, and love from God."

This is an amazing declaration of the gospel! It is
startling to think of Abraham as a wicked man, but
he was. Anyone who tries to earn acceptance, to earn
God's love, to earn respect and standing before God
by trying hard to do things for him, is a wicked person. That is what the Scriptures say. He is trying to
gain something by his own merit that can never be
gained that way. Therefore it is the height of wickedness.

Many, many Christians fall into this trap. Having
once accepted Christ and believed on him for their
eternal destiny, they spend the rest of their lives trying to gain a sense of God's approval and love through
hard, exhausting, committed, dedicated labor. But
you can never win God's love that way. You can never
do enough. You cannot earn the gift of love—but it
is yours if you take it by faith in Christ, fresh every
morning. That is what Abraham did.

In the Midst of Evil

Paul now brings in another illustration from the
Old Testament to confirm this. He says David expressed the same idea when he spoke of the blessedness of the man to whom God credited righteousness

apart from works. Paul says David is another who
gained this wonderful gift of righteousness—not by
his performance, but by his faith. In verses 7 and 8
Paul quotes David's words in Psalm 32:1-2.

> *"Blessed are they*
> > *whose transgressions are forgiven,*
> > *whose sins are covered.*
> *Blessed is the man*
> > *whose sin the Lord will never*
> > *count against him."*

The remarkable thing is that David found this gift
of self-worth before God when he was tortured by a
guilty conscience. His hands were red with the blood
of Uriah the Hittite and he was troubled with a
wrong spirit that had plunged him into deep evil as
the king of Israel.

Paul thus points outs that Abraham failed to find
righteousness by being devout and moral; he found it
when he believed in Jesus, the seed. He was called
the friend of God, not because he was such an obe-
dient servant, but because he believed in what God
said. And the bloody-handed, lustful king, David,
failed to find righteousness by being the king of Israel. In the midst of his evil he found it in Christ
when he believed God; he believed that God did not
require the sacrifice of animals, but a broken spirit
that trusted in what God had to say about the great
sacrifice that was yet to come. Thus David is called "a
man after God's own heart."

Now, would you like to be a friend of God, a man
or a woman after God's own heart? There is a way—
not by your performance, but by your trust in Jesus'
life and death and what that means for you every day.

The apostle moves on to take up *when* this happens:

Is this blessedness only for the circumcised, or also for the uncircumcised? We have been saying that Abraham's faith was credited to him as righteousness. Under what circumstances was it credited? Was it after he was circumcised, or before? It was not after, but before! And he received the sign of circumcision a seal of the righteousness that he had by faith while he was still uncircumcised (4:9-11a).

Many today are embarrassed by the Bible's emphasis upon circumcision (which removes the foreskin around the male organ). Their upbringing has taught these people that sex is dirty, and that our sexual organs are never to be discussed or mentioned. They apparently think bodies end at the waist! That, of course, represents a twisted view of human sexuality. God frequently discusses circumcision. He chose it as the symbol of this marvelous truth we are talking about, and he gave it to the Jews for a specific purpose. God is not in the least embarrassed by it, and I don't think we should be either. If we will think through this whole matter of circumcision we will gain some powerful insights into human life.

No Saving Value

Paul makes two points here. First, Abraham was circumcised fourteen years after he was pronounced righteous by faith, fourteen years after he was called "the friend of God." Therefore the ritual of circumcision cannot have any saving value whatsoever. Abraham was already God's friend fourteen years before he was circumcised. You can see how effectively that wipes out the arguments of the Jews from Paul's day on, who claim that circumcision is what makes you acceptable. This, of course, also cancels out the modern equivalent of circumcision, baptism. People are justified—made righteous, accepted in God's sight—not by being baptized, but by faith in the Lord Jesus, in his work and in his death.

I will never forget a young man who came into my study one day, Bible in hand, and announced that he had been reading the book of Genesis. He didn't know a lot about it, but he startled me by asking, "Would you circumcise me?" I blinked three or four times, then asked, "Why?" He said, "I've been reading in this Bible that if you want to know God you have to be circumcised. I want to know God, so I want to be circumcised." I patiently explained to him what circumcision meant, that it was simply a sign of something that was already true by faith. That boy became a Christian and is still growing in the Lord. As Paul made clear, it is not circumcision which saves, but faith in Christ.

The second point Paul makes is that not only does ritual have no value in saving anyone, but that the real purpose of circumcision was twofold: It is a *sign* and a *seal*. I do not want to offend anyone, but I want to point out how important God thinks this is. God personally chose the place on a man's body where this sign, this rite of circumcision, would be placed. God chose to put it on the male sex organ, and a little thought will tell us why. God wants men to remember what this ritual stands for. The most important thing you will ever know is where love, self-acceptance, standing, and significance before God is to be found. So God placed this sign—out of all the parts of the body he could have chosen—on this organ, because a man must handle it several times a day. It is a sign, therefore, impossible to overlook.

Furthermore, Paul says, it is not only a sign, but a seal. A seal is a guarantee of permanence. Once again, the rite of circumcision is an unchangeable act. Once it is done it cannot be undone. Therefore it is a guarantee of the continuity of this great truth. It is God's way of saying with visible force, "This is the ground of your life, the secret of your functioning as a human being, this great truth of acceptance before me. It will never change." Of course we no longer observe the physical sign of circumcision today (except for health reasons) but now it is "the circumcision of the heart" which applies to both male and female.

To Make Him Father

In verse 11 and 12 Paul explains *why* Abraham was made righteous. Beyond the personal salvation of Abraham himself, God had another reason.

So then, he is the father of all who believe but have not been circumcised, in order that righteousness might be credited to them. And he is also the father of the circumcised who not only are circumcised but who also walk in the footsteps of the faith that our father Abraham had before he was circumcised (4:11b-12).

The opening words in this passage should really be, "It was to make him a father of all who believe." Paul isn't saying that circumcision made Abraham a father; he is talking about what circumcision stands for, the gift of being made acceptable before God, being loved by God, a gift of worth from God. This was given to Abraham, not only for his own personal salvation, but to make him a father of many more yet to come. Remember the stars in the heavens? That promise was yet to be fulfilled.

Perhaps you are not a physical descendant of Abraham. I happen to be. I learned several years ago from the genealogist of the Stedman tribe that the Stedmans go back to Abraham—through Ishmael!

That makes me a physical descendant—but I am not boasting of that. We all are spiritual sons and daughters of Abraham when we have received worth and self-respect by believing, as Abraham did, that God meant what he said. He gives us this gift in Jesus Christ, quite apart from any merit of ours. Thus we become sons of Abraham, by faith, and he is thus the father of all who believe.

Jesus illustrated this use of the word *father* when he said to the Pharisees of his day, "You belong to your father, the devil" (John 8:44). Now, Jesus did not mean that in some way the devil had been involved in their conception. What he meant is that they were following the philosophy of the devil. They were agreeing with and controlled by the philosophy of the devil; so they were sons and daughters of the devil.

Likewise, we think and act like Abraham when we trust that God accepts us because of what Jesus is and has done for us, and not because of anything we do. In this way Abraham is our father and we are his spiritual descendants. Paul says this is true for those who are uncircumcised, and yet who keep on believing in Jesus; and it is true of the circumcised (the Jews) who also walk in the footsteps of the faith of Abraham. So Jews are not saved by being circumcised; they are saved by trusting God.

This is the great secret of life. What a change this makes in our motivation if we know that we do not have to earn God's love, God's favor, God's forgiveness. *It is already ours!* We do not have to earn it, it is ours every day. Nothing I know will set us more free than that. We do not need to take our sense of worth from other people. We do not need to maneuver and manipulate and cleverly show ourselves as people of some significance. We are set free from that. We already have the only standing that ever counts—our standing before God. So we can relax and love people without demanding anything back. That is what Christianity is all about.

9
THE FAITH OF
OUR FATHER

(Romans 4:13-25)

Faith is a simple thing, but sometimes it's hard to comprehend. Many are confused on the subject. Some think faith is nothing but mental assent to a truth—that if you believe a thing is true, then you are exercising faith. But faith is more than simply believing something is true.

Others believe faith is a feeling, a feeling of confidence. If you have confidence, you have much faith; if you do not have confidence, then you have little or no faith. Your faith depends upon how much feeling you can muster. But this is not true faith, and such a definition deceives many people.

Some think faith is actually a type of self-deception.

Mark Twain said that faith is believing what you know to be untrue. There are people who actually try to believe something they know is false. And they talk themselves into believing it and call that faith.

If you really want to know what faith is, you have to see it in action. That is why Paul, in Romans 4, brings in Abraham, the man of faith. Abraham is by no means the only man who has faith, but he is preeminently qualified as a man of faith. By looking at Abraham you can learn what faith is. In the first part of the chapter we looked at the *righteousness* of Abraham. Now we are going to look at the *faith* of Abraham.

The apostle points out four things about the faith of Abraham. First, we will look at the opposite of faith—what faith is not. Sometimes the best way to learn what a thing is, is to learn what it is not. Second, we will look at the effects of faith—what faith does, what it accomplishes. Then we will look at what faith actually is—the nature of faith. Last, we will consider the beneficiaries of faith, or those whom faith helps.

The Worthless Promise

Let us begin with what faith is not.

> It was not through law that Abraham and his offspring received the promise that he would be heir of the world, but through the righteousness that comes by faith. For if those who live by law are heirs, faith has no value and the promise is worthless, because law brings wrath. And where there is no law there is no transgression (4:13-15).

Here Paul tells us that faith is not trying to obey and fulfill some kind of law. It is not doing our best to try to live up to some standard. That is the law, and no matter what the law is or where it came from, trying our best to live up to it is not faith. In that case, Paul points out, we are not living by faith, we are living by works. It is not faith to expect God to accept and love us simply because we have tried our best to obey some standard. In fact, if we live on those terms, we will find that we cannot receive what God wants to give us. Abraham is proof that this method will never bring the gift of righteousness. If we think God is going to accept, love, and forgive us because we have tried hard to do what we think is right, we are on the wrong track. It will never work, and Paul tells us why.

First, notice that Abraham received the gift, the promise of righteousness, long before the law was given. "It was not through the law," Paul says, "that Abraham and his offspring received the promise." In fact, if we look at Galatians 3:17-18, we find that Abraham received the gift of righteousness 430 years before the law was given. So righteousness did not come by the law. That is clear.

Second, the law renders the promise worthless. "For if those who live by the law are heirs [of the promise], faith has no value and the promise is worthless." It is important to understand that. Suppose someone says to you, "If you will get up off that chair and start flying around the room, I will give you a thousand dollars." You would have to say, "Forget it! No one can fly by their natural abilities. You are asking of me something that I cannot do."

What does the law require of man? Basically, it requires something we cannot do. It asks us to love. This is all the law asks us: to love God with all our heart, strength, and mind, and our neighbor as ourselves. This is all the Ten Commandments ask, that I act in love all the time, without fail. Simple, isn't it? Jesus said love is the fulfillment of the law. When I love people, I do what the law demands. Don't say that by not being angry with them or not hurting them I am loving them. Love is a positive thing. Love is reaching out, and the law requires that I reach out in love.

If I cannot do this, the promise that comes with the law is useless. The promise is: "Do this and live." If I obey the law, God will accept me as righteous. Worth, value, and approval will be given to me because I earned them by doing what the law demanded. But if I cannot, then the promise is worthless. We cannot love everybody, and we do not. We cannot love God as we ought. It is not only that we will not, but we cannot. Therefore the law is worthless in obtaining the promise.

But Paul does not stop there. He gives another reason why you will never be able to gain righteousness by trying to meet the requirements of the law: The law brings wrath. It actually punishes you if you do not measure up. This is what we find in experience; the law brings wrath. Wrath, as we saw in Romans 1, is God's removal of all divine protection and restraints so that we are free to do what we want and have our own way. C. S. Lewis wisely said that the whole world consists of just two kinds of people: those who say to God, "Thy will be done" and those to whom God is saying, "Thy will be done."

When God removes the restraints we begin to fall apart. Wrath always results in the disintegration of the human personality. Emptiness, meaninglessness, loneliness, and worthlessness possess us because we feel abandoned and lost. We do not know where to turn, and despair and depression press down on us heavily. This always happens when wrath comes in. The law brings wrath. Thus, when we seek to live by law we suffer human disorientation (wrath) as a result.

Paul amplifies this by saying, "Where there is no law, there is no transgression." Where there is no law, people do not deliberately disobey God; they disobey in ignorance. They still die, they simply don't know *why*. There are many people today who fall into this category. I find young people who are living in immorality, living together without marriage, in all innocence of any transgression. I believe that many of them actually have no idea there is anything damaging or destructive or wrong about this. Some really think their action is not hurting them or anyone else.

This attitude is widespread in our day. What these people lack is light. They have not yet learned that what they are doing only disintegrates their personality. They do not see that it destroys them in many subtle and certain ways, and that ultimately it will lead them into death and hell. What Paul means when he says, "Where there is no law, there is no transgression," is that death and hell are taking their toll whether they know it or not. He will expand this idea in chapter 5, for there he says that sin reigned from Adam to Moses, even over those who had not yet transgressed (according to Adam's transgression). By this he means they were acting in ignorance, and yet they were falling apart.

When the law comes in, it makes me aware of what is wrong. In one sense, that only makes it worse, because then I may deliberately begin to disobey what God says, and that will bring more wrath. But the law also brings hope, because when things get bad enough we are ready to turn to what can deliver: faith in the work of Jesus Christ. This is why the law will never bring us righteousness. Sincere, dedicated attempts to obey the law are not faith. Abraham is proof of that.

Fulfilled by Faith

Next, let us look at verses 16 and 17, which tell us what faith does:

> *Therefore, the promise comes by faith, so that it may be by grace and may be guaranteed to all Abraham's offspring—not only to those who are of the law but*

*also to those who are of the faith of Abraham. He is
the father of us all. As it is written: "I have made
you a father of many nations" (4:16-17).*

Here is faith in action. If law cannot achieve righteousness, what does faith do? First, the promise comes
by faith. We actually obtain what we desire, this sense
of being approved and loved and wanted and accepted
before God himself. We are a part of his family and we
are forgiven of all the past. All this is achieved by faith,
not by seeking to earn it. The promise comes by faith.
What works could not do, faith does.

The promise includes not only personal self-worth
before God, which Abraham achieved, but it also
makes one the heir of all the world. The apostle says,
"All things are yours . . . and you are of Christ, and
Christ is of God" (1 Corinthians 3:21,23). The promise
also says you will be indwelt, as Abraham was, with the
Holy Spirit of God. Galatians 3 makes clear that
Abraham received this promise by faith; we receive it
the same way Abraham did. So faith obtains the promise.

The second thing faith does is to introduce the principle of *grace.* Law and grace are opposed to one another
in certain ways. They do not cancel each other out; they
simply do two different things. We need both; we need
law and we need grace. Do not ever say, "I am under
grace, therefore I have no need for law." The Bible
never takes that position. It is law that helps me come
to grace, and without it I never would come. But law
and grace do not have the same functions. It is grace
that guarantees the promise.

Now what is grace? There are many ways to define
it. I love this one:

God's Riches At Christ's Expense

It is enrichment we don't deserve. It is all the richness of life—love, joy, peace, and the fulfillment of the heart's longing—given to us as a gift. There is an old hymn that puts it well:

> *"Do this and live!" the law demands, But gives me neither feet nor hands. A better word his grace doth bring. It bids me fly, but gives me wings.*

The law condemns; grace enables. If you and I had to earn our standing before God—not only at the beginning of our Christian life, but every day throughout—we would certainly fail somewhere along the line. If it depended upon us, somewhere we would blow it and lose the whole thing. But if it comes by grace, if it is purely a gift, and does not depend upon us at all but upon God alone, then it is guaranteed to all Abraham's offspring. So faith brings in the principle of grace which guarantees the promise to all who believe.

Now we come to the heart of the passage in verses 17 through 20. We are ready to consider what faith actually is.

> *He {Abraham} is our father in the sight of God, in whom he believed—the God who gives life to the dead and calls things that are not as though they were. Against all hope, Abraham in hope believed and so became the father of many nations, just as it had been said to him, "So shall your offspring be." Without weakening in his faith, he faced the fact that his body was as good as dead—since he was about a hundred years old—and that Sarah's womb was also dead. Yet he did not waver through unbelief regarding the promise of God. . . . (4:17-20).*

Paul gives us three things that tell us what faith is. The key, he says, is the *object* of faith. Next, he shows us the *obstacles* to faith. And then he tells us the *objectives* of faith—where faith will bring us.

The Quality of Our Faith

Abraham, Paul says, believed God. God was the object of his faith. The quality of our faith depends upon the object in which we have trusted. The amount of faith I have has nothing to do with it. This is why Jesus told us that even if we have only a little faith, like a grain of mustard seed, it will work. The object of our faith is the important thing.

I may leave for work tomorrow and go out to the driveway with the utmost faith that when I get into my car and drive into the street my car will work just as it was working today. But it may be that while it was parked someone took off the hubcaps and removed the lug bolts from the front wheels and then put the hubcaps back on so I cannot see any difference. That may have happened. And though I have the utmost confidence that my car is going to work properly, when I get onto the street and turn the corner, sooner or later the front wheels are going to fall off. I might end up dead—killed by faith!

On the other hand, I may have become worried a bit by what I have just said, and perhaps I go out to my car and take off the hubcaps and examine the lug bolts to make sure they are there. And even then I may not be too confident; I may start my car and drive it rather timidly down the driveway, still thinking that something might go wrong. But if no one has tampered with it I am perfectly safe—even though I have little faith—because the *object* of my faith is strong. This is why we should not talk about our faith; we should talk instead about the God in whom our faith is fixed. This is what Abraham looked at. It is not a question of how little or how big our faith is; it is a question of how big our God is! What kind of a God is he?

Two things about this God helped Abraham tremendously. First, he is the God who gives life to the dead—the God who makes dead things live, the God who brings to life again things that once were alive, vibrant, full of life, but which have died and become hopeless. Second, he is the God who "calls things that are not, as though they were." He calls into existence things that do not exist. He is a creative God. The book of Genesis records how God said, "Let there be . . . " and there was. Over and over, for a week, God said, "Let there be . . . " and there was. After six days he rested. This is the kind of God Abraham had—the God who gave life to the dead and who called into existence things that did not exist. In this God he fixed his faith. Abraham's faith worked because the object of his faith was capable of doing whatever he said.

Obstacles

Now let us look at the obstacles to faith. Whenever we are called to exercise faith, there will be obstacles. Abraham teaches us this. There are horrendous obstacles, and Abraham faced two of them. First, there were hopeless circumstances. "Against all hope, Abraham in hope believed. . . . " It also says in verse 20, "Yet he did not waver [or stagger] through unbelief regarding the promise of God. . . . " That is, the promise itself was the second obstacle to faith because it had such staggering possibilities. It was too good to be true! That God would make him heir of all the world and give him a standing before God that he did not deserve was beyond belief. It was too good to be true, so that was an obstacle to faith. Isn't that interesting? There are two obstacles to faith: hopeless circumstances and staggering possibilities. Let us see what Abraham did with them.

What were the hopeless circumstances Abraham faced? Paul tells us there were two: Abraham's body and Sarah's womb. Abraham's body was a hundred years old and was sexually dead. The promise of God hung on the fact that there must be a child born to Abraham and Sarah. Through that child all the nations of the world would be blessed by Abraham. And, more important yet, through that child would come the Seed, Jesus Christ, whom Abraham saw and rejoiced in and who would make possible the gift of righteousness. Everything hung on the birth of a baby. Abraham looked at the circumstances and saw his hundred-year-old body and the barrenness of Sarah's womb. She was ninety years old and had never had a baby. They had been trying for years and years and no baby had come. These were the hopeless circumstances.

Now, here is the beauty of Abraham's faith: He faced the facts. I love that. Paul says, "Without weakening in his faith, he faced the fact. . . . " Many of us think faith is evading the facts—escapism, some kind of dreamy idealism that never looks at facts, a kind of unrealistic adventuring in which you hope everything is going to work out. It is never that! Abraham looked at the facts—his dead body and the barrenness of Sarah's womb—and he faced them head-on. He sat and thought about it, and he saw how hopeless the situation was. There was no chance at all! His body was a hundred years old and Sarah's womb was ninety years old and had never borne children. She was far past the age of childbearing. It was hopeless.

There was no hope, yet Abraham believed in hope. How? When he looked at his dead body he remembered he had a God who raises the dead. And when he thought about Sarah's barren womb, he remembered he had a God who calls into existence the things that do not exist. That would take care of everything, wouldn't it? And so, against all hope, he believed in hope, because of the God in whom his faith was fixed.

Then he did one other thing. It is not mentioned here, but this has always intrigued me. He told Sarah what God had said. I have often wished I could go back in history and observe certain times, and this is one of them. I would love to have been a bug on the tent wall when Abraham came in to tell Sarah this news! As he comes in, she says, "Well, dear, your eggs are ready. What have you been doing?"

"Oh, I've been having devotions, and what a wonderful time I had! God told me something."

"Well, what was it?"

"Well, I don't really know how to put this; you'd better sit down. God told me something very startling that is going to happen to us."

"That's interesting," she says. "What is it?"

Just like a man, Abraham blurts it out: "You're going to have a baby!"

"*What?*"

"That's what God said. You're going to have a baby."

"What, *me?*"

"Yes, you."

"Abraham, did you stop at the wine shop on your way home this morning?"

And Sarah laughed. It says so in Genesis. Sarah laughed, "Ha! God said I'm going to have a baby!" But then Sarah did something else. God had said something to Abraham that also applied to Sarah, and Abraham must have told her. I am convinced Sarah must have made a little plaque and put it over the kitchen sink and meditated on what God said: "Is there anything too hard for God?" When God says he will do something, is there anything too hard for him? And you know, when Sarah began to feel pregnant, her faith laid hold of this promise again. When the baby came, Sarah was a woman of faith, because she had been thinking of the God for whom nothing is too hard. There is the faith of Abraham. That is how he handled the hopeless circumstances.

How did he deal with the staggering possibilities? It is unbelievable that all nations should be blessed through him. He would be heir of the world, he would be called the friend of God. Could it be? But Abraham remembered that he had a God who gives life to the dead and a God who calls into existence things that do not exist. And so he believed. Staggering as the possibilities were, they did not stagger Abraham because of the God in whom he believed.

Faith Grows

In verses 20 through 22 we find the *objectives* of faith. The first is in verse 20:

> . . . *but {he} was strengthened in his faith and gave glory to God.*

His faith was made strong. Faith grows, just as Jesus said it would. If you have faith like a tiny grain of mustard seed, but the object of your faith is trustworthy and has promised to do something, then exercise your faith and it will grow. Obey! Abraham did; and as he believed and obeyed, he was strengthened in his faith and he gave glory to God. Faith never glorifies man; it glorifies God. It is God who acts, not man. What is accomplished is not something we do on behalf of God; it is God who does it by us and through us, on his own behalf. God, therefore, is thanked; and God is glorified. So faith grows, and faith glorifies.

In verse 21 Paul says Abraham also was . . .

> *fully persuaded that God had power to do what he*
> *had promised. This is why "it was credited to him*
> *as righteousness."*

Faith grounds us on the truth, as it did Abraham.
He was fully persuaded. This is the faith that was credited to him as righteousness. Faith grasps the promise.
Faith lays hold of what God has offered. As Abraham's
faith grew, he grasped the promise and found himself
loved and accepted by God, a friend of God.

Finally, verses 23 through 25 deal with the beneficiaries of faith:

> *The words "it was credited to him" were written not*
> *for him alone, but also for us, to whom God will*
> *credit righteousness—for us who believe in him who*
> *raised Jesus our Lord from the dead. He was deliv-*
> *ered over to death for our sins and was raised to life*
> *for our justification (4:23-25).*

This happened two thousand years before Paul, but
Paul says God did not write those words for Abraham
alone. For whom were they written then? For us today.
We look at the faith of Abraham and say, "That was
extraordinary faith." Paul says it wasn't; it was ordinary
faith. Anyone can exercise such faith if they want to.

I can have righteousness, too. I can be a friend of
God, accepted before him, with worth and value in his
sight—not just once as I begin my Christian life, but
every day, taking it fresh from his hand. I am forgiven
of my sins, restored, every day afresh and anew—a
thousand times a day if I need it. All that Abraham
had—the promises of being heir of the world, the indwelling of the Spirit—all are ours as well. This verse
says the gift of righteousness is for those "who believe
in him who raised Jesus our Lord from the dead." He is
still the God of resurrection, the God who can raise

from the dead. "He was delivered over to death for our sins and was raised to life for our justification." So we live by his death and by his life.

Now if we believe in the God who raised Jesus from the dead and we are ready to live on the basis of his death and his life for us, we, like Abraham, are heirs of all the world. All these things are ours, Paul says. The indwelling of the Spirit is granted to us moment by moment, and day by day, all our life long. And we, like Abraham, are the friends of God.

If I have a God who can raise from the dead and who can call into existence the things that do not exist, I am going to be a very exciting person to live with. I will never know when a thing that is dead and dull and lifeless may be touched by the grace of God and brought to life again. When something that I cannot possibly hope for—something which does not now exist, but which will be called into existence by the God who calls into existence the things that do not exist—when such a thing is promised by a God like this, life is an adventure. Do we have that kind of faith?

10
REJOICING
IN HOPE

(Romans 5:1-2)

In Romans 5 the apostle Paul traces the results of having been justified by faith. We can see this from the opening word of the chapter: "Therefore. . . ." As a result of what he has already said, Paul comes to certain conclusions.

Therefore, since we have been justified through faith, we have peace with God through our Lord Jesus Christ, through whom we have gained access by faith into this grace in which we now stand. And we rejoice in the hope of the glory of God (5:1-2).

That little word "rejoice" is the key to this whole fifth chapter. We find it again in verse 3: "Not only so, but we also rejoice in our sufferings. . . . " Have we gone this far yet? This is a higher stage of Christian growth and development. Finally, in verse 11 we find that the apostle, with his very logical mind, says, "Not only is this so, but we also rejoice in God. . . . " This is the third level of Christian growth.

There is the outline of the whole chapter: learning to rejoice at these various stages—rejoicing in the hope of glory, rejoicing in present sufferings, and rejoicing in God. As a Christian, if I really understand my theology, I will be rejoicing, even in the midst of suffering.

As I look around at Christians, sometimes I wonder if we ever grasp this idea. Some of us look like we have been marinated in embalming fluid. We never seem to rejoice. But Christian teaching and doctrine is designed to produce a spirit that cannot help but rejoice. It isn't something artificial— screwing on a smile and pretending that I am happy when I am not. When we really understand Christianity, it will produce a truly rejoicing spirit. If I am a glum bum, I should study the fifth chapter of Romans and it will turn me into a glad lad!

First, we learn to rejoice in our spiritual position; then, to rejoice in our present troubles; and finally, we rejoice in God himself, our powerful Friend. For the moment, we will look at the first two verses only.

Therefore, since we have been justified through faith, we have peace with God through our Lord Jesus Christ, through whom we have gained access by faith into this grace in which we now stand. And we rejoice in the hope of the glory of God.

The first thing we learn as a Christian is that we are justified by faith. To help us understand what that actually means, the apostle brought in the example of Abraham, who was justified by faith. Those two terms, "justified" and "faith," are explained to us and demonstrated for us in the life of Abraham. To be "justified" means that Abraham was declared to be the righteous friend of God. What we need to understand is that Abraham didn't earn that. He was given that at the beginning of his relationship with God, when he believed God about the coming of a promised seed.

The War is Over

Then, Paul says, there are three ways by which you can test whether you really do believe God's promise and have been justified by faith. Since we have been justified by faith, the first result is that we have peace with God. As we think about our lives and our relationship with God, if we really have believed that God justifies the ungodly, we will have peace with God. I am a Christian. That means I am in the family, I belong to the family of God. The war is over. All the conflict between me and God is ended; I am at peace with him.

I was in Honolulu when World War II ended. We had gone through the excitement and joy of V-E day some months before, when the war had ended in Europe, but that was a long way from the South Pacific. Though we were glad that the fighting in Europe had ended, we still had a war to fight. Out in the South Pacific there were many bloody battles yet to come. But I will never forget the day it was announced that peace with Japan had been signed in Tokyo Bay. All over the world, World War II was at an end. In Honolulu the people simply poured out into the streets. All over the city lights that hadn't burned for years went on. There was dancing and shouting and music and laughter, with thousands of people jamming the beaches and streets of the city, rejoicing because they were at peace.

That is something of what happens in the heart when we understand that we have been justified by faith. The war is over, we are at peace with God. All conflict has ceased. I think there are at least four things that are immediately true when we are at peace with God.

Lost Fears

The first is that we lose our fear of God. There is something in all of us that instinctively fears God. I remember how awesome God seemed to me as a boy. I thought of God as a heavenly policeman, always watching me, a stern and forbidding judge, ready to correct me and straighten me out. I will never forget the joy that came into my heart when I realized that God was no longer my judge—he was my Father. When one has been justified by faith, he no longer fears God as a judge. According to this book and the promises of Scripture, God no longer must function as a judge in relationship to us. He is now a loving, tenderhearted, compassionate father. As a father, of course, he does discipline. That is what love does. But God is no longer a judge. That beautiful picture our Lord gave us in the story of the prodigal son is the picture of God as we learn to see him. Having been justified by faith, we immediately lose our anxious fear of God.

Second, we lose our fear of death. If we have been justified by faith, we are no longer afraid to die. When I was young I lived for a while in the Red River Valley of North Dakota in the little Scottish settlement named after Ayr, Scotland—Ayr, North Dakota. It was a Presbyterian settlement and held to the old custom of ringing the bell of the church when someone died. I can still remember lying in my bed, listening to the tolling of the bell, knowing that someone had died and feeling the cold clutch of fear in my heart as I faced the possibility of my own death. Someday I would die. It could even happen while I was a boy. I knew it could happen to me, and I felt the fear of death.

Certain psychologists and psychiatrists are now admitting that the basic fear behind all other human fears is the fear of death. The conflict with which we constantly live is this shadow of the end that hangs over us all, this awareness that some day this life is going to end. Hebrews speaks of that. It says, Jesus came "so that by his death he might destroy him who holds the power of death—that is, the devil—and free those who all their lives were held in slavery by their fear of death" (Hebrews 2:14-15). So when I come to understand that I have been justified, given a righteous acceptance by a loving father, I immediately lose that fear of death. I am no longer afraid of what lies beyond. I know it is not judgment, but glory.

Third, when I have peace with God, I have the answer to the attacks of doubt and fear the devil is still able to bring into my life. Surely this is one of the things that troubles many young Christians. They start out their Christian life with a sense of rejoicing and an experience of peace. But after a while there will come a time when all they have been believing and resting on and rejoicing in seems to turn dull and cold and unbelievable. They don't know what has happened. They think they have just been kidding themselves about Christianity, and now they have awakened to the cold reality of life. They do not understand that the devil, through his angels, has access to us through our thoughts. He can insert these troubling doubts and fears into our minds without our being aware of it—even against our will, at times.

I know there are some who think that after one has been a Christian awhile he should reach a point when he never again has any doubts. But we never reach that point. Some people think that pastors never have any doubts about their salvation or their relationship with God. On my own experience that is not true.

When I was a young pastor, a dear ninety-year-old Presbyterian pastor, Dr. Francis Russell, was a tremendous help to me. Just a couple of years before Dr. Russell died I received a call from him, asking me to come and see him. I found him in deep distress over his personal salvation. He told me, "I feel like God is angry with me. If I were summoned into his presence now there is nothing I could offer to him." I had to help that dear, godly old man, and remind him again that he had been justified by faith in the work of Christ. I reminded him that his salvation has nothing to do with what he was like, but with Jesus, and what *he* had done. This is how we can deal with these doubts and fears if we have believed in our justification by faith.

If you do not have that sense of peace, the way to get it back is not by working on your feelings, but by reviewing your justification. Go over the facts again, remind yourself of what God has declared, and what kind of a God he is—Abraham's God, who can raise the dead to life and call into existence things that do not exist. He is able to perform what he has promised. Then your faith will be restored and you can handle these doubts and fears.

Fourth, if we have peace with God, we have an answer to the accusation of our own consciences when we sin. I know that many young Christians, in that glory and first flush of love in their relationship with the Lord, really think they are not going to sin again. Sin seems to them an impossible thing. Their hearts are so caught up with the love God has shown to them, that they cannot imagine themselves going back and doing some of the things they once did. But sooner or later they will be back doing some of those things. Old habits will reassert themselves; old ways of thinking will return. Perhaps they will not go back to all that they did formerly, but they will go back to some. They will sin again. Or it may be that after years of Christian life and service, they will fall into some terrible sin they thought they never would or could do again.

What do you say then to your accusing conscience when it asks, "Are you a Christian? Could you possibly be a Christian and act like this?" That is where justification by faith comes in. You remind yourself at that time: "My standing and my acceptance by God does not depend upon me. Even my sin does not cancel it out. The whole essence of the gospel is that God has found a way to put aside my sin, in the work of his beloved Son on my behalf." That is why you read, at the close of chapter four, "He was delivered over to death for our sin and was raised to life for our justification."

These are the ways you can test whether you really have believed it: Do you have peace with God? Are you freed from the fear of God and the fear of death? Do you have an answer to the doubts and fears and attacks that come from the enemy, those "flaming arrows of the evil one" that Paul speaks of in Ephesians 6? Do you have an answer to the accusations of your own guilty conscience when you fall, or sin? Here is where the answer lies: You have been justified by faith.

Notice that Paul is careful to remind us again that our justification is through the Lord Jesus Christ. It is never through ourselves. We have no merit before God ourselves. We never deserve this, we never earn this, and no matter how long we have served God as a Christian and have lived a clean and moral life, we can only stand on the ground of the work of the Lord Jesus on our behalf. That is why Paul insists on saying this again and again. He knows our prideful flesh. He knows that after we have cleaned up some of the bad areas of our lives we will begin to take credit for it and think that we have deserved something from God. So he faithfully reminds us that we are not deserving in this matter at all. The first mark of our justification by faith, then, is that we have peace with God.

Access to the King

The second mark is found in the next verse:

> . . . *through whom we have gained access by faith into this grace in which we now stand (5:2).*

We have access to continued grace, enabling us to stand in the midst of pressures, problems, trials, and difficulties. This is a constant supply, because we have instant access to God himself, the God of all grace. That is the second way we know we are justified by faith—we see that we have this instant access to the grace of God—to the throne of grace, as the writer of Hebrews puts it.

A beautiful picture in the book of Esther illustrates this. Esther, a lovely Jewish maiden, was a captive in the land of Persia. The king, seeking a bride, found

her and made her his queen. After Esther ascended to
the throne as queen, a plot was hatched against the
Jews. Unwittingly, the king signed a decree that
meant death for all Jews in Persia. Esther's godly
uncle, Mordecai, said it would be necessary for her to
go to the king and tell him what he had done. Esther
knew that was a dangerous thing, because the law
said no one could come before the king without first
being summoned. There were no exceptions—even
for a queen—for this was the law of the Medes and
the Persians which could not be changed. Unless the
king extended his golden scepter to that person, he
must die. Yet Esther knew she must dare to take her
life in her hands and go before the king.

The story says she fasted for three days and three
nights before she went. I am sure that was to prepare
her heart and her courage. It does not say what else
she did during that time. With a wife, four
daughters, and a mother-in-law in my home, I have
observed women getting themselves ready for some
years now, and I'm sure that one of the things Esther
was doing was fixing her hair. It probably took three
days and three nights to get it ready! Then we are told
that she dressed herself in robes of beauty and glory,
and stepped into the audience hall of the king, appearing all alone before him. The king was so smitten
with her beauty that his heart went out to her. He
stretched forth his scepter and accepted her. She had
abundant access to the king.

This pictures what Paul is telling us. Who would
dare stand before the God of all the earth, the God of
majesty and power and greatness and glory, unless he
had been given access to the King? The wonder of
this promise is that by being justified by faith, we
have access to his presence. Esther received from the
king's hand all that she needed to handle this

problem which threatened her life. That is what this portrays for us. Dressed in robes of beauty and glory that do not belong to us—for they are the garments of Jesus—we have access to the King, to receive from him all that we need to handle any threat that comes into our lives. We have continual acceptance before him. Our strength does not come from our circumstances; we get it from our continual access to the power and presence of God in the midst of danger or difficulty, trouble or pressure. The writer of Hebrews puts it this way:

> *Therefore, brothers, since we have confidence to enter the Most Holy Place by the blood of Jesus . . . let us draw near to God with a sincere heart in full assurance of faith (Hebrews 10:19,22).*

Something Beyond

Now look at the third thing that comes as a result of being justified by faith:

> *And we rejoice in the hope of the glory of God (5:2).*

That means that as we look at life ahead, even though life comes to an end—and it will—that is not the end of the story. We confidently anticipate that something lies beyond. We rejoice in the hope of the glory of God.

Hope here is not a word that means a mere possibility, a good chance. Hope, as it is used in the Scriptures in this way, is a ringing certainty, based upon the words of Jesus himself.: "If I go and prepare a place for you, I will come back and take you to be with me that you also may be where I am. . . . Because I live, you also will live" (John 14:3, 19). That is the certain hope of everyone who has been justified by faith. If you really have been justified by faith you know that you have the promise of God that he will do this, and that he is able to do what he has promised.

That promise is given to us regardless of our conditions on earth. It may be tough here. For some people it is tough. There are some Christians in other parts of the world who know nothing of the freedom and the joy of relationships that we have in this country. They are persecuted, they are in danger, they wake up every morning with the dreary expectation of living one more day under some watchful, hostile eye. Life may be cold and hard, it may be filled with pain and sorrow, but the minimum promise to all who are justified by faith is that there is a glory beyond death that is certain.

I have a friend who lives in the Midwest. He lives in the country, and one stormy morning, in the dead of winter, he looked out his window and saw the mailman drive up and leave something in his mailbox. Wanting to see what it was, he dressed warmly and went out into the bitter cold. With the snow swirling about him, he walked about a quarter of a mile down the lane to where the mailboxes were located. He opened the mailbox and, to his disappointment, saw that all that was there was a seed catalog. But he opened it and began to thumb through it.

You know, there is nothing like a seed catalog to capture the beauty and brilliance of flowers and vegetables. As he stood there in the snow, suddenly he felt as though spring had come. He could taste the crunch of a cucumber and smell the fragrance of those red roses and feel the juice of a red-ripe tomato running down his chin. It seemed as though winter faded for the moment and he was caught up into the beauty of spring and summer. Surely that is something of the experience that we get at times when we read the Scriptures. Here in the midst of "the winter of our discontent," something of the glory that is waiting beyond, the hope of the glory of God, breaks through.

I will never forget reading, as a young Christian, the words of Samuel Rutherford, that dear old seventeenth-century Scottish Covenanter who lived at a time when the English church was persecuting believers in Scotland. He was a dear and godly man who had come to know and love the Lord Jesus and to understand these great truths in the Scriptures about the inner strengthening that comes through faith. As he was lying on his deathbed, he received a summons from the king of England to come to London and appear on trial for his life. He knew he was dying, and he sent back this word by the messenger of the king: "Go and tell your master I have a summons from a Higher Court; and ere this message reaches him, I'll be where few kings and great folk ever come." That was the spirit of the man. He wrote many letters that reflect the glory of his faith and expectations. Anne Ross Cousin has gathered them for us. Some of them are arranged as hymns. One of her hymns was D. L. Moody's favorite, and it is mine also:

> *The sands of time are sinking,*
> *The dawn of heaven breaks;*
> *The summer morn I've sighed for—*
> *The fair, sweet morn awakes.*
> *Dark, dark hath been the midnight,*
> *But dayspring is at hand,*
> *And glory, glory dwelleth*
> *In Immanuel's land.*

O Christ, He is the fountain,
The deep, sweet well of love;
The streams on earth I've tasted,
More deep I'll drink above.
There to an ocean fullness
His mercy doth expand,
And glory, glory dwelleth
In Immanuel's land.

The bride eyes not her garment
But her dear Bridegroom's face;
I will not gaze at glory
But on my King of grace,
Not at the crown he giveth
But on His pierced hand;
The Lamb is all the glory
Of Immanuel's land.

That is the first stage of the Christian life—just the beginning. That is what we get, without fail, when we are justified by faith. But it is just the start. Then we go on to handle life and its suffering, and finally, we end up rejoicing in God. But everyone who has put faith in what Jesus Christ has done on his behalf—not in what he himself has done—has come to a place of complete assurance, continual acceptance, and confident anticipation. When we know we have been justified by faith we will have these in our life.

11
REJOICING
IN SUFFERING
(Romans 5:3-10)

We have just seen the first stage, or level, of Christian growth—the rejoicing in hope that comes by being justified by faith. That rejoicing comes immediately. We rejoice because we will be with the Lord. We have a hope for the future, a hope beyond death. But Paul goes on:

> *Not only so, but we also rejoice in our sufferings, because we know that suffering produces perseverance; perseverance, character; and character, hope. And hope does not disappoint us, because God has poured out his love into our hearts by the Holy Spirit, whom he has given us (5:3-5).*

It is clear from this that Christians are expected to suffer. We may not like it, but it is a fact. In his letter to the Philippians, the apostle puts it very plainly, "For it has been granted to you on behalf of Christ not only to believe on him, but also to suffer for him" (Philippians 1:29).

Those who think that becoming a Christian will exempt them from suffering have been seriously misled, for the Scriptures themselves teach that we should expect suffering. The Greek word for "suffering" basically means *tribulation*, something that causes distress. It can range from minor, daily annoyances to major disasters that sweep down out of the blue, leaving us stricken and shaken.

According to Romans 5, the proper Christian response is to rejoice: "Not only so, but we also rejoice in our sufferings." Here is where many people balk. They say, "I can't buy that! Do you mean to say that God is telling me that when I am hurting and in pain, going through mental and physical torment, I am expected to be glad and happy and rejoice in that? What kind of a nut is this Paul, anyway? It's not human, not natural!"

There are many who feel this way. I think we can easily identify with the attitude of the lady whose pastor went to see her when she was going through trouble. She kept complaining and grousing and griping. He stopped her and said, "I don't think you should talk that way. Christians are not to do that." She was very upset. "Why, I don't understand, Pastor. When God sends us tribulation, he surely expects us to tribulate a little bit!"

Unanimous Testimony

Most of us would feel the same way. We feel like tribulating . . . and we do. But it is not only Paul who tells us to rejoice; this is the unanimous testimony of every writer of the New Testament. All tell us to rejoice in suffering. First Peter 4:12 says, "Do not be surprised at the painful trial you are suffering, as though something strange were happening to you. But rejoice. . . . " Suffering is normal, and our normal response is to be rejoicing. James 1:2 says, "Consider it pure joy, my brothers, whenever you face trials of many kinds." There it is again: joy, rejoicing. Even the Lord Jesus told us, in the Sermon on the Mount, "Blessed are you when people insult you, persecute you and falsely say all kinds of evil against you because of me." What does he say to do? "Rejoice and be glad, because great is your reward in heaven" (Matthew 5:11-12). God's call to rejoice in suffering is found everywhere in Scripture.

Let us take a closer look at what this really means. There are certain things it does not mean. First, it is clear from Scripture that rejoicing in suffering is not a form of stoicism. It is not simply a "grin-and-bear-it" attitude, or "tough it out and see how much you can take," or "just hang in there until it's over and don't let anything get you down," or "keep a stiff upper lip." Many feel that if they do that, they are fulfilling the Word and "rejoicing in suffering." But that is not it. Non-Christians can do that. Many pride themselves on how much they can take. Sometimes people who are not Christians will put us to shame by the things they bear without complaining. Rejoicing in suffering is not merely being stoical.

Furthermore, we are not expected to enjoy the pain. Some think "rejoicing in suffering" means that you must enjoy your pain and hurt, that somehow Christians ought to be glad when terrible tragedy occurs and their hearts are hurting. But that isn't what Paul is saying. Those who feel that way are called masochists. They like to torture themselves. You may have met people like that, folks who are not happy unless they are miserable. If you take their misery away from them, they are really wretched, because it is their misery that gives them a sense of contentment. That is a twisted, distorted view of life, and it is certainly not what Paul is saying.

Nor is he saying that we are to pretend we are happy. Some think this passage says that when you are in public, you should put on an artificial smile and act happy, even if your heart is hurting like crazy. But Christianity is never phony. Phoniness of any kind is a false Christianity. Neither the apostles nor the Scriptures ever ask us to be unreal. Scripture clearly tells us to have a genuine sense of rejoicing.

Still, you may not be able to rejoice right at the moment of trial. Hebrews 12 helps us there. It says, "No discipline seems pleasant at the time, but painful. Later on, however, it produces a harvest of righteousness and peace for those who have been trained by it" (Hebrews 12:11). At the moment of hurt you will not feel like rejoicing, but it should soon follow that you do rejoice in your suffering.

I heard a man some years ago put this very well. He had gone through great physical trouble, and one of his legs had been amputated. That did not arrest the course of his disease, and he ultimately died because of it. Just a few days before his death I visited him in the hospital. He said something I never forgot because it so perfectly expresses what Christian rejoicing in suffering means. He said, "I never would have chosen one of the trials that I've gone through, but I wouldn't have missed any of them for the world!" Now that is saying it. He realized his suffering had done something of supreme value; therefore, even though he wouldn't have chosen it, he wouldn't have missed it, either. He is not alone; would you or I have chosen it? I doubt it! But that attitude is rejoicing in suffering.

Inside Information

How do you get to the place where you can rejoice in suffering? The apostle's answer is, "We rejoice in suffering because we know. . . . " We can rejoice because we know something. It is not just because it is such a great feeling to be hurt—it is because of something our faith enables us to know, a kind of inside information that others do not share. Worldlings lack it totally. Something that we know will cause us to rejoice in our suffering. What do we know? Paul tells us, "Knowing that suffering produces. . . . " Suffering does something, accomplishes something. It is productive. It is of value. We know it works, and that is what makes us rejoice.

Watch a woman in labor; watch the expression on her face. If you have any empathy in you, you cannot help but feel deeply hurt with her because she is going through such pain. And yet, there is usually joy also because she knows that childbirth produces children. It is the child that makes it all worthwhile. Thus suffering produces something worthwhile.

What does suffering produce? The apostle says it produces four things. First, suffering produces *perseverance*. In some versions the word is patience. The Greek word literally means "to abide under, to stay under the pressure." Pressure is something we want to get out from under, but suffering teaches us to stay under, to stick in there and hang with it. We use some of these expressions today, and I think they are appropriate. Perseverance is the opposite of panic, of bailing out. The best translation I can think of is the word "steadiness." Suffering produces steadiness.

When I was a boy in Montana, I helped a man break horses. I worked in a corral with three-year-old horses that had never had saddles on their backs. I was always interested in watching the horses when they first felt a saddle thrown on their back. That must be frightening to an animal. They don't know what in the world is happening to them. Some horses will react angrily, rearing back and trying to get away—even striking out with their forefeet at their trainer. Their nostrils flare, their eyeballs roll, and they panic! Others will just stand there trembling, shaking like a leaf. They won't move, they're so afraid. They don't know what is happening to them.

I think Christians respond that way, too. Do you remember when you became a Christian and first went through a trial? How easily you panicked and cried out to the Lord, "What's gone wrong?" You were in a panic over what was happening, fearful that it would wreck everything and destroy your hopes and dreams. You were just like the disciples in the boat on the Sea of Galilee when the storm raged. They panicked. They came to the Lord and shook him and said, "Wake up! Don't you know we're about to perish?" And the Lord did as he does with some of us. He stood up and said, "Don't panic." Then he said to the storm, "Peace, be still." And quiet came.

That is what suffering does. It steadies us. We go through a time like that and we're anxious and afraid; then the Lord stills the storm and we think, "Thank God that's all over. I'll never have to go through that again! I've learned my lesson!" And two weeks later there is another storm. But this time we've been through it once, so we steady up a bit. We do not get quite so fearful.

We learn something—we learn about ourselves, first. We learn we are not as strong as we thought we were. We learn we don't have the stick-with-it we thought we had. We wanted to bail out much sooner than we thought we would.

Then we learn something about the Lord—we learn how gracious he is. We learn he can handle events in ways we could not dream of nor anticipate. We see him work things out in ways we never could have guessed. So the third and fourth times a trial comes, we are steadier. We don't panic; we don't bail out. We stay under and let it work itself out. That is what Paul says here. Suffering produces steadiness. If we did not suffer, we would never learn that quality.

Proven Reliability

Second, not only does suffering produce steadiness, but steadiness produces *character*. The Greek word for "character" carries with it the idea of being put to the test and approved. It is the idea of being shown to be reliable. Steadiness produces reliability. We finally learn that we will not be destroyed, that things will work out. Steady up, and people start counting on us. They see strength in us, and we become more reliable people.

We have all seen tire advertisements on television in which a car equipped with four tires is put through horrendous tests—driven through desert sands, bogs, swamps and marshes, driven over rough, hard, cobblestone roads, over roads with holes and chuckholes, over boards studded with nails. The tire is twisted and pulled and stretched in every direction, and we are amazed at what it can take. After the test they hold up the tire, and it looks as if it had never been out of its wrapping! Then the ad comes: "Buy

Sock'em Tires! They're tested, proven!" Now that is what this word "character" means. God is strengthening us so he can hold us up and say, "He's approved, he's tested."

God is in the process of making veterans. A veteran has been through something and has been tested and proven. Here is a passage by Paul that I have always loved from the *Living Bible*:

> I think you ought to know, dear brothers, about the hard time we went through in Asia. We were really crushed and overwhelmed, and feared we would never live through it. We felt we were doomed to die and saw how powerless we were to help ourselves; but that was good, for then we put everything into the hands of God, who alone could save us, for he can even raise the dead. And he did help us, and saved us from a terrible death; yes, and we expect him to do it again and again (2 Corinthians 1:8-10).

Now, that is a veteran speaking. He has been through some tough things, but he knows God can take him through anything, and he will. He is not saying, "It's all over." No, he is saying, "There's more coming, but God will take me through." That is a veteran.

Years ago I asked a nine-year-old boy, "What do you want to be when you grow up?" I'll never forget his answer. He said, "I want to be a returned missionary." He did not want to be just a missionary, but a returned one—one that has been through it with it all behind him. Here Paul tells us God is in the process of building returned missionaries.

Third, we find that reliability also produces something. Suffering produces steadiness, steadiness produces reliability, and reliability produces *hope*. So now we are back to hope. In verse 2, Paul spoke of "rejoicing in hope," the hope of sharing the glory of God, a hope for the future beyond death. But here is hope that we will share the glory of God—which is God's character—*right now*. We have the hope that God is producing the image of Christ in us right now. That is a great thing! This hope is certainty, not just possibility.

We are being changed; we see ourselves changing. As we grow more like Jesus, we become more thoughtful, more compassionate, more loving. We are being mellowed. We are becoming like Christ— stronger, wiser, purer, more patient. To our amazement, a certainty grows in our hearts that God is doing his work just as he promised. He is transforming us into the image of his Son.

Confidence from Hope

That brings us to the fourth step Paul mentions, that hope does not disappoint us. I like the King James translation better. It says, "Hope maketh not ashamed." That is a figure of speech called "litotes," which is the use of a negative to express a positive idea. Paul does this in Romans 1:16 when he says, "I am not ashamed of the gospel of Jesus Christ." What does he mean? He means he is proud; he is confident and bold. I think that is the term we ought to use here. Hope makes us confident. Hope, or certainty, produces confidence and boldness.

I once met a man who had been shot by his own son. He survived this awful and traumatic time, and then began to stand up before groups of men to explain how God used that situation to get his attention. He began to study and to grow. Hearing him, I could understand that a man who previously had been ashamed to speak of Christ was now confident and bold. What the Lord had shown him, and how the Lord supported and sustained him through this terrible, tragic time, meant so much to this man that he did not care what anyone thought about it. He shared openly what God had brought him through. We lose our fear of ridicule and shame and we speak up out of the reality of our experience of what God has brought us through.

Paul goes on to explain why hope does not disappoint us. He says it is "because God has poured out his love into our hearts by the Holy Spirit, whom he has given us." Now, to my mind, this is one of the most important verses in Romans. It is a significant verse because it adds a thought we have not seen in this book up to now. It is the explanation, above all else, of how to rejoice in suffering. This is the first mention in Romans of the love of God. Up to now Paul has not said anything about the love of God; but now it is "God has poured out his love into our hearts by the Holy Spirit, whom he has given us."

We must be careful to see how Paul presents this concept because the love of God is the subject he develops in verses 6 through 10. That connection is important. These last verses have been extracted from their context and used for evangelistic preaching so many times that we have forgotten what they originally meant. Paul uses them here in connection with suffering.

> *God has poured out his love into our hearts by the Holy Spirit, whom he has given us. You see, at just the right time, when we were still powerless, Christ died for the ungodly. Very rarely will anyone die for a righteous man, though for a good man someone might possibly dare to die. But God demonstrates his own love for us in this: While we were*

still sinners, Christ died for us. Since we have now been justified by his blood, how much more shall we be saved from God's wrath through him! For if, when we were God's enemies, we were reconciled to him through the death of his Son, how much more, having been reconciled, shall we be saved through his life! (5:5-10)

The argument here is extremely important. It will explain how to rejoice in suffering. I know Christians who are suffering but are not being made steady and reliable and confident. Instead, they are becoming bitter and resentful and angry, even to the point of denying their faith. Suffering, you see, does not produce these qualities automatically. We can go through suffering as a Christian and be filled with anger and rage and resentment against God. What makes the difference?

Evidence of Love

As Paul explains here, the difference lies in seeing our suffering as evidence of God's love, and not his wrath. Then we will experience that love even in suffering. The Holy Spirit will lavish on us a love of God so rich and radiant and glorious that we will not be able to do anything but rejoice in our suffering. But if we see our suffering as evidence of God's wrath, we will be frustrated, angry, and miserable. That is why Paul brings in this description of God's love for us.

Anyone who has gone through any degree of suffering knows that in the moment of pain and hurt it is easy to feel that God does not love you. It is easy to feel rejected, unloved. We are so used to thinking that love is something which blesses and warms and takes care of us, it is almost impossible for us to think we are being loved when we are hurting. It is hard for us to believe that the one who is bringing the hurt is doing it out of genuine love. We feel broken, worthless, and forgotten. That is why we need to understand the argument in verses 6 through 10.

Paul says there is a place where every Christian knows that God loves him, even though he himself feels worthless, useless, and forgotten. What is that place? It is the cross. In the cross of Jesus Christ we always see two things. First, we see ourselves. We see that, as Paul puts it here, we are helpless. If there were any other way to get to God, then there never would have been a cross. But the cross is God's testimony that there is no other way. That is why the verse says, "At the right time, in due time, Christ died." At that time in history God amply demonstrated to all the world that man could not save himself.

The great Hebrew prophets had spoken, and that did not help. Greek philosophers had taught, and that did not help. The Romans had come in with their military might and imposed law and order over the course of the whole world of that day, and that did not help. But at the right time, Christ died on the cross so that men could see how helpless and powerless they were to save themselves.

As we look at the cross we see how ungodly we are. We are not like God, we do not act like God. We have the capacity to do so, but we do not. We even want to at times, but we do not. We see in the cross just how unlike God we are. We see that we are sinners, destroying ourselves and others. We find ourselves lawless and selfish, and we know it was man's sin—our sin, yours and mine—that nailed Jesus to that cross. It was not his own sin, but yours and mine. There we learn that we are enemies of God, enemies sabotaging God's plan to help us, wrecking

everything he tries to do to reach us. For years we
fight back and resist God's efforts to love us and to
draw us to himself.

We are the enemies of God. And yet we know, if
we are Christians, that in the place where man's inadequacy is so fully demonstrated, we also have the
clearest testimony that God loves us. "God so loved
the world that he gave his only begotten Son." Jesus
came to break through all our despair, weakness,
shame, sorrow, and sin, all man's ruin and disaster.
He came to demonstrate a God who loved mankind
and would not let it perish.

Now we come to the force of Paul's argument. If I
clearly knew God's love when I became a Christian—
when I was an enemy and helpless and powerless—
how much more can I count on God's love now that I
am his child? Even though I am suffering, even
though I do not feel loved right now, even though it
seems as though God is against me, how much more
can I count on God's love for me right now!

Paul is arguing from the greater to the lesser. If
God could love me when it was so plain that I did not
deserve it, how much more must I count on his love
now that I know I am dear to him and loved by him.
Therefore, this suffering is not coming into my life
because God is angry with me; it comes because God
loves me. It comes from the heart of a Father who is
putting me through something I desperately need to
enable me to grow into the kind of a person I desperately want to be. And he loves me enough that he will
not let me off, but will take me through it. Therefore
it is not his anger I experience, but his love.

That is what Hebrews 12 argues, isn't it? If we
have been disciplined by the fathers of our flesh—and
we know *they* love us—why can't we believe that God
loves us when he puts us through times of testing,

pressure, and suffering? When I see this, then I can rejoice because I know suffering will produce the things that make me what I want to be. There is a hymn that expresses this idea beautifully. It goes like this:

> *When we have exhausted our store of endurance,*
> *When our strength has failed ere the day is half done,*
> *When we reach the end of our hoarded resources,*
> *Our Father's full giving is only begun.*
>
> *His love has no limit, His grace has no measure,*
> *His power no boundary known unto men;*
> *For out of His infinite riches in Jesus*
> *He giveth, and giveth, and giveth again!*
>
> *—Annie Johnson Flint*

("He Giveth More Grace," copyright 1941, 1969 by Lillenas Publishing Co.)

12
REJOICING
IN GOD

(Romans 5:11-21)

The one clear mark of a true Christian is that he always rejoices. Three times in Romans 5 believers are given reasons for rejoicing. First, we rejoice in our spiritual position. "Having been justified by faith, we have peace with God through our Lord Jesus Christ. We have access by faith into this grace wherein we stand, and we rejoice in hope of the glory of God." That is our spiritual position. The moment we believe in the Lord Jesus, we can rejoice in the hope of sharing the glory of God.

Then we are to rejoice in our growing conformity to the character of Christ. This is produced by suffering. Suffering helps us become like Jesus. As we suffer, knowing we are undergirded, protected, and covered over by the love of God shed abroad in our hearts by the Holy Spirit, we learn to rejoice in our sufferings.

In verses 11-21, we learn to rejoice in our great and glorious God. Verse 11 tells us:

> *Not only is this so {Paul has said that twice before in this chapter}, but we also rejoice in God through our Lord Jesus Christ, through whom we have now received reconciliation.*

In my book *Authentic Christianity*, I call this rejoicing "an unquenchable optimism." Christians always have grounds for rejoicing. No matter what happens, we have a ground for rejoicing. The three kinds of rejoicing described in Romans 5 represent three levels of maturity. They are not necessarily chronological levels, but they are levels of understanding and responding to truth that reflect a continually growing and deepening maturity. The third level is rejoicing in God through our Lord Jesus Christ, through whom we have now received the reconciliation.

Notice again how Paul, as he so frequently does, reminds us that everything comes to us comes "through our Lord Jesus Christ." Christ is the way to God. He himself said so: "I am the way, the truth, and the life. No man comes to the Father but by me." Therefore, when we see the greatness of Christ, we have seen the greatness of God. It is he who reveals the Father. Remember how John begins his Gospel?

> *In the beginning was the Word, and the Word was with God, and the Word was God. . . . The Word became flesh and lived for a while among us. We have seen his glory, the glory of the one and only Son, who came from the Father, full of grace and truth (John 1:1,14).*

That is the way we see God. When we see the greatness of Jesus, we see the greatness of God. When we see and know the love of Jesus, we know the heart of God. Therefore, we are to rejoice in God through our Lord Jesus Christ.

Record of Achievements

How do you do that? How do you see the greatness of Christ? Paul says it is by understanding the reconciliation. If you want to know how great a person is, you look at the record of his achievements. What has he done? From verse 12 of Romans 5 to the end of the chapter is a record of the greatness of Christ, his achievement of what Paul calls "the reconciliation."

This passage is one of the most theologically important in all of the Bible. In this passage is the clearest statement in the Bible on what is called "original sin," that is, the blight that has been passed on to our whole race as the result of the sin of our father Adam. Here too is the complete answer to those who doubt the historicity of Adam and Eve. There are some who claim that the first chapters of Genesis are merely legend, or myth, that Adam and Eve were not real people. But this chapter shows that is false. All through the passage, Adam, as a real person, is contrasted to and compared with the Lord Jesus. This section also lays the groundwork for all that Paul will say in chapters 6, 7, and 8. So it is tremendously important.

I have found that if we get involved in the details of the passage—and it is easy to do—we invariably get lost in the argument and lose the main point, which is the greatness and the glory of the Lord Jesus, the reason we can rejoice in God through him. So instead of dwelling on the details of the argument, I want to summarize it for you.

There are four movements in this section. First, in verses 12-14 Paul begins with us "in Adam," which is where we start as a race. Then verses 15-17 contrast this with what we are if we are "in Christ." Verses 18 and 19 summarize these thoughts, and the chapter closes with a brief explanation of how the law fits in (verses 20 and 21).

Verse 12, then, shows us where we begin, "in Adam."

> *Therefore, just as sin entered the world through one man, and death through sin, and in this way death came to all men, because all sinned—*

Paul is making a comparison here, which the Greek text makes clear. He is saying, "Just as sin entered the world through one man, and death through sin, *even so through one man* death came to all men, because all sinned." That's the Stedmaniac version of this verse.

Two Evils

Paul's argument begins with two undeniable, indisputable facts: the universality of sin and the universality of death. We cannot deny these. Everywhere we look there is evidence that what he says is true, that we are victims of the twin evils of sin and death.

There are some who may not accept the idea of sin. There are people today who do not like this word *sin*. Call it anything we like, the fact remains there is clear evidence wherever we look that something has gone wrong with humanity. Call it karma, destiny, fate, evolutionary darkness, or whatever—but it is certain that something is wrong. G. K. Chesterson said, "Whatever else may be said of man, this one thing is clear: He is not what he is capable of being."

I think any line of evidence will substantiate that. Some kind of twist has come in, something that we cannot explain—a taint, a moral poison that makes us act in irrational ways—so that even when we know something is wrong or hurtful, we want to do it anyway.

I needn't go any further than my own heart to find evidence of that. I know some things would destroy me and my family, and yet at times I catch myself wanting badly to do them. And so do you, so don't feel so pious! That is what is called "original sin." Adults aren't the only ones who suffer from it; the striking and remarkable thing is that it is found in babies. Sin is there at the beginning of life; babies are born with it, which is conclusive proof of what Paul is saying here. It has gripped the race.

My grandson comes over to our house frequently and tears up the place. It takes us two days to get it back in shape after a visit from him. His mother tells us that if she says to him, "Now, eat your food," that's the one thing he doesn't want to do. So she has learned how to make him eat his food. She says, "Now, don't eat your carrots," and he gobbles them up. Anything prohibited, that is what he wants to do. No one had to teach him that. We never sent him to school to learn how to disobey. Even when he was only two years old, he knew how to resist instruction and command; he wanted to do what he ought not to do.

Perhaps this universal tendency to evil has been stated most clearly by a secular agency. The clearest statement on original sin I have ever read comes from a report of the Minnesota Crime Commission. In studying humanity the commission came to this frightening and factual conclusion:

*Every baby starts life as a little savage. He is com-
pletely selfish and self-centered. He wants what he
wants when he wants it—his bottle, his mother's
attention, his playmate's toy, his uncle's watch.
Deny him these wants, and he seethes with rage
and aggressiveness, which would be murderous,
were he not so helpless. He is dirty. He has no mor-
als, no knowledge, no skills. This means that all
children, not just certain children, are born delin-
quent. If permitted to continue in the self-centered
world of his infancy, given free reign to his impul-
sive actions to satisfy his wants, every child would
grow up a criminal, a thief, a killer, a rapist.*

This is a clear statement on the universality of sin
and of the fact, as Paul says here, that by one man,
sin entered the world, and along with sin came death.
Everyone acknowledges the universal presence of
death. We look at a newborn child and say, "Here is
someone starting to live." But it is equally true to say
of that child, "Here is someone who is starting to
die." Death is at work in that child from the moment
of birth. We are born to die. This is the story of our
race. We do not need to argue it; it is inescapable.
Later on in this passage Paul says, "Death reigned."
Still later on, he says, "Sin reigns." So in these two
forces introduced into humanity, we have a pair of
royal tyrants who rule over men. King Sin and his
evil and cruel consort, Queen Death, hold in their re-
morseless hands every human being, without exception.

Through One Man

How did sin and death get control of our race? The
apostle answers: through one man. That's the key to
this whole section. Again and again Paul reiterates
that phrase: through one man, by one man. Paul is

contrasting two men, Adam and Jesus. But in either case, what comes to us comes from one man, either Adam or Jesus.

Through Adam sin and death gripped our race. We sin because we are sons and daughters of Adam, and we die because we are sons and daughters of Adam. We don't die for our own sins. Normally, we would die for our own sins; but, as Paul goes on to argue, there are even some—babies, for instance—who haven't deliberately sinned at all, and yet they still die. Therefore, Paul traces the reign of sin and death back to Adam. This is the argument of verses 13 and 14.

> *For before the Law was given, sin was in the world. But sin is not taken into account when there is no law. Nevertheless, death reigned from the time of Adam to the time of Moses, even over those who did not sin by breaking a command, as did Adam, who was a pattern of the one to come (5:13-14).*

Paul's argument is simply this: Death is the punishment for breaking a command. In the Garden of Eden, God said to Adam, "Do not eat of the fruit of the tree of the knowledge of good and evil. In the day that you eat thereof, you shall surely die." Adam broke that specific, clear-cut command; he ate of the fruit. That was not merely a little incident, a peccadillo; Adam actually was choosing to be an independent creature and denying his dependence upon the God who made him. It was an act of rebellion; it was an act of idolatry. He enthroned himself as a god, in the place of God. Adam broke the command and, as a result, death and sin passed upon all his descendants.

So Paul says death is the result of breaking a

command—and you need a law to be able to break a command. Perhaps we have driven down our street for years and never had to stop at a certain intersection because there was nothing that required it. Then one day a stop sign is erected. Now the law has come in. From that time on, failing to stop at that intersection is to break a command. If we don't stop, we are subject to a penalty, even though we have been driving through that intersection without stopping for years. But when the law comes in we break a command if we fail to stop.

In order to have death, Paul says, there had to be a command to break. But people were dying long before the law was ever given. People died from the time of Adam to Moses, even people who never had a command to break. How could that be, if death is the result of breaking a command? Paul's conclusion is: The whole race actually sinned when Adam sinned. We broke the command in Adam. Adam broke a direct command and we were present in him; therefore we die as he died because of a broken command.

At this point many people say, "Well, that isn't fair! God is punishing us for Adam's sin!" But this misunderstands the nature of our humanity. We are not individuals quite separate from others, but we are tied in together, all a part of one great bundle of life; we share life together. We recognize this when we speak of "the brotherhood of man" and when we say, "No man is an island." But at other times we choose to think we have a right to stand alone, as though no one else exists. Whether we understand it or not, this passage declares that when Adam sinned, he plunged the whole race into disaster. We are all born with sin at work in us and, as a result, death is taking its toll. We sinned in Adam, and we die because of him.

Pattern and Contrast

The most important phrase in this paragraph is the last one: Adam was a pattern of the one to come. The apostle will now show us how Adam is a kind of picture of Christ; and yet there is a great contrast between them. The verses that follow draw both a comparison and a contrast. First, verse 15:

> *But the gift is not like the trespass.*

The gift every human being is always looking for is righteousness, a sense of worth, which comes only as a gift from the Lord Jesus. The trespass is Adam's disobedient act in the Garden of Eden. But the gift, Paul says, is not like the trespass.

> *For if the many died by the trespass of the one man, how much more did God's grace and the gift that came by the grace of the one man, Jesus Christ, overflow to the many!*

Adam brought a single experience of death to all people. We only die once, don't we? Adam brought that death to us. But Christ brought a repeated and ever-growing experience of life to all who are in him. That is the contrast. We can take life from Jesus a thousand times a day. We can take the gift of worth over and over again. Whenever our spirit feels put down, crushed, insignificant, inadequate, or insecure, we can be renewed, we can take again the gift of life and righteousness from him. Jesus Christ is greater than Adam; for though the trespass of Adam brought death once, the sacrifice and the death of Jesus brings life a thousand times. Verse 16:

> *Again, the gift of God is not like the result of the one man's sin: The judgment followed one sin and brought condemnation, but the gift followed many trespasses and brought justification.*

Adam's single trespass brought death. Adam trespassed once and brought death to all who were in him. Christ died once and, despite thousands of trespasses, brought justification to all who are in him. That is the contrast. Adam trespassed once and brought death to all. Jesus died once and brought life—despite thousands of trespasses. One trespass brought death; the death of Jesus brought forgiveness for thousands of trespasses. All my life, as many times as I sin, I cannot out-sin the grace of God. No matter how many trespasses are involved in my record, there is freedom in Christ and forgiveness for all of them.

Now let's look at verse 17:

> *For if, by the trespass of the one man, death reigned through that one man, how much more will those who receive God's abundant provision of grace and of the gift of righteousness reign in life through the one man, Jesus Christ.*

Adam's transgression permitted death to reign over the whole race. This is talking about more than just the funeral at the end of my life. True, that funeral happens because of Adam's trespass, but there is more to it than that. Not only does death come to us finally because of Adam, but it reigns throughout our lives because of Adam. Paul is talking about forms of death other than the mere cessation of life.

What is life? Life is love, joy, and excitement. It is vitality, enrichment, power; it is fulfillment in every direction, in every possibility of our being. Death is the absence of life. Death is emptiness, loneliness, misery, depression, boredom, and restlessness. How much of your life is made up of death? Most of it, perhaps? Some people never seem to have anything but death in their lives. Death reigns because of Adam's transgression.

Paul says that Christ's death provides such abundant grace and loving acceptance, available again and again and again, that all who are in him can reign in life . . . now! I can have life in the midst of the pressures and circumstances and suffering and troubles. My spirit can be alive and joyful—gaining fulfillment and delight. Life in the midst of death! We are to reign in life now. Love, joy, peace, glory, and gladness fill our hearts even in the midst of the heartaches and pressures.

Paul draws this parallel so that we might see how much more we have in Jesus than we ever had in Adam. What we lost in Adam, we regain in Jesus— plus much more. Just as a climber on a mountaintop can dislodge a pebble which rolls on and accumulates others until it begins an avalanche that will move the whole side of a mountain, so Adam's sin in the Garden of Eden dislodged a pebble that has built into an avalanche of sin and death which has swept through our entire race. But, Paul tells us, Jesus has launched another avalanche of grace, and he can amply counteract all that Adam has brought.

Verses 18 and 19 give a summary. First, verse 18:

> *Consequently, just as the result of one trespass was condemnation for all men, so also the result of one act of righteousness was justification that brings life for all men.*

Death—judgment or condemnation—comes to us not because of our own sins, but because of Adam's. It is a gift from Adam. What a terrible gift it is! And thus the acceptance and worth that we need to have, the love that we desperately crave and must have in

order to function, is also a gift, a gift from the Lord
Jesus Christ. We can have all that we want, anytime
we need it. Verse 19:

> For just as through the disobedience of the one man
> the many were made sinners, so also through the
> obedience of the one man the many will be made
> righteous.

Some claim we are righteous because God declares
us righteous. But here it is stated that we are *made*
righteous in Jesus Christ. Paul is saying that when
we were in Adam, sin and guilt were not an option—
we had no way of choosing. We sin because that is
part of our nature. And so, when we are in Christ,
having worth and love is not something that we have
to earn—it is a gift from the Lord Jesus. It is part of
our new, true nature.

The Law Was Added

In verses 20 and 21, the apostle briefly deals with
the place of the law:

> The law was added so that the trespass might in-
> crease. But where sin increased, grace increased all
> the more, so that, just as sin reigned in death, so
> also grace might reign through righteousness to
> bring eternal life through Jesus Christ our Lord.

Someone might raise the question, "Why then did
the Ten Commandments have to be given?" Paul's
answer is, "The Ten Commandments never were
given to make men do right." That is what we think
they were given for, but they were actually given to
show us how wrong we already are, and to make us
sin more, to increase the trespass. Isn't that strange?
As in the example of my grandson, the law makes you
want to do wrong even more. It increases the trespass.

But a strange thing happens at that point. Paul tells us that the worse we get—the more we fling ourselves into the rebellion, sin, and evil that we know to be wrong—the closer we are to being broken, to coming to the end of ourselves and discovering the grace of restoration, cleansing, and forgiveness in Jesus Christ.

I listened recently to a tape by Charles Colson in which he told of his experience in prison after the Watergate crisis. In that dark and lonely place, crammed in with forty other men, he found a brother in Christ. The two of them met and began to pray for others in that prison. They didn't know what God could do—they almost despaired that anything could happen—but as they began to pray, God began to work. They found that the Spirit of God swept through that prison in a remarkable way. Men were broken. Hardened, violent, brutal men—who had spent their lives in resistance to right, truth, and good, and had given themselves over completely to hardness, cynicism, and brutality—began to break and to find forgiveness.

Do you know there is a spiritual awakening going on in our prisons today? I read that in one year, in the Los Angeles County jails, 256 prisoners received the Lord. Prisoners are open to Christ because the law has driven them into trespass to such a degree that they are ready to hear the gospel. Sometimes this happens without outward rebellion. Sometimes men become frustrated, hard, and cynical. When that happens we learn the grace of God will abound more and more, for the increase of sin only increases the grace of our Lord Jesus.

The point of all this is that the one who breaks through is Jesus. Adam ruins us all. Only Christ can set us free. Sin and death will never loosen their filthy hold on us except at the command of Jesus Christ. Therefore, the One to whom we look is the Lord Jesus, the One who broke the terrible death grip on us and set us free—Jesus, the head of a new race, the beginning of a new humanity. *Jesus is Lord.*

As we see him thus, we discover what the Scriptures say: that the blessed Lord, who broke through death and sin, has come to live within us, to give himself to us, and to infuse us with his strength and purity, his wisdom and power. All that he is is available to us. Thus we rejoice in God through our Lord Jesus Christ, who has made for us the reconciliation.

13
CAN WE GO
ON SINNING?

(Romans 6:1-2)

Let me ask you a question. Now that you are a
Christian—now that you understand that the grace
of God forgives your sins, past, present, and future,
that the sacrifice of Jesus Christ on your behalf settles
the debt for sin, no matter when sins occur— do you
then have the right to go on sinning, living as you
were, knowing that the grace of God will cover those
sins?

That is a highly relevant question; many people
today are asking it, and many are saying that we *can*
go on sinning. Many claim that they have the right
to go on living in a blatantly sinful way because, they
say, their sins are forgiven. A man in our congregation

admitted to me that he was a homosexual but claimed that he did not need to make any change in his life because, as a Christian, his sins were forgiven. This is not an out-of-date question, but one we all wrestle with and must resolve. The apostle Paul faces this question in the sixth chapter of Romans.

In chapters 6 and 7 he interrupts his argument temporarily to deal with two very practical questions. In chapter 6 Paul responds to those who ask, "What about the sins of believers?" In chapter 7 he takes up the demands of the Ten Commandments. Then, in chapter 8, he again picks up his argument and begins to carry on by describing the tremendous results of being in Jesus Christ (as opposed to Adam).

We will study only two verses of chapter 6 in this chapter. As we have seen before, Paul always states the truth first in a kind of nutshell, in a pithy statement of what he wants to say. Then he takes up his argument, step by logical step, and explains and expounds it until it is perfectly clear. That is what he does here. The whole truth that answers the question, "Can we go on sinning?" is dealt with in the first two verses of chapter 6. Paul says,

> What shall we say, then? Shall we go on sinning so that grace may increase? By no means! We died to sin; how can we live in it any longer? (6:1-2)

This is the whole argument, right there: We died to sin; how can we live in it any longer?

An Appropriate Question

Let us observe three things about this brief statement. First, notice the question is logical. Shall we go on sinning that grace may increase? That is a good question to ask. If my teaching or preaching does not arouse this question in someone's mind, there is probably something wrong with my teaching, for it is the kind of question that ought to be asked at this point. There is something about the grace of God and the glory of the good news that immediately raises this issue. If sin is so completely taken care of by the forgiveness of Christ, then we don't really need to worry about sins, do we? They are not going to separate us from Christ, so why not keep on doing them? It is a perfectly logical question. It was raised everywhere Paul went, and it is a question that must be faced.

But second, notice that it is not only logical; it is also natural. That is because sin, basically, is fun. Isn't it? Oh, come on—admit it! Sin is fun. We like to do it. Otherwise we wouldn't keep on doing it; we wouldn't even get involved in it. We know sins are bad for us. Our minds tell us, our logic tells us, our experience tells us: Sin is bad for us. Nevertheless, we like to sin. Otherwise we would not. Therefore, any suggestion that we can escape the penalty for our sin and still enjoy the action arouses a considerable degree of interest. It does in me, anyway.

We must understand that the apostle is talking about a lifestyle of sin, not just a single failure or two. He is talking about Christians who go on absolutely unchanged in their lifestyle from what they were before they were Christians. The word for "go on sinning" is in the present, continuous tense. It means the action keeps on happening. The question is, "Can we go on sinning?" Verses 15 and following deal with the effects of a single act of sin in a believer's life and what happens when we fail even once. We will come to that in due course. But here Paul is talking about habitual practice, or something that frequently

occurs in a believer's experience, something that was
there before he became a Christian. Can we go on living this way?

Finally, notice that this question is put in such a
way as to sound right and even pious. Shall we go on
sinning, so that grace may increase? This suggests
that our motivation for sinning is not just our own
satisfaction—we are doing it for the glory of God, so
that grace may increase. God loves to show his grace.
Therefore, if we go on sinning, he will have all the
more opportunity. What a chance for God to show
his grace! It is clear that this question is not asked by
a complete pagan or by a worldling, but by someone
who seems intent on the glory of God.

Having said that, we come now to the answer, the
positive answer of Paul.

> *What shall we say then? Shall we go on sinning so*
> *that grace may increase? By no means!*

Paul immediately reacts with a very positive statement, bluntly put: "By no means!" Or, as it is literally in the Greek, "May it never be!" Absolutely not!
It is interesting to me to see how other versions translate this phrase. The King James Version sounds hor-
rified: "God forbid!" Phillips seems to catch this same
note of horror: "What a ghastly thought!" The New
English Bible puts it very simply, "No, no." So here
is a no-no in the Christian experience. Can we sin?
No-no. I gather from all this that the apostle Paul
simply does not agree with this philosophy that we
can go on sinning and be forgiven. Why? In his inescapable logic, Paul answers in just four little words:
"We died to sin."

> *We died to sin. How can we live in it any longer?*

Here is the whole truth. The rest of the chapter is but an exposition of what Paul means. We will take that exposition step by step because there is tremendous understanding involved in it. But Paul does not make any logical advance on his original statement. When we get to the end of the chapter, he has simply made clear what he means by "We died to sin." There is the whole argument, and if we understand what he means, we will see why he asks, "How can we go on living in it any longer?"

What It Doesn't Mean

Now let's look at this phrase, "We died to sin." First, it does not mean that sin is dead in me. It does not mean that, as a Christian, I have reached the place where I cannot sin.

Some years ago I was living in the city of Pasadena. One day I went to get a haircut. I soon found the barber was a Christian. As we began to talk, he started to tell me about his Christianity. He told me that seventeen years earlier he had been "sanctified," as he put it, and he was no longer able to sin. For seventeen years he had lived without sin. He made it very clear that he had done no sin at all.

As I began to discuss this with him I brought in certain other passages, and we got into an argument. The longer we went, the hotter he got—all the while he was cutting my hair. He worked himself up into such a lather that I finally said to him, "Look, if you can get so upset and angry when you have no sin in you, what would you be like if you were a sinner like the rest of us?" It was two weeks before I dared to appear in public after that haircut! Surely such a claim to total sinlessness carries its own rebuttal.

So this passage does not mean that sin is dead in

us; nor does it mean, as some have supposed, that we should die to sin. There are movements and churches based upon this idea. They say Paul is teaching us that we ought to die to sin. One can attend meetings, conferences, and camp meetings where he will be exhorted to die to sin. We are told this is the way to come to a victorious life. We are told we ought to begin to crucify ourselves and die to sin. Now I submit that Paul is not saying we ought to do this; he is telling us it has been done. *We died to sin.* It has already happened!

Third, neither does Paul mean that we are dying to sin. Some take it that way. They say this means the Christian is gradually changing and growing. The more he does so, the more he dies to sin, there will come a time when he will outgrow all his evil. But it does not mean that at all. Once again, we must face the flat statement the apostle makes: We died to sin. It is past tense. It has already happened.

If we go back to chapter 5, we have that great contrast with what we were in Adam and what we are now in Christ. "In Adam," he says, "we will sin. There is no way we can escape it; Adam has passed on the taint of sin and death as his heritage." Therefore, in Adam, we will sin. We all do. But then he says, "If we are in Christ (and the implication is clear that we are), we will not go on sinning." Look at verse 21 of chapter 5:

> . . . *so that, just as sin reigned in death, so also grace might reign through righteousness to bring eternal life through Jesus Christ our Lord.*

Now whatever else those words mean, it is certain that what happens in Christ cancels out what happened in Adam. If death and sin come to us from Adam, then life and deliverance come from Christ.

You can see already one reason why Paul would add, "If this is true, how can we go on sinning?" We need to understand his line of argument. When you become a Christian, if you have by grace received the gift of God—which is Jesus himself—and the gift of righteousness which he brings, then you are no longer in Adam, but in Christ.

And yet, having said that, we have to face the fact that Christians—who are no longer in Adam but are now in Christ—do sin, and they do die. Chapter 5 told us that sin and death are the results of Adam's transgression. That, I think, brings us to what we need to understand—the nature of our humanity.

The first thing the Scriptures tell us about ourselves is that the most important part of us is our spirit. We *are* spirit; we *have* bodies and souls, but we are spirit. That may sound a bit spooky. After all, we can see our bodies and at least feel our souls. But how do we detect our spirit? We have been brainwashed by the world to believe that only those things which can be seen and felt are real—and who can see or feel a spirit? So we have a struggle. But the Scriptures tell us that basically, down deep, the very nature of our being is spirit, even as God is Spirit. You can't see your spirit, nor can you feel it; but that is who you are.

Made to Hold Something

The Scriptures help us to understand the nature of that spirit by a beautiful symbol. Since we cannot see our spirit, we have to view it through a symbol, a visual aid. The most common visual aid in Scripture to describe our human spirit is that of a vessel. You can think of your spirit as a little cup inside of you, made to hold something.

The Scriptures tell us that in the beginning this

cup was made to hold none other than God himself.
All the greatness and glory of God could be poured
into that tiny human cup. That is what Adam was, as
he came fresh from the hand of God, a cup filled with
God himself. But in the Fall that cup was emptied,
and filled again with a kind of poison. A satanic twist
began to poison all our humanity. We find that when
the poison Adam brought in fills our spirit, it spreads
into the soul. Now the soul is the realm of our experience. It is the functioning of the mind (the reason),
the will (the power to choose), and emotion (the
power to feel). Scripture tells us that this poison has
touched us in all those areas, so that we do not think
rightly, we do not feel rightly, we do not choose
rightly. That is why things go wrong wherever
human beings are involved.

What the spirit and the soul feel will be expressed
finally in the body's action. That is the way we are
made. What the body does always reflects what the
spirit and soul are doing. That is, if we have fear (one
form of evil and death within us), it will express itself
in several ways. Shyness or timidity may be one way;
anxiety and worry, another; bluster and boasting,
still another. All these reflect the fear inside.

If we feel angry and hostile, it comes out in sharp
words or even violent actions. We poke someone in
the jaw, or we yell at the top of our voice, or storm
out of the house and slam a door. All this reveals what
is inside, what is filling the cup of the spirit. If it is
self-love that is there, as it certainly is, it comes out
in greed, possessiveness, and selfishness, or through
sexual promiscuity, satisfying self, exploiting
another person. Or it may be ambition, power-
hunger, whatever. All of this comes out from within.
This is saying nothing more than what Jesus himself
told us in Mark 7.

> *What comes out of a man is what makes him 'un-*
> *clean.' For from within, out of men's hearts {that*
> *is a word for spirit}, come evil thoughts, sexual*
> *immorality, theft, murder, adultery . . . {Ho,*
> *you say, you haven't got me yet! Well, hang on!}*
> *. . . greed, malice, deceit, lewdness, envy, slan-*
> *der, arrogance and folly. All these evils come from*
> *inside and make a man 'unclean' (Mark 7:20-*
> *23).*

Paul says the same thing Jesus said. It all depends on what fills the cup of the spirit. If it is Adam's life, then that is what will come out. There is nothing we can do to stop it. All we can do is try to pretend it is something else; and we are all adept at doing that.

But what happens when that spirit fully and truly turns to Christ, when it receives the gift of God's grace, the gift of worth? Then, according to this argument in Romans 5, the tie with Adam is broken. The spirit is emptied of its satanic content—sin— and it is filled again with the Holy Spirit, who releases to it the life of Jesus. That is what the Holy Spirit has come to do. Our human spirit, our essential nature, is no longer in Adam, in any sense at all. It is now in Christ. We are tied to Christ. That is the teaching of Scripture from beginning to end, from Genesis to Revelation.

But the problem comes because our souls and bodies, which have functioned for years under the control of sin, are still going on in the same old way, living according to those patterns built up under the reign of sin. Our habits, thoughts, and actions are already established along wrong lines. That is where the evil and sin in a believer's life come from. His spirit is freed from sin; his soul and body are yet under its control.

Righteousness Is Inevitable

It is a struggle to reeducate the soul and the body, and we fail many times until we allow the Holy Spirit to bring them under the control of Jesus Christ dwelling in the cup of our spirit. But it will happen, and it must happen, Paul argues. If Christ is in the cup of the spirit, then just as we could not evade sin because we were in Adam, so in Christ we cannot evade righteousness.

The life of Jesus is more powerful, more persistent, more insistent than the life of Adam ever was. That is the meaning of all the "much mores" in this section. If we had to sin in Adam, then for the very same reason we must begin to practice righteousness in Christ. It is not something we can help; it will just happen. That is why Paul asked the question, "Having died to sin, how can we live in it any longer?" Why, it is impossible. It is not a question of should we; it is a question of can we. His answer is, "No, it can never be."

Right next door to us is a home built a number of years ago which has been inhabited now by two different families. The first was a rather difficult family, the kind of people who would never keep a yard or house in order. Soon after they moved in, the brand new home began to show the effects of their style of life. The yard was littered with trash and garbage. The lawn died for lack of care. When it was replanted, it withered again. To enter their house was to enter a shambles. It was never clean or in order.

But then these neighbors moved out and new ones moved in. It wasn't long until it became obvious that a different kind of people lived there. They cleaned up the house and painted it. The yard was cleaned up, the lawn was dug up and replanted, and it has been cared for adequately ever since. Things are completely different. What happened? It is impossible there would not be a change, because there was a change in those who dwelt inside. This is what Paul is telling us here. There has to be a change because Christ has entered our spirit.

Self-Deceived

Now someone asks, "What if a Christian does go on sinning, living in sin, claiming forgiveness, but goes on without any change in his life whatever?" What about that? There are people who do this. The answer, in light of this Scripture, is simple. These people simply reveal that they have never truly been justified by faith. They are not Christians. Let's put it as bluntly as the apostle himself put it. They are deceiving themselves and others. Though they may do so with good intent, and with utter sincerity as far as they know—nevertheless the case is clear.

It is impossible for your lifestyle to continue unchanged when you become a Christian. It is simply impossible, because a change has occurred deep in the human spirit. Those who protest and say they can go on living in sin reveal that there has been no change in their spirit; there has been no break with Adam. They are still in the same condition.

The apostle makes that plain in a couple of places. The first is in Ephesians:

> For of this you can be sure: No immoral, impure or greedy person—such a man is an idolater—has any inheritance in the kingdom of Christ and of God. {He is not a Christian yet. He is claiming to be, but he is not. And lest we be fooled by his claims, the apostle goes on to say,} Let no one deceive you with empty words, for because of such things God's wrath comes on those who are disobedient (Ephesians 5:5-7).

In very much the same terms, Paul puts it again in
1 Corinthians:

> *Do you not know that the wicked will not inherit*
> *the kingdom of God? Do not be deceived: Neither*
> *the sexually immoral nor idolaters nor adulterers*
> *nor male prostitutes nor homosexual offenders nor*
> *thieves nor the greedy nor drunkards nor slanderers*
> *nor swindlers will inherit the kingdom of God.*
> *And that is what some of you were. {They were;*
> *they are no longer. Some of them are still struggl-*
> *ing, and some of them do occasionally fail and go*
> *back to some of these things. But there's a vast dif-*
> *ference. They no longer are that way at heart; there*
> *has been a break, a change in their lifestyle.} But*
> *you were washed, you were sanctified, you were jus-*
> *tified in the name of the Lord Jesus Christ and by*
> *the Spirit of our God (1 Corinthians 6:9-11).*

I think Paul is clear and fully answers the question,
doesn't he? He says there is great hope for those
caught up in any of these things. There is a way of
deliverance. It is not a way that permits going on
with the same style of life. Jesus Christ came to free
us from sin, not to allow us to continue in it.

The question we must face about ourselves is,
Have we really begun to hate sin deep inside—our
own sin, the things we do wrong and, for the moment, choose to do? Have you begun to hate it? Do
you want to be free from it, to be delivered, want its
power broken in your life? You can only want that
because there has come into your heart a new Spirit;
into the cup of your human spirit has come the grace
of the Lord Jesus Christ. And from that vantage
point, he is beginning to assert control of his purity
throughout your whole life. You cannot settle for sin
any longer.

In the rest of the chapter Paul helps us to understand more about how this works, but here he makes the principle itself unquestionably clear. Can we go on sinning? May it never be!

14
THE TRUE BAPTISM OF THE SPIRIT

(Romans 6:1-14)

When a person becomes a Christian, when he really, truly receives Jesus Christ as Lord, something happens that makes it impossible for him to go on living a lifestyle of evil, because he died to sin. The apostle now uses two marvelous visual aids to help us understand this. One of them is baptism, and the other is grafting (as a plant or a branch is grafted into a tree). Here is what he says about baptism:

What shall we say, then? Shall we go on sinning so that grace may increase? By no means! We died to sin; how can we live in it any longer? Or don't you know that all of us who were baptized into

Christ Jesus were baptized into his death? We were therefore buried with him through baptism into death in order that, just as Christ was raised from the dead through the glory of the Father, we too may live a new life (6:1-4).

When I was a boy in Montana I had a horse that could smell water from farther away than any animal I ever saw. You could be riding across the dry, parched plains, when suddenly he would prick up his ears, lift his head, and quicken his pace, and you knew he smelled water somewhere and was heading for it. Some people are like that. Whenever they read these passages and see the word "baptism," they smell water. You can just see them prick up their ears, lift their heads, and head for it. But there is no water here. This is a dry passage.

More Potent Than Water

This passage deals with how we died to sin, how we became separated from Adam and were joined in Christ. No water can do that. That requires something far more potent than water. It is, therefore, a description of the baptism of the Holy Spirit (as it is called elsewhere in the Scriptures). John the Baptist, who made his reputation because he baptized in water, said, "I indeed baptize you with water, but there comes One after me, greater than I, who will baptize you with the Holy Spirit." That is what Paul is talking about here—the baptism of the Holy Spirit, which places us into Christ.

In 1 Corinthians 12:13, Paul says exactly the same thing: "For we were all baptized by one Spirit into one body—whether Jews or Greeks, slave or free—and we were all given the one Spirit to drink." Notice how he emphasizes that *all* believers were baptized into one body. We were placed into Christ. You are not a Christian if that is not true of you. Therefore, people today who say you need to undergo the baptism of the Holy Spirit *after* you become a believer do not understand the Scriptures. There is no way to become a believer without being baptized with the Holy Spirit.

The baptism of the Spirit happened first, historically, on the day of Pentecost, when the Holy Spirit came upon 120 people who were gathered in the temple courts. It fused them into one body, joining them to the head, which is Jesus. Thus the church was formed, one body in Christ, all members one of the other and members of the Lord Jesus himself. That is the baptism of the Holy Spirit. It is not something *felt*; it is not something we can know through our senses when it takes place; it is something the Spirit does to our human spirit. Yet this baptism is essential to becoming a Christian. It is part of the process by which we share the life of Jesus Christ.

Notice some things that Paul says about the baptism of the Spirit. First, he says that we are expected to know about it: "*Don't you know* that we were all baptized into Christ, into his death?" He expects these Roman Christians, who had never met him or been taught personally by him, to know this. It is something new Christians ought to know.

Shadow on the Sand

Now, how would they know this? Here is where water baptism comes in. Water baptism teaches, by symbol, the meaning of the baptism of the Spirit. The one is the shadow, or figure, of the other. The people to whom Paul was writing had been baptized in water after their conversion and regeneration, and Paul supposes that their water baptism had helped them to understand the reality of what the Spirit had already done to them.

Some time ago, my fellow pastor, Ron Ritchie, told me of an experience he had one Easter Sunday during a baptism service in the ocean near his home. You really have to love Christ to be baptized in the frigid waters of the Pacific! A woman came up to him and asked him to baptize her nine-year-old daughter. Ron was reluctant to do so without finding out whether the girl really understood what was happening, so he began to question her and to teach her about the reality behind water baptism. He was gesturing as he talked to her, and noticed the shadow of his hand as it fell on the sand. So he said to the little girl, "Do you see the shadow of my hand on the sand? Now that is just the shadow; the hand is the real thing. And when you came to Jesus, when you believed in Jesus, that was the real baptism. You were joined to him, and what happened to him happened to you. Jesus was alive; then he died, was buried, and then he arose from the dead. And that is what happened to you when you believed in him."

He pointed to the shadow on the sand and said, "When you go down in the water and are raised up again, that is a picture of what has already happened." The girl immediately caught on and said, "Yes, that is what I want to do because Jesus has come into my life." So water baptism is a shadow, a picture, a symbol worked out for us to teach what happened to us when we believed in the Lord Jesus.

Notice also that the apostle explains how we died to sin. The Spirit took us and identified us with all that Jesus did. Now, I do not understand that, because that means the cross is a timeless event. The Spirit of God is able to ignore the two thousand years since the crucifixion and resurrection and somehow identify us, who live in this twentieth century—as he has all believers of past centuries—with that moment when Jesus died, was buried, and rose again from the dead. We participate in those events. That is clear.

But I do not think we need to struggle with this, because something similar has already been referred to in chapter 5. There we were told that by being born into this human race we became part of what Adam did. Way back at the dawn of history, Adam sinned, and we sinned in Adam. I do not fully know how that is true, but I certainly believe it. Every evidence of history demonstrates it to be true. This is not theological fiction; it is fact. Adam sinned, and so we sin. Adam died, and men ever since have died.

The apostle is now saying that what was true in Adam has now been ended; now we are in Christ, by faith in Jesus Christ. Once Adam's actions affected us; but now Christ's actions become ours as well. Christ died, and we died; Christ was buried, and we were buried with him; Christ rose again, and we rose with him. So what is true of Jesus is true of us.

Here Paul is dealing with what is probably the most remarkable and certainly the most magnificent truth recorded in the pages of Scripture. It is the central truth God wants us to learn. We died with Christ, were buried, and rose again with him. That union with Christ is the truth from which everything else in Scripture flows. If we understand and accept this fact, then everything in our lives will be different. That is why the apostle labors so to help us understand.

Notice one other thing about this paragraph—the purpose for which all this happened. Paul says, "We were therefore buried with him through baptism into death *in order that*, just as Christ was raised from the dead through the glory of the Father, we too may live a new life." Remember, Paul is answering the question, "Can a believer go on sinning?" His answer is, "Absolutely not." We cannot because we have died, have been buried, and have risen again with Jesus; and therefore we too may live a new life.

Nectarines and Peaches

Verses 5 through 10 introduce a new figure and reveal a deeper revelation of what has happened to us. Paul now uses the figure of *grafting*.

> *If we have been united with him in his death, we will certainly also be united with him in his resurrection (6:5).*

In other words, you cannot pick and choose. You cannot die with Christ and not be risen with him. If you died with him, you must be risen with him as well. Paul uses a word from botany here. The word "united" means "to graft a branch into another." If you have fruit trees, you may have done grafting. Perhaps you have taken a branch from a nectarine tree and grafted it into a peach tree. The branch is tied into the tree in such a way that the life from the trunk of the tree flows into the branch and they grow together until finally you can't tell the difference between the graft and the natural branch. The life is fully shared. This is the figure Paul is using here to describe our tie with the Lord Jesus. His life becomes our life. We are no longer in Adam, in any sense. The tie is totally broken. We are now in Christ, and he is our life from now on.

This is important for us to understand. To help us further, Paul now gives us both sides to this parallel—death and resurrection. Verses 6 and 7 explain what it means to die in Christ; verses 8-10 explain what it means to be risen with him. Verses 6 and 7:

For we know that our old self was crucified with him so that the body of sin might be rendered powerless, that we should no longer be slaves to sin—because anyone who has died has been freed from sin.

In this parallel, Jesus was crucified and we were crucified too. Our old self, the old man, the man who was in Adam, is dead, and the tie has been broken. All that we were as a natural-born human being ended when we believed in Jesus.

Paul refers to the essential "you," the spirit within. Biblical psychology tells us that basically we are spirits, as I have already discussed, dwelling in human bodies. Your body is not you. Even your soul, which is produced by the union of the body and the spirit, is not wholly you. You are your spirit.

Until the Cross

Next, Paul explains that Jesus was crucified in order that the sin which was in his body on the cross should come to an end, that this body be rendered powerless with respect to sin. You say, "Now, wait a minute. There's something wrong here. There was no sin in Jesus." That is true. Scripture is careful to teach us that in Jesus there was no sin. He did not sin; there was no sin in him until the cross. But this tells us an amazing thing about our Lord when he was on the cross. There, Paul says, he was "made sin" for us. Sin, in the believer, is located in the body. (I will expand upon that in a moment.) Therefore, it was described in Jesus in terms of the body. His body became possessed and controlled by sin. That is why his body died. And by his death his body was thus rendered powerless with regard to sin.

Why do we bury a corpse? We bury it because it is useless, inert, inactive. There is nothing it can do any longer, and so we bury it. That is why Jesus was buried—to prove that the sin in his body was ended. The body was useless, unresponsive. Paul says that is what happens to us. When our spirit has died in Christ, then the body of sin will be rendered powerless.

What does Paul mean by this term "body of sin"? He means the physical body dominated and controlled by sin. In Adam, sin filled the whole of man—his spirit, his soul, and his body. Therefore, his descendants had to sin. That is why, before I became a Christian, even when I tried to be good, I couldn't. Something always went wrong and I ended by fouling up in some way. I was a slave to sin, and no matter how much I wanted to be different, I couldn't be.

But now that bond has been broken. In Christ my spirit is freed. It has been united with Jesus; it has risen with him, and it is free from sin. This explains that rather interesting passage in 1 John 3:9, which says, "No one who is born of God will continue to sin, because God's seed remains in him; he cannot go on sinning, because he has been born of God." John is talking about the spirit, the essential me. In that sense, it is proper to say of believers, "We cannot sin."

What Paul makes clear in Romans 6 is that sin remains as an alien power trying to dominate and control our bodies and our souls. It is the presence of the spirit in the body that produces the soul, just as electricity in a light bulb produces light. The soul is our conscious experience and is produced moment by moment as we live, as light comes from a light bulb moment by moment. Paul makes it clear that in Christ our spirits were freed from sin. They do not sin, and cannot sin, because they are linked with

Christ so that we may be able to control the sin which is in the body.

From here on, we do not have to sin. If we do, it is because we allow it to happen. But we are no longer slaves to sin. Throughout the rest of this account Paul deals with this theme. The body is the means by which we are tempted to sin. There is nothing inherently sinful about our bodies—they are perfectly all right—but somehow an alien power remains in them, and that is where we are tempted all our life long. The body is the seat of sin.

Sin in the Body

I think I can illustrate this for you. When you sit at the table to eat, you are satisfying a normal appetite that God gave to your body. It needs food; it needs to replenish its energy. There is nothing wrong with eating. But when we get to the table and find plenty of food on it, each one of us has something within us that makes us want to eat too much. We often eat more than we should. We say that we have a weight problem. What we really have is a sin problem. Sin within us wants to take a natural function of the body and push it beyond what it ought to do— and thus it becomes sin. That is why, when we sit at the table, many of us are going to sin by becoming gluttons and gourmands. A gourmand is someone who eats greedily, who delights in luxurious food, who lives for the taste of food. We are all tempted this way because sin, as a principle, is still in control of the functions of the body. But our spirit opposes it, and we do not have to give in. That is the point.

From time to time the body requires rest. The body of Jesus grew weary and needed rest. But there is in us a principle that wants to overindulge, and we become lazy, slothful, apathetic. We want other people to work and to serve us while we rest. This is so natural that it is even hard to know when we go over the line.

The mind, that amazing instrument, reasons and logically deduces and produces an amazing variety of inventions and technological advances. Yet the mind, with its ability to think and reason, can easily move beyond what it should into evil thoughts and prideful reactions, and attitudes of jealousy and lust. We can sin with our minds.

Consider the tongue, that member of the body that is so little, James says, yet can be set on fire by hell. With our tongues, designed to be that by which we bless God, we curse him instead. The tongue is like the rudder of a ship. It turns the whole life in a wrong direction because of our words.

Consider the glands and hormones. Physiologists tell us that they are linked somehow with our actions. Just as the brain is linked with the mind, so the glands are linked with our emotions. They are often responsible for the way we feel. They pour out hormones into the bloodstream and affect the body. Some hormones make us overreact. Instead of experiencing normal fears designed to protect us from evil, we become paranoid, worried, filled with anxiety. Or we become lustful and indulge in wrong attitudes. We become angry, so that we hate and feel jealousy. We indulge in what the Bible calls "inordinate affections." Even our loves become twisted. That is sin in the body—no longer in the spirit, but in the body. I do not have to describe this in terms of our sexual appetites. These are normal, legitimate, valid appetites, made by God to be satisfied; but something within us wants to satisfy them too soon, or with the wrong person, or sometimes in the wrong way.

That is where evil comes from—the body, not the spirit. I hope this is clear, because it is a very important picture, and one that governs the rest of the book of Romans (as well as all the New Testament). The regenerated spirit cannot sin. It is born of God and it cannot sin. It has been set free from sin in order that we may begin to exercise control over the body of sin, so that it may be rendered inactive; we no longer need to be slaves to sin.

Not only have we been set free to refuse sin, but a new *power* to resist sin has been given to us:

> *Now if we died with Christ, we believe that we will also live with him. For we know that since Christ was raised from the dead, he cannot die again; death no longer has mastery over him. The death he died, he died to sin once for all; but the life he lives, he lives to God (6:8-10).*

Once we have reckoned ourselves dead to sin with Christ, there is nothing left but to go on to life. Jesus does not go back into sin; he does not go back into death. Sin and death are over, as far as we are concerned, because that is what is true of Jesus. He lives now, and he lives under the will and by the power of God. Therefore, Paul says, the same thing is true in our lives. Not only do we need to recognize that we died to sin with Christ, but also that his life is in us now. His power is available to us. When we decide not to sin, we have the power to carry it out, because Christ is living in us.

The Two-Step

It all comes down to the two simple steps described in verse 11. This is the first time in the book of Romans that we are asked to do anything; this is the first exhortation in all of Romans. Up to now, everything Paul has written has been about what God has done for us. Now in verse 11 we are asked to do something. What is it?

> *In the same way, count yourselves dead to sin but alive to God in Christ Jesus.*

When you are tempted, there are two things to do. First, remember that you do not have to obey sin. You are free to refuse it, free to say, "No, you don't have the right to use that part of my body for a sinful purpose." And second, remember his power in you to enable you to offer that same part of your body to God, to be used for his purposes. Now that may mean a struggle, because sin is very strong. When we start to turn away from evil in our bodies, the habits of our lives are so deeply ingrained that often it is very difficult, and we struggle. But we have the power not to sin because we have God himself within us, the living God.

A group of ex-homosexuals living in San Rafael, California, has a great ministry with those still involved in homosexuality. I was struck by this paragraph from one of their papers. The writer is describing how tough it is to turn from these evil practices and be different once you have been deeply involved in them. He says:

> *This very weekend one of our brothers said to me, "How can I last through even one more year of this?" I said in response, "How can I last one more week?" But I will last, and so will he. For we have each other, and the sharing and fellowship and caring are God's ingredients to healing— long-lasting healing—that will impart strength beyond endurance, as God does it in his time, and in his way.*

That says exactly what Paul says in Romans 6. There will be a struggle; it is not always easy, but we have the strength to do it and we have the right to do it. We have the freedom not to sin and the desire not to sin. That is what God has brought to us in Christ.

Now you will see how the rest of this fits in. Paul is describing the two steps we are to repeat over and over in dealing with evil in our lives. First, in verses 12-13a, Paul explains how to count yourself dead to sin:

> *Therefore do not let sin reign in your mortal body so that you obey its evil desires. Do not offer the parts of your body to sin, as instruments of wickedness . . .*

Step number one is to reckon yourself dead to sin, to recognize it no longer has power over you. Step number two is found in verse 13b: Offer yourself to God.

> *. . . but rather offer yourselves to God, as those who have been brought from death to life; and offer the parts of your body to him {your tongue, your mind, your stomach, your hands, your feet, your sex organs—offer them to God} as instruments of righteousness.*

That is the way to win over temptation. Then Paul closes with this fantastic statement in verse 14. This, to me, is one of the greatest verses in all Scripture:

> *For sin shall not be your master, because you are not under law, but under grace.*

Why does Paul bring in the law? He brings it in because he is dealing with one of the most basic problems of the Christian struggle, the thing that often depresses and discourages us more than anything else—the sense of condemnation we feel when we momentarily yield to sin. The law produces condemnation. The law says that unless I live up to this standard, God will not have anything to do with me. We have been so influenced by this idea that when we sin, even as believers, we think God is angry and does not care about us. We also think that way about ourselves, and become discouraged, defeated, and depressed. We want to give up. "What's the use?" we ask.

But Paul says that is not true. We are not under law. God does not feel that way about us. We are under grace, and God understands our struggle. He is not disgusted with us; he is not angry with us. He understands our failure. He knows there will be a struggle and there will be failures. He also knows he has made full provision for us to recover immediately, to pick ourselves up and go right on climbing the mountain. Therefore we don't need to be discouraged, and we shouldn't be. Sin will not be our master because we are not under the law and condemnation, but under grace. And even though we struggle, if every time we fail we come back to God and ask his forgiveness, and take it from him, and remember how he loves us, and that he is not angry or upset with us, and go on from there, we will win.

I will never forget how, as a young man in the service during World War II, I was on a watch one night, reading the Book of Romans. This verse leaped out of the pages at me. I remember how the Spirit made it come alive, and I saw the great promise that all the things I was struggling with as a young man would ultimately be mastered—not because I was so smart, but because God was teaching me and leading me into victory. I remember walking the floor, my heart boiling over with praise and thanksgiving to God. I walked in a cloud of glory, rejoicing in this great promise: "Sin shall not have dominion over you, for you are not under law, but under grace."

Looking back across these more than forty years since that night, I can see how God has broken the grip of things that mastered me then. Other problems have come in, with which I still struggle. But the promise remains: "Sin shall not have dominion over you. You are not under law, but under grace."

15
WHOSE SLAVE
ARE YOU?

(Romans 6:15-23)

Surely believers ought not to sin, but unfortunately, they do. In verses 1-14 of chapter 6, we looked at the answer to the question, "Can I go on living as I once did? Can I continue a lifestyle of sin, just as though nothing had really happened to me, except that I will go to heaven when I die?"

Paul's answer is: "Absolutely not! You cannot do that; if you do, it is proof that you never really participated in the death and resurrection of Jesus." In other words, you are really not a Christian. Anyone who goes on in an unchanged life after having professed that he has come to Christ is simply giving testimony to everyone that he really has not been

changed in his heart at all. Paul has just declared,
"For sin shall not be your master, because you are not
under law, but under grace."

In verse 15, he raises the question again, but in a
slightly different way:

> *What then? Shall we sin because we are not under*
> *law but under grace?*

Now the question is not "can we" but "shall we?"
Paul is asking whether a Christian should choose to
sin occasionally because of the momentary pleasure
involved.

Every one of us faces that situation from time to
time. Sometimes we run up against some especially
delicious temptations. At times, we are all confronted with the suggestion, "Why not give in? After
all, I'm not going to hell because of this. My salvation rests on Christ and not on me. And actually,
God is not going to reject me because of this, for the
law does not condemn me any longer. I am not under
law. It is love that will discipline me; law will not
condemn me. I can be forgiven; I can be restored—so
why not sin?" I have heard many Christians talk that
way, and I have felt the full force of this confrontation
in my own life. Since we are not under law, but under
grace, why not give in and enjoy a sin? Do you see the
thrust of the apostle's question?

In the verses that follow, Paul answers that question, beginning with an emphatic "No. By no
means!" If I, as a Christian, go on and sin deliberately, even if it is only occasionally, I must face what
sin will do to me. We believers must face the full results of what will happen when we choose to do what
we know is wrong, even though we have been set free
in Christ and need not do these things.

Paul's answer is threefold. Shall we sin because we

are not under law but under grace? By no means!
First, sin makes one a slave (verses 16 through 19).
Second, sin will make one ashamed (verses 20 and
21). Finally, sin will spread death throughout our
whole existence (verses 22 and 23).

Made to Be Mastered

Let's look at the first part of Paul's answer. In verses 16 through 19 he tells us that sin will make slaves
out of us:

> *Don't you know that when you offer yourselves to
> someone to obey him as slaves, you are slaves to the
> one whom you obey—whether you are slaves to sin,
> which leads to death, or to obedience, which leads
> to righteousness? But thanks be to God that,
> though you used to be slaves to sin, you whole-
> heartedly obeyed the form of teaching to which you
> were entrusted. You have been set free from sin and
> have become slaves to righteousness. I put this in
> human terms because you are weak in your natural
> selves. Just as you used to offer the parts of your
> body in slavery to impurity and to ever-increasing
> wickedness, so now offer them in slavery to right-
> eousness leading to holiness (6:16-19).*

Paul goes into the common experience of the world
of his day to give us a picture of what humanity is
like. He uses the word "slaves" to describe us. In
doing so, he is dealing with a profound psychological
fact: Human beings are made to be mastered. Someone has to master us.

Several years ago in Los Angeles I saw a man walking down the street with a sign hung over his shoulders. The front of it said "I'M A SLAVE FOR
CHRIST." On the back it read, "WHOSE SLAVE
ARE YOU?" It is a good question. All of us are slaves

to one or the other of these two masters—sin or righteousness. We have no other choices. By the very nature of our humanity, we are made to serve and to be
controlled by forces beyond our power.

We think we are creatures of sovereign choice, but
we are not. Our choices are narrow and limited. The
great question is: Who controls the choices in that
narrow band? What forces are at work to limit us to
such a narrow range throughout our lives? The answer is that something beyond us controls these
choices. God is at work; Satan is at work. We are
given a limited ability to choose.

Paul then speaks of these two kinds of slavery. He
says that we Christians have been set free from slavery
to sin. Once we *had* to sin. Before we came to Christ,
there was no choice; no matter whether we chose
what we thought was good or chose what we thought
was wrong, we ended up making a choice that led to
evil. There was no other way. Even the right things
we tried to do were tainted with evil, with selfishness.

Well then, what happens when we sin as believers?
Now we are free, and yet we go back and choose to do
something wrong. We are confronted with this
temptation to give way for the moment and indulge
ourselves in some sin. Most of us try to kid ourselves
into believing it is not very serious. "It won't hurt us
anyway," we reason, so we make the choice.

Paul says, "Let's look at what happens. First of all,
don't you know that you have set in operation a basic
principle of life?" The principle is this: If you yield
yourself to sin, you become sin's slave. Jesus stated
this in John 8:34—"Verily, verily, I say unto you
[that is a little formula that means he is stating basic,
fundamental, absolutely foundational truth],

whosoever committeth sin is the servant of sin"
(KJV).

No Ultimate Control

Now, what does this mean in practice? A slave, of
course, is someone who is not in ultimate control of
his own actions, someone who is at the disposal of
another person, someone who has to do what that
other person says. When we choose to tell a lie, we
give one of the clearest evidences of this principle in
our lives. Have you ever noticed what happens when
you tell a lie?

A man said to me one day, "I told what I thought
was a little white lie. I thought that would handle
the matter. But you know, I found out that I had to
tell 42 other lies—I counted them—before I finally
woke up to what I was doing and admitted the whole
thing and got out from under." We can't tell just one
lie. We are not in control of the events. If we choose
to tell one lie, before we know it, we have to tell
another.

The same is true with anger. I decide I am going
to put a little sharpness in my voice when I answer
someone. I want to cut him down just a little. I don't
want it to go too far—after all, I do like him—I just
want to hurt him slightly. So I do. What happens?
He answers back in kind. So I cut a little deeper, and
before I know it, I am embroiled in an argument and
a battle that I did not want. It happened because I
became a slave to sin. Sin pushed me further than I
wanted to go. There was no way I could escape.

Second, sin not only takes me further than I desire
to go, but it also infects others with the same attitude. Notice how it works. I wake up in the morning feeling surly and grouchy, and I snap at someone.

Then the other person snaps back, and soon the whole household reflects my attitude. I choose to do something a little shady in my business, and soon others begin to do the same thing. So sin begins to spread, like an infection. Years ago I heard a little rhyme:

> *I said a very naughty word, only the other day. It was a truly naughty word I had not meant to say. But then, it was not really lost, when from my lips it flew; My little brother picked it up, and now he says it too.*

That is the way sin begins to spread. Part of the slavery is that when I yield myself to something (and do so two or three times, so that it gets out of control and goes beyond what I wanted before I wake up to what is going on), it becomes difficult to change. Something resists every opportunity I take to change, because a habit has begun. Someone said to me the other day, "It's easy to quit smoking; I've done it dozens of times!" What a testimony to the power these things have to grip and control us! Paul is right: We become slaves of that which we obey.

In verse 20 and 21 Paul continues:

> *When you were slaves to sin, you were free from the control of righteousness. What benefit {or what fruit} did you reap at that time from the things you are now ashamed of?*

Each of us can look back in our lives at something we are ashamed of. It leaves a stain in our minds when we think about it. Shame is the awareness of unworthy actions and irreparable damage that we do to others, and our painful feeling about them. We have all felt shame. Sin—no matter what it is or how small it seems—always leads to shame, a shame that stains and blots our memories. We all know what it is like—those shameful deeds that we would like to forget, but can't; hurtful words that we wish we had never said; strained relationships that go on for years, so that whenever we meet certain people we feel uncomfortable.

This is the inevitable fruit of sin, something of which Paul reminds us many times. In Galatians he says, "Do not be deceived [don't kid yourself]: God cannot be mocked. A man reaps what he sows. The one who sows to please his sinful nature, from that nature will reap destruction. . . ." I can't drop the seed of evil into my heart without reaping from it the harvest, the fruit of corruption. But "the one who sows to please the Spirit, from the Spirit will reap eternal life" (Galatians 6:7-8). That is exactly what we see here in Romans 6.

The End of Light

The third reason we should not give way to sin is found in verses 21 to 23:

> *Those things result in death! But now that you have been set free from sin and have become slaves to God, the benefit you reap leads to holiness, and the result is eternal life. For the wages of sin is death, but the gift of God is eternal life in Christ Jesus our Lord (6:21-23).*

Life and death are the two results. When Paul talks about death here, he is talking about something that you experience right now while you live. Death is both physical and moral; the one is a picture of the other. Physical death always involves darkness, the end of light and life. It involves limitation, for a corpse is helpless—what can it do for itself? And it involves, ultimately, corruption—the corpse begins to decay and stink; rottenness sets in.

When we sin as believers, these same elements are present. There is, first of all, darkness. I can look back in my own life and see how, as a young Christian, there were times when I struggled and struggled to understand passages of Scripture. I could not seem to grasp them; they were closed to me. Others understood them and seemed to be rejoicing in them, but I could not—until God, in his mercy, began to deal with me about things that I was doing that I knew were wrong. Finally, God led me to the place where I could be free. I would repent and turn from these things and come into the freedom that God had given me in Christ. Then I would discover that the Scriptures began to open up, and light came into my darkness.

I meet Christians all the time who do not seem to understand the Word of God. I do not know if this is always the explanation, but in many cases it is because they are deliberately allowing things in their lives that they know are wrong. They do not realize that these things spread death. Darkness sets in, and they cannot see the light. Paul reminds us in 2 Corinthians 4:4, "The god of this age has blinded the minds of unbelievers, so that they cannot see the light of the gospel of the glory of Christ."

Besides this darkness, sin produces other limitations too. Remember the account in the Old Testament about Moses in the wilderness? He became angry one day when the people tested him and frustrated him. God told him to speak to the rock and it would give water. Instead, in his anger, Moses struck the rock with a rod. That was just a little thing, a momentary blowup. For a few seconds, he lost his temper. But God said, "Moses, because you have done this, you will not be able to enter the Promised

Land. When the people enter the land, you must stay behind because you have done this thing."

I am not suggesting there are things we do that forever limit the opportunities God gives us. But I know that as long as we cling to things that we know are wrong, justifying them and refusing to enter into the freedom that God gives us, there is loss of opportunity. That is why many Christians never seem to discover the adventure of serving God. They sit with folded arms, watching other people having fun and excitement, while nothing opens for them. Often it is because of this very thing— the choices of sin that they make. Death means a lessening of our freedom and delight in the things of God and an increase in boredom and banality. Sometimes our lives become utterly nauseating to us. Have you ever felt that way? Sometimes your whole Christian experience almost stinks in your own nostrils. That is a sign of the death brought in by sin.

Now throughout this account, Paul stresses over and over again the words "set free." "You have been set free," he says. "You no longer are the slaves of sin. When you came to the Lord Jesus, a change occurred; you have been freed. You are no longer a slave to evil, but a slave to righteousness." Paul says, "Just as you used to offer the parts of your body in slavery to impurity and to ever-increasing wickedness, so now offer them in slavery to righteousness and holiness."

Now that you have been set free from sin and have become slaves to God, all this business of being limited, of experiencing death and shame, is totally unnecessary. That is the tragedy of sin in a believer's life. We do not have to experience death in our lives; we have it only because we choose it, although we were free to choose otherwise.

Useless Unless Used

Years ago a member of our family was learning to ride a bicycle. She learned how to balance herself and pedal down the street. And she did very well at it. But the only way she could stop herself was by running into something, and I was constantly picking her up out of the bushes and off the sidewalk.

One day, while I was helping her, I said, "You don't have to run into things to stop; there is another way to do it. A provision has been made so that you can stop this bicycle without having to run into things." I showed her that all she had to do was to reverse the pedals and the coaster brake would bring her to a stop. But I had shown her that before, so that this time she replied with just a bit of sarcasm, "Well, I am sure relieved to know that!"

I realized she didn't need me to tell her there was another way to stop. What she *did* need was to actually use it when it was time. What good is it to have a provision for stopping if you never use it? You might just as well not have it.

The question the apostle raises in this passage is this: "What good is it to be set free from sin by Jesus Christ and have every opportunity and every possibility of walking in holiness (wholeness) and in righteousness (a sense of worth, a sense of security and assurance that you are loved by God and are valuable to him), if, at the moment of choice, we ignore these things and go right on as though we were slaves to sin?"

As I travel across America, I often notice how our cities are filled with churches. And those churches are often filled with Christians. This country would appear to have a fantastic opportunity to witness a new quality of life—a quality of life so uniquely different from that of the world that people ought to be stopping us on the street to ask, "What goes with you? How can you have such peace in your eyes? How can you have such love in your heart? Why are you so different?" Instead, with our cities filled with churches and our churches filled with people, all the world sees is the same old tired reactions which are so familiar to them.

The challenge of Romans 6 is this: Christ has made us free, free to be kings, free to have a sense of worth, free to be secure in our own personhood, knowing who we are before God. He set us free to be whole people, untorn by conflicting interests. With a single eye we can live to the glory of God, free from the control or the blame or the censure—or the praise—of men. We are free at last to respond to the greatest calling a man or woman can have—the call to know God.

This is what the closing verse means. "The wages of sin is death, but the gift of God is eternal life." Jesus described that eternal life in John 17:3—"Now this is eternal life: that they may know you, the only true God, and Jesus Christ, whom you have sent." Here we are, called to this kind of living, called to this quality of existence . . . and yet, because of the foolishness of our hearts and the weakness of our faith, we choose to give way to momentary indulgences that lock us into slavery, shame, and death.

May God help us set sin aside and live as the free men and women God has made us to be! As Paul said in Galatians 5:1, "It is for freedom that Christ has set us free. Stand firm, then, and do not let yourselves be burdened again by a yoke of slavery." We have been freed from the slave market; now we are to walk as new men.

16
FREE TO
WIN OR LOSE

(Romans 7:1-6)

Romans tells us that God's solution to man's problem is to begin a whole new race. He does not use halfway measures, or try to patch up the old; he does not try to improve what is there until it becomes good enough to live with. He cuts man right off at the root and begins a new race.

But the wonder and the glory of it is that he starts the new race within the shell of the old. Outwardly, we remain unchanged. Our bodies are still subject to decrepitude, decay, and death. Yet within, a new man has begun if we have exercised faith in Jesus Christ. God's solution is to end the curse of Adam and to release within us the power of a new life, the

life of Jesus himself. When we put our faith in our
Lord and what he has done, we enter into an identifi-
cation with his death and his resurrection. The death
of Jesus cuts us off from the old Adam with whom we
all began life. The resurrection of Jesus, Paul says,
introduces us to a whole new power—the life of
Jesus, available to us.

This radical transformation will change our attitude, outlook, and value system, and therefore it
will change our lifestyle. But we can still sin as believers, if we choose to. If we do, however, we cannot
escape the enslavement that sin will bring. It will involve us more deeply than we would like; it will
spread darkness and corruption throughout our lives;
it will lead us to do things of which we will be terribly ashamed. Though we can choose to sin, we will
not escape its consequences. We will not be condemned to hell but we will be chastised unto repentance.

Chapter 7 deals with still another question before
the apostle Paul more fully develops this wonderful,
glorious gospel. The question is this: Does the law
help us, as believers, to handle the problem of sin?
The answer is both yes and no. Yes, the law does help
us—but only up to a point. It will help us to define
the problem. But no, the law is no help at all when it
comes to delivering us. In fact, it will only make
things worse.

Paul deals with the last part of this question first.
In verses 1 through 6 he shows the necessity of being
freed from the law in order to handle the problem of
sin. We cannot handle our sins with the law hanging
over our heads; we must be freed from that. This is a
pertinent problem today. Every Christian rejoices in
what he reads in the Scriptures about our identifica-
tion with Christ and in these tremendous terms—

"freed from sin," "dead to sin," and "alive to God," "alive to righteousness," wholeness, power. Yet our experience tells us that we do not often achieve this. We are aware that we all have a problem with sin. We still like it, and we still do it. We experience what Paul says we will experience (enslavement, death, darkness, unhappiness, and shame) as a result of our sin. This is true for every believer in Christ today. Churches everywhere are filled with Christians who are struggling with this.

What is wrong? Basically, it is the problem that Paul describes in Romans 7. We still have not learned how to handle the law. We still want regulations and detailed instructions to follow so we can be freed from our problems. Yet, when we try, even with the best of intentions, it still doesn't work. That is what Paul deals with in this chapter. Now, let's see what he has to say in verses 1-3:

> *Do you not know, brothers—for I am speaking to men who know the law—that the law has author-ity over a man only as long as he lives? For ex-ample, by law a married woman is bound to her husband as long as he is alive, but if her husband dies, she is released from the law of marriage. So then, if she marries another man while her hus-band is still alive, she is called an adulteress. But if her husband dies, she is released from that law and is not an adulteress, even though she marries another man.*

This is a simple illustration taken right out of life. This situation occurred again and again in Paul's day, and it occurs frequently in ours. It is intended to clarify our relationship to the law. But before we get into the illustration and its application, let's first notice that Paul carefully underlines for us to whom

this passage is addressed. In the first verse, he says,
"Do you not know, brothers—for I am speaking to
men who know the law. . . ." In other words, if we
are to understand this paragraph, we must know
something about the law—its function, its purpose,
and its effect. If we don't we will end up confused.

What Do You Know?

We must take a moment to ask ourselves if we understand the law. First, do we realize that "the law"
refers to a standard of conduct, or behavior, which is
expected of men? There are other uses of the word
"law." Sometimes it is used in reference to a principle
that governs our lives, such as the law of gravity. But
here Paul is talking about a standard of conduct that
we are expected to live up to.

The most obvious and perfect expression of that
standard is the Ten Commandments, which tell us,

> *You shall have no other gods before me.*
> *You shall not make for yourself a graven*
>   *image. . . .*
> *You shall not take the name of the Lord your God*
>   *in vain. . . .*
> *Remember the sabbath day, to keep it holy. . . .*
> *Honor your father and your mother. . . .*
> *You shall not kill.*
> *You shall not commit adultery.*
> *You shall not steal.*
> *You shall not bear false witness against your*
>   *neighbor.*
> *You shall not covet. . . .*
> *(Exodus 20:3-17 RSV).*

That is a standard of conduct. That is the law Paul
talks about here—the law that was given to Israel.

But Paul has already explained in chapter 2 that,

in a wider sense, the law is relevant to men everywhere. Have you ever heard people talking about their experiences and relationships with others? Listen for a while, and you will hear a phrase like this: "I don't think that is fair." What do these people mean? What is it that determines whether a thing is fair or not? It is obviously some unspoken standard of conduct or behavior that both the speaker and the listener have in mind which is universally understood.

Some put it this way: "I think this is the right thing to do." There again is an unspoken standard of behavior. Someone says, "I'm going to get even!" How do you know when you are "even"? There is clearly a measure, a standard in mind. So, as Paul points out in chapter 2, the law really is everywhere; it is embedded in the heart. There is an undescribed, unspoken standard of conduct to which we all refer. Every man everywhere thinks in these terms, no matter what his background. Now, that is the law. It is the unspoken agreement we all understand and to which we must measure up. This is what Paul calls "the law."

Let's see what more we can know about the law. The purpose of the law is to condemn failure. It never pats us on the back when we do right. It takes for granted that we ought to do right anyway, and it never says "thank you" for doing right. But if we do wrong, the law condemns us. In one way or another, it points out and punishes wrongdoing. It does this in the laws of our land, in traffic laws, and even in our so-called "moral" laws. Evil and wrongdoing always take their toll. Therefore, the nature of law is to condemn failure.

Why does the law discourage people? If law condemns—and no one likes to feel put down and condemned—then the effect of the law, invariably, is to

discourage, to produce a sense of defeat, and ultimately, a sense of despair. That is what the law does.
That is why, in our land and in all the nations of the
earth, law produces a sense of despair. That is a major
problem with which people wrestle today.

People under Law

No one likes to despair, so we react in various
ways. There are certain invariable signs that reveal
how people are still under the law. Paul wrote to
those believers in Christ still under the law. In their
minds, at least, they thought they had to live under
the law, and there are certain signs of people who live
like that.

One of the first signs is that they are always proud
of their record. You say, "Wait a minute! I thought
you said the law's effect was to make you discouraged
and defeated. Someone who is proud of his record is
not discouraged and defeated." Well, that is a diver-
sion. The law is making them discouraged, and they
don't like it. In certain areas of their lives they see
defeat, so they attempt to get people's attention off
this area and onto areas where they feel they have suc-
ceeded. That is why they are always pointing out the
areas of their success and boasting about how well
they are doing. They want to keep us from looking at
that other area where they are failing. The law reveals
failure. Therefore, one of the first marks of a person
who is living under the law is that he is always pointing out how well he is doing. Isn't that strange?

Another mark of people living under the law is
that they are critical of others. This is another diver-
sionary tactic. Why are people critical of others?
Well, if I succeed in getting my friends' eyes fastened
on other people, they won't look at me. And I feel
justified because I think the faults I point out in

others aren't the same faults of which I am guilty. God plays some amazing tricks with us. He so blinds our eyes, or allows Satan to do so, that invariably the things for which we criticize others are the very things of which we are guilty. But we don't know it! The law produces a sense of failure and defeat, and we constantly adjust to it and compensate for it by criticizing others.

Another mark of those under the law is that they are always reluctant to admit any error or fault. I was interested in Chuck Colson's characterization of former President Richard Nixon. One of Nixon's problems was that he could never admit he was wrong. In fact, in *Born Again* Colson said that even when Nixon obviously had a cold—nose running, face red, sneezing, all the symptoms of a cold—he would never admit it. That is the mentality of those who are under the law. They feel very heavily the standard of conduct they are expected to have, so they pretend they are living up to it, even though they aren't. They hate to admit defeat because that means they must change.

Another symptom of those under the law is that they suffer times of inner boredom and depression, and often show symptoms of depression, discouragement, and defeat. The law is doing its work of condemning, and that sense of condemnation produces depression. Did you know this? Remember, you can't understand this passage unless you know what the law does. If you know this, you can see it is a major problem in the church. This is what has gone wrong with so much of the American church today.

Her Tie to the Law

Let's go back now to the illustration Paul uses. You and I are the woman in his little story. She has two husbands, one following the other. Now, the point of this story is not that the woman has two husbands. Although that is important, it is not the major point. What Paul is getting at here is what the death of the first husband does to the woman's relationship to the law—not what it does directly to the woman herself, but what it does to her tie to the law. Notice that verse 2 tells us the place of the law in this story:

> *For example, by law a married woman is bound to her husband as long as he is alive, but if her husband dies, she is released from the law* of marriage [or, the law of her husband].

Notice three factors here: the law, the woman, and the husband. It is the law that binds the woman and her husband together. The law is outside their relationship, saying, "You two must stay together because you are married." The law is not the husband, as it is often interpreted to be.

If the first husband dies, Paul says, the woman is released from *the law*. Not only is she released from her husband, but she also is released from the law. If her husband dies, the law can say nothing to her as to where she can go and what she can do and who she can be with. She is released from the law. The death of the husband makes the woman free from the law.

Now, who is this first husband? According to the context, it is quite clear. We have been looking at it all along. The first husband is Adam, the old life into which we were all born. We were linked to it, married to it, and couldn't get away from it. Like a woman married to an old, cruel husband, there is not much we can do about it. While she is married she is tied to that husband. The law says so. In verse 3, Paul says:

*So then, if she marries another man while her hus-
band is still alive, she is called an adulteress. But
if her husband dies, she is released from that law
and is not an adulteress, even though she marries
another man.*

Now, that is plain, isn't it? The woman cannot
have two husbands at once. She cannot have a second
husband while she is married to the first. She is stuck
with number one and she has to share his lifestyle. As
we have already seen, that lifestyle is one of bondage,
corruption, shame, and death. That is why we who
were born into Adam have to share in the lifestyle of
fallen Adam. It fits perfectly, doesn't it?

Now, if this woman, while she is married to her
first husband, tries to live with another—for her husband's lifestyle is sickening to her—she will be called
an adulteress. Who calls her that? The law does. The
law says, "You are a hypocrite." That, you see, is the
spiritual counterpart of the physical term "adulteress." The law condemns her; it points out her failure; it calls her an adulteress. It is only when the first
husband dies that she is free from that condemnation
of the law and thus can marry again. When she does,
the law is absolutely silent; it has nothing to say to
her at all.

You Also Died

Now look at verse 4:

*So, my brothers, you also died to the law through
the body of Christ, that you might belong to
another, to him who was raised from the dead, in
order that we might bear fruit to God.*

What a fantastic verse! Here is the great and marvelous declaration of the gospel of our Lord Jesus.
Notice how Paul draws the parallel: "So . . . you

also." We fit right into this. The key thought here is "you died to the law through the body of Christ." The body of Christ refers to the death of the Lord Jesus on the cross. He died in a body. He came to take a body upon himself, so that he might die.

Paul refers to what the Scriptures say in many places—that on the cross the Lord Jesus was made sin for us. He took our place, as sinful humanity, on the cross. I don't know how, but he did. In other words, *he became that first husband.* It is extremely important to grasp this. On the cross, he became that first husband, that Adamic nature to which we were married. And when he became that, he died. And when he died, we were freed from the law, just as the woman was released from the law of marriage when her first husband died.

So the law has nothing to say to us anymore. We are free to be married to another. Who is this? It is Christ risen. Our first husband is Christ crucified; our second husband is Christ risen from the dead. We now share his name, we share his power, we share his experiences, we share his position, his glory, his hopes, his dreams—all that he is, we now share. We are married to Christ, risen from the dead. The law therefore has nothing to say to us. Isn't that clear?

Paul then goes on:

> *For when we were controlled by the sinful nature, the sinful passions aroused by the law were at work in our bodies, so that we bore fruit for death. But now, by dying to what once bound us, we have been released from the law so that we serve in the new way of the Spirit, and not in the old way of the written code (7:5-6).*

While we were married to sin (the old Adamic life), we often tried to act as though we were married to someone else. We tried to act righteous and loving and kind. Many of us did. We really tried to behave ourselves, but we found we couldn't. The law refused to go along with us. The law judged us. It said, "You are really not that way, you are just acting like that. You are pretending." The law called us hypocrites, and it was right. That is what we were. We were religious hypocrites, attempting to give the impression that we were okay, right, loving, moral, kind, and good, when we weren't at all. Inside, our attitudes were selfish and hostile and loveless. We were pretending. And the law saw through it and named us what we were: hypocrites!

No Longer Hypocrites

But, according to this, we died to the law through the death of our first husband. When Jesus was crucified, that first husband died. And now we are free from the condemnation of the law. We are married to another—Christ risen from the dead. So now, when we seek to be righteous and to do righteous things, to be loving and kind, we are no longer hypocrites. This is the point Paul wants to make. We can be what we really are. We are tied to Jesus. His life is now ours, and we are acting according to our true nature.

We are married to a new husband. And because we share his life and power, we not only are able to be what he is, but we are also free from any condemnation or failure in our struggle along the way. We don't always act right, but the law doesn't condemn us. The law's purpose was to condemn, and we can't be condemned anymore because we are not hypocrites. We are doing what we were designed to do. We have a new identity. No longer bound to our failures, we can admit them and forget them. We don't have to have them clinging to us; we no longer have to believe that God is unhappy with us because we don't always live exactly right. He has made provision for this. It is not a fraud when we go back to God again and again, and accept forgiveness from his hand.

Therefore, it is not law that straightens us out, it is love. We no longer need the law to straighten us out, for we have love to do so. We are free to fail and still be loved. But we are also free to win in the new power given to us. The next question Paul asks is, "Is the law worthless, then, and contemptible?" His answer, of course, is no. Some Christians talk that way about the law, but Paul never does. There is a place for it, and it is valuable in a certain way, but it can do nothing to deliver us from evil. Only our relationship to love can do that.

17
THE CONTINUING STRUGGLE

(Romans 7:7-25)

The gospel of Jesus Christ is able to set men free. This is its central declaration: Christ has come, he has died, he has risen again, and he has entered our hearts through the Holy Spirit so that we who believe might be free.

This is what the gospel is all about—freedom! Freedom from self-centeredness, freedom from hostility and bitterness, freedom from anxiety and all kinds of fears, freedom from bondage to evil habits of any type. This is the freedom Christ has come to give us. He has come to release us, to free us to be the men and women God has designed us to be, living in the midst of (as Paul describes it) "a generation of crooks and perverts," yet being lights shining in the darkness. As we have seen all the way through this book and especially in Romans 5 and 6, this kind of life is totally possible in Jesus Christ. Yet there are at least two ways we can miss it, even though we are Christians.

Paul has dealt with one of these in Romans 6. In the last half of Romans 6 he pointed out that, even though one is a Christian, he can give himself over to the bondage and slavery of sin. He can continue to give way to sin. He may think it is not worthwhile to fight or he may enjoy the pleasure sin gives him, so he keeps on doing wrong things. This is what theologians call "antinomianism," which means, simply, "against the law." Antinomianism reflects an attitude that unfortunately is common among us—the idea that God, in his grace, will forgive us, so why not indulge in sin? "Let's go ahead and sin because we know God will forgive."

The answer to this attitude is found in Romans 6:15-22. The Scripture says that if you live on that basis, sin will enslave you, it will shame you, it will limit you, it will defile you, it will spread corruption and death in your life. And though you may be a Christian, you will have a miserable Christian life because you cannot give way to sin without being enslaved by it.

The second way we can miss God's freedom is exactly the opposite: handling this problem of sin by trying our best to do what God wants. By discipline and dedication of heart, and the exercise of determined will power, we try our best to do what God asks, to live according to the law, and to fulfill the requirements of the law.

This attempt takes many forms. Sometimes it means taking certain steps to overcome certain problems. Such a program may sound good, because it is an appeal to do that which is right, but it is what the Scriptures call legalism, the exact opposite of antinomianism. It is a wholehearted attempt to do what God wants—with the end result that we become defensive, self-righteous, critical of others, proud of our own record. Furthermore, we become unaccountably bored, discouraged, depressed, and even frequently despairing. That, basically, is the story of Romans 7.

We have already seen in Romans 7:1-6 that there is no need to be like this. Legalism is not the answer; we are not under the law, but under grace. Romans 7 is a commentary on Paul's great declaration of Romans 6:14: "Sin shall not be your master, because you are not under law, but under grace." Not only are we freed from sin, but from the law as well. The law condemns us, but we are no longer under law if we are resting in Christ. Therefore, the law does not serve any useful purpose in delivering us from sin.

To Drive Us to Christ

That raises the question: "What, then, is the purpose of the law in a Christian's life? Is the law really contemptible and worthless? Ought we to just dispense with it?" There are many Christians who say, "I'm a Christian, saved by grace. The law has no meaning to me at all. The law was given to Moses for the Israelites, but it doesn't apply to a Christian. Let's dispense with it." But Paul never speaks this way, and neither does Jesus. In fact, Jesus tells us in the Sermon on the Mount that if anyone disparages the law, changes it, or waters it down in any degree whatsoever, he is under the curse of God. The law abides forever.

We must clearly understand what Paul is teaching here about the function and purpose of the law. We must know (1) that the law simply *cannot* deliver us from sin; but (2) it can always do one thing well—even with Christians: It can expose sin in us and drive us back to Christ. This is what the law is for, and this is the story of Romans 7:7-25.

This section divides into two parts. In verses 7-13, Paul discusses how the law exposes sin and "kills" the believer. That is the term he uses: The law kills us. Then, in verses 14-25, he takes up exactly the same theme—how the law exposes sin and kills us—but this time it is not explained, it is experienced. In the first section Paul tells us how it works; in the second section he tells us how it feels. Ours is a feeling generation; this passage therefore ought to strike a responsive chord in many hearts, for Paul describes exactly how it feels to be under the law as a Christian.

In verses 7 through 11, the apostle begins to describe his own experience in relationship to the law:

> *What shall we say, then? Is the law sin? Certainly not! Indeed I would not have known what sin was except through the law. For I would not have known what it was to covet if the law had not said, "Do not covet." But sin, seizing the opportunity afforded by the commandment, produced in me every kind of covetous desire. For apart from law, sin is dead. Once I was alive apart from law; but when the commandment came, sin sprang to life and I died. I found that the very commandment that was intended to bring life actually brought death. For sin, seizing the opportunity afforded by the commandment, deceived me, and through the commandment put me to death (7:7-11).*

This is Paul's experience. It is clear he is describing something he himself went through. But also note that Paul employs the past tense throughout this passage, which suggests he is describing his experience before he became a Christian. This probably happened not long before he became a Christian, and many commonly experience it today. Paul, as we know, was raised in a godly home. He was a Jew, raised in the city of Tarsus. As a typical Jewish son, he was taught the law from birth. So when he says he lived "apart from the law," he does not mean he didn't know what it was. He simply means a time had to come when the law came home to him. "The commandment came," he says.

We have all had that experience. We have read much Scripture that was just words to us—beautiful words, perhaps, but we didn't understand them. Then, years after, something we went through made those words come alive. This is what Paul is talking about here. He knew the law from birth, but he did not understand what it was saying until he went through a certain experience. Here he describes that experience, one he had before he became a Christian.

Protected from Temptation

Like many today, Paul was protected and sheltered in his home, kept from exposure to serious temptations. He was reared in the Jewish culture, which also sheltered those around him. He grew up relatively untroubled with problems of blatant sin. There are many people like that in our churches today. They have grown up in a home where they have been protected and sheltered. They have run with a crowd of friends who, likewise, have been kept from exposure to various temptations. They have not fallen into evil.

Many young people, like Saul of Tarsus, think they have handled the problem of sin. What about keeping the law? It's not hard! Hardly any severe temptations come under these circumstances. These people don't struggle along this line. They have the world by the tail—they can handle it, they think. As Paul describes it, "They are alive apart from the law."

But then comes a time when they are exposed to blatant sin. They are thrust into a different lifestyle, a different crowd of people. They move out on their own and suddenly find themselves removed from the shelter, protection, love, and cultural defenses that have been theirs from childhood. Perhaps the new crowd—as a way of life—does things that these sheltered young people have been taught are wrong. Now, for the first time, they feel the force of the law's prohibition. The law says, "Thou shalt not covet, commit adultery, murder, steal" or whatever it may be. And yet the crowd around them says, "Let's do it—it's fun!" For the first time, they begin to feel the prohibition of the law. Then a strange phenomenon happens. Something about that situation arouses within them a strong desire to do the prohibited things. Maybe they are able to resist for awhile, but eventually they find themselves pressured, pushed by something within that wants very badly to do these things.

This is what Paul discovered. It was the tenth commandment, "Thou shalt not covet," that got to him. He thought he had been keeping all the law because he had not done some of the external things prohibited in the other commandments. But this one commandment talks about how you feel inside, your desires, your imagination, your ambitions. It says, "Thou shalt not desire what another has." Paul found himself awakened to this commandment and discovered that he was coveting, no matter where he turned. When the law came, he found himself aroused by it, brought under its power. It precipitated an orgy of desire. Many of us have felt this same way.

Power at a Touch

Not long ago I had an opportunity to go up into the Colorado Rockies for a conference. As I came out of my hotel, the man who was to drive me there was waiting in his powerful, shiny new Lincoln Continental. I got into the car, and to my amazement he started driving without turning on the engine—or at least that's how it seemed to me. I suddenly realized that the engine had been running all the time. It was so quiet I hadn't heard it. As we moved up into the Rockies, the power of that engine became obvious. We traveled up the steep grades in those great mountains with ease because of the power released by his touch on the accelerator.

That is something like what Paul is describing here. Sin lies silent within us. We do not even know it is there. We think we have hold of life and can handle it without difficulty. We are self-confident, but only because we have never really been exposed to a situation that puts pressure upon us—we have never had to make a decision against the pressure of the commandment, "Thou shalt not. . . ."

But when it happens, we suddenly find ourselves filled with attitudes that almost shock us—unloving, bitter, resentful thoughts, murderous attitudes—we would like to get hold of someone and kill him, if we could. Lustful feelings surface that we never dreamed were there, and we find we would love to indulge them if only we had the opportunity. We find ourselves awakened to these desires. As the great engine surges to life at the touch of the accelerator, so this powerful, idling beast within called sin springs to life as the law comes home to us.

Now, is this the law's fault? No, Paul says, it isn't; he goes on in verses 12 and 13,

> *So then, the law is holy, and the commandment is holy, righteous and good. Did that which is good, then, become death to me? By no means! But in order that sin might be recognized as sin, it produced death in me through what was good, so that through the commandment sin might become utterly sinful.*

This is what the law is for: to expose the evil force in every one of us, a force waiting only for the right circumstance to spring into action, overpower our will, and carry us into things we never dreamed we would do.

According to this passage, sin's great power is that it deceives us. We think we have life under control, but we are fooled. Sin is simply waiting for the right occasion when—like a powerful, idling, engine—it roars into life and takes over at the touch of the accelerator of the law . . . and we find ourselves helplessly under its control.

The law is designed to expose that sin so we begin to understand this evil force we have inherited. The law shows up sin for what it is, something exceedingly powerful and dangerous, something stronger than our will power that causes us to do things we resolved not to do.

Present Tense Experience

In verses 14-25, the same experience is described again, but this time in terms of how we feel when it happens. There is only one major difference between this section and the previous one. Here Paul switches to the present tense. This is significant because it means he is now describing his experience at the time he wrote this letter. This, then, is a description of the law as it touches the Christian's life. It does exactly the same thing as it did before we became a Christian, only now we have it from the point of view of the believer who is deceived by the sin still within.

> *We know that the law is spiritual; but I am unspiritual {that is, carnal, fleshly; and Paul gives us now an excellent definition of carnality}, sold as a slave to sin. I do not understand what I do. For what I want to do I do not do, but what I hate I do (7:14-15).*

Some have been convinced, from this verse alone, that Paul was a golfer! If you have ever tried golf, you know that this is the very thing that happens. What you want to do, you do not do. What you do not want to do, that is the very thing you do. Of course, Paul has a much greater problem than playing golf. The key to this whole passage is verse 14: "The law is spiritual," Paul says. "It deals with my spirit. It gets right at the very heart of my being." Fundamentally, as we have seen, human beings are spirits. The law is spiritual, and it touches us in that area. "But I am carnal," Paul says. "I can't respond to it. I am sold as a slave to sin."

Now, this always raises a problem. Compare this with chapter 6, verse 17, where Paul speaks of slavery and says, "But thanks be to God that, though you used to be slaves to sin, you wholeheartedly obeyed the form of teaching to which you were entrusted. You have been set free from sin and have become slaves to righteousness." If he could write that to the Romans, surely it was true of him as well. Yet how could he write that he had become in Christ a slave to righteousness, and just a few paragraphs later write, "I am carnal, sold under sin, a slave to sin"? It is in

his human spirit that he is made a slave to righteousness, while in his soul the struggle with sin goes on.

In spite of what many have said, Paul is not confused here. He is simply describing what happens
when a Christian tries to live under the law. When a
Christian, by his dedication, will power, and determination, tries to do what is right in order to please
God, he is living under the law. And Paul is telling
us what to expect when we live like that—for we all
try to live that way from time to time. Sin, you see,
deceives us. It deceived Paul as an apostle, and he
needed this treatment of the law. It deceives us, and
we need it too.

Paul then tells us what happens. There are two
problems, which he gives us in verse 15: "I do not
understand what I do. For what I want to do I do not
do. . . ." That is problem number one. I want to do
right—there are things I would love to do, but I cannot do them. The second problem is: ". . . but what
I hate I do." There are some things I don't want to
do—yet I find myself doing those very things.

In the verses that follow, Paul takes the second
problem first, and shows us what happens.

> *And if I do what I do not want to do, I agree that
> the law is good. As it is, it is no longer I myself
> who do it, but it is sin living in me (7:16-17).*

That phrase, "it is no longer I who do it," is extremely important. Paul makes the statement twice
in this paragraph, and it explains how we can be delivered from this condition.

> *I know that nothing good lives in me, that is, in
> my sinful nature {or my flesh}. For I have the de-
> sire to do what is good, but I cannot carry it out.
> For what I do is not the good I want to do; no, the*

evil I do not want to do—this I keep on doing.
Now if I do what I do not want to do, it is no
longer I who do it, but it is sin living in me that
does it (7:18-20).

Let's examine this carefully. Paul says that as a Christian, redeemed by the grace of God, he now has something within him that wants to do good, that agrees with the law, that says the law is right. Something within says that what the law tells him to do is right, and he wants to do it. But also, he says, there is something else in him that rises up and says, "No!" Even though he determines not to do what is bad, he suddenly finds himself in such circumstances that his determination melts away, his resolve is gone, and he ends up doing what he had sworn he would not do. Have you ever felt that way?

The "I" and the "Me"

So, what has gone wrong? Paul's explanation is, "It is no longer I who do it; it is sin living in me." Isn't that strange? This indicates a division within our humanity. There is the "I" that wants to do what God wants, and there is the sin which dwells in "me," which is different than the "I." We must understand what this is.

As we have seen, human beings are complicated creatures. We have a spirit, a soul, and a body. These are distinct, one from the other. What Paul suggests here is that the redeemed spirit never wants to do what God has prohibited. It agrees with the law that it is good. And yet there is an alien power, a force that he calls sin, a great beast lying dormant within his soul and body. When it is touched by the commandment of the law, it springs to life, and so Paul does what he does not want to do.

Jesus himself agrees with this. On one occasion he said, "If your right hand offends you, cut it off." He did not mean that one should actually chop off his right hand, because that would be a violation of other texts that indicate that God made the body and made it right, and it is morally neutral. What he means is that we should take drastic action because we are up against a serious problem. He indicates there is a "me" within us that runs our members, that gives orders to our hands, our feet, our eyes, our tongue, our brain, our sexual organs, and controls them. That "me" is giving an order to do something wrong; but there is another "I" in us who is offended. That "I" does not like it, does not want it. And so Jesus says, "Cut it off."

In a moment we are going to see how this happens, what it is that cuts off the "me" and thus enables us to handle the problem. Man is made in such a way that his will power is never enough; sin will win, and we will do the evil we swore not to do.

Now, in verses 21-23, look at the other side of this problem.

> *So I find this law at work: When I want to do good, evil is right there with me. For in my inner being I delight in God's law; but I see another law {another principle} at work in the members of my body, waging war against the law {or principle} of my mind {my agreement with the law of God} and making me a prisoner of the law {principle} of sin at work within my members.*

Here is the same problem exactly. I know what is right and want to do right, and determine and swear to do it—only to find that under certain circumstances all that determination melts away and I fail. I do exactly what I did not want to do. So I come away angry with myself. "What's the matter with me? Why can't I do what is right? Why do I give way when I get into this situation? Why am I so weak?" This is right where we live, isn't it? This is what we all struggle with.

The heart's cry at that moment is,

> *What a wretched man I am! Who will rescue me from this body of death? (7:24)*

What is this? Right here we arrive at the place where the Lord Jesus began the Sermon on the Mount: "Blessed are the poor in spirit, for theirs is the kingdom of heaven." Blessed is the man who comes to the end of himself. Blessed is the man who has arrived at spiritual bankruptcy, who cries, "What a wretched man I am!" Why? Because this is the point—the only point—where God's help is given.

This is what we need to learn. If we think we have something in ourselves that can work out our problems, if we think our wills are strong enough, our desires motivated enough, that we can control evil in our lives by simply determining to do so, then we have not yet come to the end of ourselves. And the Spirit of God simply folds his arms and lets us go ahead and try it on that basis. We fail, and fail miserably—until, at last, out of our failures, we cry, "O wretched man that I am!" Sin has deceived us; and the law, as our friend, has come in and exposed sin for what it is. When we see how wretched it makes us, then we are ready for the answer, which comes immediately:

> *Thanks be to God—through Jesus Christ our Lord! (7:25)*

Who will deliver me from this body of death? The Lord Jesus has already done it. When the law has brought us to feelings of wretchedness and discouragement and failure, we are to respond by reminding ourselves immediately of the facts about ourselves in Jesus Christ. Our feelings must be answered by facts.

Free Sons of God

We are no longer under the law. That is a fact. We have arrived at a different situation; we are married to Christ, Christ risen from the dead. This means we must no longer think, "I am a poor, struggling, bewildered disciple, left alone to wrestle against these powerful urges." We must now begin to think, "No, I am a free son of God, living a normal human life. I am dead to sin, and dead to the law, because I am married to Christ. His power is mine, right at this moment. And though I may not feel it, I have the power to say 'No' and walk away and be free, in Jesus Christ."

I recently met a Canadian pastor with a burden on his heart to get the Word of God into the Soviet Union. He joined an organization (among several that exist today) which transports Bibles there. His first experience crossing the border with a load of Bibles in the trunk of his car was thrilling. He wasn't going to try to smuggle them in; he was just counting on God to somehow get him through.

He and a friend loaded the boxes of Bibles into the car, and as they drove to the border, all his resolve and courage began to drain away. Within a mile or so of the border his friend asked, "How do you feel?" He replied, "I feel scared." So they stopped alongside the road and simply told the Lord how they felt. "Lord, we are scared. We didn't get into this situation because we want to be here. It isn't we who want to get this Word into Russia; it is you. This is your project, and this is your situation. We are willing to take whatever risks you ask, but you have got to see it through. We are scared and we don't know what to do. We don't have any wisdom, we don't know how to handle this situation when we get to the border, but we expect you to do something."

As they prayed this way, totally bankrupt, wanting to do good, unable to do it but committing the matter to the Lord Jesus, they felt the inward sense of the Spirit of God witnessing to them that God would act. They didn't know how or what he would do, but they felt a sense of peace.

They drove on to the border. When the guard asked for their papers, they gave them to him. He examined them, then said, "What do you have in the trunk?"

"Some boxes."

"Let me see them."

So they opened the trunk, and there were the boxes. They expected surely that his next question would be, "What's in them?" But he didn't ask it. He simply said, "Okay," shut the door, gave them their papers, and on they went.

This is what this passage describes for us. This is the way we are to live, the way we are to face every challenge, large or small. "Thanks be to God, it is through Jesus our Lord."

Some teachers say this passage in Romans 7 is something a Christian goes through just once. He then gets out of it and moves into Romans 8, never to return to Romans 7 again. Nothing could be further from the truth! Even as mighty a man as Paul went through it again and again. This describes what every believer will go through many times, because sin has the power to deceive us and to cause us to trust in ourselves, even when we are not aware we are doing so. The law will expose that evil force and drive us to this place of wretchedness that we might then, in poverty of spirit, cry out, "Lord Jesus, it is your problem; you take it." And he will.

The chapter ought to end with the exclamation in verse 25: "Thanks be to God—through Jesus Christ our Lord!" The next sentence is the summarizing verse that introduces Paul's explanation in chapter 8. Here, then, is the way of deliverance for Christians. We *do* need the law. Every time sin deceives us into self-trust we need it. But the law will not deliver us from sin; the law will only bring us, again and again, to the mighty Deliverer. His life and power within us sets us free, without condemnation.

18
NO
CONDEMNATION

(Romans 8:1-4)

The eighth chapter of Romans is the favorite of many—and not without reason. This is one of the most significant chapters in the Scriptures. Someone has called it "the brightest jewel in the treasure chest of the Word of God." I like to think of it as a great mountain rising above all the surrounding hills and capturing all attention. Yet Paul does not introduce any new thoughts here until verse 17. In the chapter's opening words he simply gathers up what he has been saying and brings it into focus.

To understand this chapter we must ignore the division between chapters 7 and 8. I believe the text of the Scriptures is inspired by God, "breathed out" by him—but I wonder if the chapter divisions were put in by the devil! Many times they come right at a place where they actually obscure truth. Sometimes these divisions break the continuity of a thought and take it out of the context, so that we are likely to miss something tremendously important. That is certainly true here. The first two verses of chapter 8 ought to be linked with the closing verse of chapter 7. They are really all one sentence. When you read them that way, it will help explain the struggle and darkness in Romans 7. It is a struggle that does not have to go on, and Paul resolves it with this one, great, flashing word of relief:

> *Thanks be to God—through Jesus Christ our Lord!* (7:25)

Then the rest of verse 25 belongs with the opening verses of chapter 8. It explains what he means when he says, "Thanks be to God—through Jesus Christ our Lord!"

> *So then, I myself in my mind am a slave to God's law, but in the sinful nature a slave to the law of sin.*

That summarizes all that he has been talking about in chapter 7. But don't stop there, for there should be no break between that and verse 1 of chapter 8 . . .

> *{But} there is now no condemnation for those who are in Christ Jesus, because through Christ Jesus the law of the Spirit of life set me free from the law of sin and death.*

Chapter 8 ought to open with the word "But." It introduces a contrast that shows the way out of the struggle of chapter 7.

Linked by the Body

What is Paul saying in this passage when it is all taken together? First, he makes clear there is a struggle in the Christian life, a struggle between what he calls "the sinful nature" and the Spirit. I am not sure I like that term "sinful nature" too well, however. The Greek word is "flesh," and, as the word is used in the Scriptures, it not only means the body, but it also means the sin that finds its seat in our bodies. It is by the body that we are linked to our father, Adam. God made a body for Adam that is like ours—with two eyes, two ears, a nose, and so on, and we have these characteristics because Adam had them. But we also have inherited from Adam the principle of sin.

This principle is hard to define. In some way, it describes the access the devil has to our humanity. It is the means by which Satan is able to implant in our minds his "fiery darts," as Paul calls them in Ephesians. These might be obscene and lustful thoughts, selfish attitudes, or hostile, bitter feelings toward others—and they come into our minds suddenly, unbidden, when we least expect them. They come from this root of sin in our bodies, the flesh.

Every Christian must expect to be caught up in a struggle between the flesh and the Spirit. Paul describes this struggle in Galatians 5:17.

> *For the sinful nature {or flesh} desires what is contrary to the Spirit, and the Spirit what is contrary to the sinful nature {the flesh}. They are in conflict with each other, so that you do not do what you want.*

This really is a verse of hope. Paul says the Spirit struggles against the flesh, so that we *cannot* do the

things that we would. This is what Paul is describing
in Romans 7:25—"I myself in my mind am a slave to
God's law." That is, as he said earlier, "I want to do
good, I believe in it. I delight in God's law in my
inner being. I am changed; I agree that the law is
good. But I find I can't do it."

In his mind he is awakened to the value and the
righteousness of God's law, that this has come about
through the Spirit in his life. How else can we ever
come to the place of agreeing that God is good and
holy, his Word is right and the law is good, except
by the Spirit of God in us? It is only when a man is
filled with the Holy Spirit that he can talk like that.
Therefore, it is the Holy Spirit, within Paul's human
spirit, agreeing with God's law. But set against that
is this sin in his flesh that takes hold of him and
makes him a slave to the law of sin, even though he
does not want to be.

How does he break this hold? He breaks it, as he
says, by relying upon a new view of himself that is
true because he is in Jesus Christ. This is what Romans 8 declares. The life of Jesus in him, released to
him by the Holy Spirit, sets him free from the law of
sin and death.

But there is a struggle to believe that great fact. If
you have ever watched an alcoholic, or perhaps have
struggled with alcoholism yourself, you know the
struggle is intense. An alcoholic can come to the
place where he can see everything evil happening to
him because of alcohol. He wants to quit; he determines to quit. He knows he is going to lose his wife,
his children, his reputation, and everything if he
doesn't quit. I have seen these people resolve never to
drink again. Yet, in a moment of temptation, the
very struggle of Romans 7 comes in, and suddenly
they find themselves overpowered by sin. They give

in, and they hate themselves for doing it.

Those who struggle with homosexuality feel the same way. Habits have settled in and they find it very difficult to say no, even though they want to. Born again, they want to be delivered—but they find their new identity in Christ hard to believe.

And it is not only sins like these that can grip us. A hot temper or a habit of overeating can do the same thing. Perhaps right now you are saying, "For dinner I am going to have just a very light meal." And someone will spread out a beautiful roast and apple pie and, before you know it, your resolve is gone—and so is the food.

This is a problem of the will, isn't it? Our wills are weak, and we know it. This is what Paul is describing here. This is the struggle of the Christian life. It comes again and again, *but it does not have to continue.* Some Christians resent the fact that the struggle is there at all. They have a false idea of Christianity. They think Christianity means God takes away all temptation so they never have to struggle again. Unfortunately, that is not true; and many people have been hurt and have become angry with God because he does not do that. I have seen young Christians become extremely upset because they thought they were free from struggle and then found they weren't.

The text tells us this struggle can cease only when we reckon on who we really are in Christ. What we need is a new self-image; this is what will deliver us. When we see who we really are, we can say "no" to the flesh and "yes" to the Spirit—and discover a whole new way of life.

No Condemnation

The second major thing the apostle says is that not only is there a struggle, but (and this is very important) the struggle is without condemnation. Though we may struggle at times, Paul says there is no condemnation to those who are in Christ Jesus. The reason there is no condemnation is given in one little phrase: "in Christ." That goes right back to our justification by faith. We came out of Adam, we are in Christ, and God will never condemn those who are in Christ.

Now, we have to understand what "no condemnation" means. What is Paul talking about? Certainly the most basic element here is that there is no rejection by God. God does not turn aside, he does not kick us out of his family. If we are born into the family of God by faith in Jesus Christ, the Holy Spirit has come to dwell within us and he will never, never leave us. No matter what we do, he will never leave us. God will never cut us out of his family or treat us as anything less than sons and daughters.

One of the most beautiful stories of the Scriptures is that of the prodigal son who left home, got into deep trouble, wasted his life in riotous living, and ended up in the pigpen. On this subject Dr. Vernon McGee asks, "Do you know the difference between the son in that pigpen and the pig? The difference is that no pig has ever said to himself, 'I will arise and go to my father.'" He is right; only sons say that. Thus there will be no condemnation, no rejection, by God. He will always treat me as his child, not as his enemy.

The second thing "no condemnation" means is that God is not angry with us when struggle comes into our lives. We want to be good; we want to stop doing bad. But when the moment of temptation comes, we find ourselves overpowered and weak, and we give way. Then we hate ourselves. We go away frustrated, feeling, as Paul described, "What a wretched man I am! What's the matter with me? Why can't I do this thing? Why can't I act like I want to?" But though we may condemn ourselves, God does not. He is not angry with us about that. He sees us, as the Scriptures show us, as a child in his family, learning to walk.

No father ever gets angry with his little son because he doesn't get right up and start running the first time he tries to walk. If the child falls and stumbles and falters, the father helps him; he doesn't spank him. He lifts him up, encourages him, and shows him how to do it right. And if the child has a problem with his feet—maybe one foot is twisted or deformed—the father finds a way to relieve that condition and help him learn to walk. This is what God does. He is not angry when we struggle. He knows it takes a while—quite a while, at times. And even the best of saints will, at times, fall. This was true of Paul, it was true of all the apostles, and it was true of all the prophets of the Old Testament. Sin is deceitful and it will sometimes trip us. But God is not angry with us when it does.

Now, a word of caution. When we deliberately decide to sin, and like it, then he will punish us. This is the discipline of a father described in the closing part of chapter 6. When we deliberately give ourselves back into sin once we have been set free from it, then, as a loving disciplinarian, God will correct us and punish us until we begin to see what has happened. He does this out of love, just as an earthly father would. But that is a different condition than the one we are facing here. Here Paul is describing those times when we want to do good, and we are trying to do good. But we are weak, and in a moment of temptation we fail. And we fail again and again. Still there is "no condemnation to those who are in Christ

Jesus." Even when we are being punished as disobedient sons, we still are not rejected. This remains true
no matter what happens to us.

Why are we not condemned? The answer Paul
gives in verse 2 is beautiful:

> . . . *because through Christ Jesus the law of the
> Spirit of life set me free from the law of sin and
> death.*

Paul was not left with a continuing, constant
struggle; God came in and did something about it.
God reminded him of what he knew to be true, and
he began to believe it. When he began to think of
himself as God thought of him he found he had power
to say no to sin.

In summary, Paul actually brings out three reasons
in this whole passage why there is no condemnation.
First, look back at verse 18 of chapter 7: "I know that
nothing good lives in me, that is, in my sinful nature. For I have the desire to do what is good." His
heart is right, that is clear. Then again, in verse 22,
"For in my inner being I delight in God's law." Paul
really wants to do right, his heart is right; therefore
there is no condemnation. The basic desire is to be
good—and God will not and does not condemn that.

Second, and obviously connected with this, Paul
explains that sin has deceived and overpowered him.
It is also too much for us. We can't handle this wild
beast raging within us when it is awakened by the demands and prohibitions of the law. God does not condemn us for that; he knows it is more than we can
handle. He lets us discover that fact by our own experience, but he does not condemn us when we do.

Third (and this is the most important), God has
already made provision in Christ for our failure. He
knows that our very struggle is driving us back to

Christ. When I have come to the place of saying, "What a wretched man I am!" the only thing left, if I want any escape at all, is to ask, "Why am I thinking of myself in this way? God says I am different." Reckoning on the difference that has come to me in Christ, I can rise up to act differently. This is the way out. God knows my failures are driving me to this moment; and as a loving father he is patiently waiting for it to come. Therefore God will not condemn me.

The Spirit of New Life

We have seen two clear declarations so far: One, there is struggle in the Christian life; two, the struggle is "without condemnation." The third major thing Paul says is that provision has been made for victory. The law of the Spirit of life in Christ Jesus has set us free from the law of sin and death. This is why Paul cries, "Thanks be to God—through our Lord Jesus Christ!" This law of the Spirit of life is what God has already said he has done for us in Christ. He has cut us off, made us different creatures, brought us into Christ, and married us to him. We are no longer the same as we were. When we believe that, we release the Spirit of life within us.

When we fail and are angry with ourselves, our natural way of thinking goes something like this: "I'm a mess, a hopeless, helpless mess! Why can't I stop this thing that is hurting me so, and hurting others too?" We are all wrapped up in our own feelings and think we deserve to be whipped and punished, and cast into hell.

At that point God says to us, "Your view of yourself is wrong! Your wretchedness is only a temporary condition to which you are giving in. The truth is, you have been set free. You are married to Christ.

Your human spirit has been indwelt by the Holy
Spirit and it cannot sin. It has not sinned and does
not sin. You have been deceived by the sin in your
flesh, and it has taken over and led you into this mess.
But that is not who you fundamentally are. Don't believe that about yourself anymore. There is fresh forgiveness from God and the righteousness of Christ
waiting for you. You are in Christ; this is who you
are."

Take his forgiveness, believe it, thank God for it,
and go on, knowing your struggle will end.

Of course this does not mean God has ended all
temptation in our lives. The law of sin and death, like
the law of gravity, goes on working all the time. But
the moment you believe what Jesus Christ says about
you and what he has done for you, a new law comes
into effect. This new law is stronger than the law of
sin and death; it even uses that law to accomplish its
end.

When I was a boy, I discovered there was a law at
work that affected my eyesight. It is what I later
learned to call the law of myopia, which is near-
sightedness. It was in my members, right in my eyes,
so that I could not see what other people could see.
Finally, I went to a doctor about it, and he told me
what was wrong—and he prescribed glasses for me to
correct the problem.

Later I discovered a new law, the law of contact
lenses—two little pieces of plastic which I could put
in my eyes every morning and which would keep
working all day long. All I had to do was put them
in. They did not eliminate the law of myopia— they
actually used it. But the result was that I saw perfectly, with 20/20 vision. Now, if I got self-confident
and decided I didn't need those contact lenses anymore ("I can handle this situation without them!")

and took them out, immediately the law of myopia would take over and I would have the same old problem again. But if I put the lenses in, the law of contact lenses would cancel out—overcome—the law of myopia, and I could see perfectly.

This is what Paul is telling us here. God has given us a new image of ourselves. We are not what we feel we are. When we believe this, we can be set free at any time—any time when by faith we reckon that what God says is true. This is our provision for victory.

Basis for Victory

The fourth major point Paul makes in this brief paragraph is given in verses 3 and 4. He reviews the basis for victory:

> *For what the law was powerless to do in that it was weakened by the sinful nature, God did by sending his own Son in the likeness of sinful man {flesh} to be a sin offering. And so he condemned sin in sinful man {the flesh}, in order that the righteous requirements of the law might be fully met in us, who do not live according to the sinful nature but according to the Spirit (8:3-4).*

This is a beautiful description of the good news in Jesus Christ. There is nothing new here; we have had it all before.

Paul says the law is powerless to produce righteousness. It cannot do it. It cannot make us good in any way. It can demand and demand and demand, but it cannot enable and it never will. This, by the way, is why nagging a person never helps. Did you know that? Nagging is a form of law, and God will not let the law nag us because it doesn't help. It only makes it worse. If you try to nag your husband or wife or child, you will find the same thing happens there. Nagging only makes a person worse. Why? The reason, Paul says, is that the law stirs up the power of sin. It releases this force, this beast within us, this powerful engine that takes over and carries us where we don't want to go.

So nagging, or any form of the law, will never work. This is not because there is anything wrong with what is being said; it cannot work because of the weakness of the flesh. Paul says in 1 Corinthians 15:56, "The sting of death is sin, and *the power of sin* is the law." The law keeps sin going; it stirs it up.

To break through this vicious circle God sent his own Son. There is a beautiful tenderness about this. He sent "his own Son." He did not send an angel, he did not send a mere man—he sent his own Son as a man, in the likeness of sinful flesh. Notice that! He did not send him in the likeness of *flesh* (a mirage), but in the likeness of *sinful flesh* (in the flesh but without sin). Jesus had a real body, a body like yours and mine. Since sin began in the body, it has to be judged and broken in the body. Therefore, Jesus had a body. But it was not a *body* of sinful flesh, it was the *likeness* of sinful flesh. It was like our sinful bodies, in that it was subject to infirmities (Jesus grew weak and tired, hungry and weary), but there was no sin in him. Paul preserves that distinction very carefully here.

In that body of flesh, without sin, he became sin. As we read here, he was sent "as an offering for sin." In the mystery of the cross, (which we can never, never understand, no matter how long we live) the Lord Jesus, during the hours of darkness, gathered up all the sins of the world—the terrible, evil, foul, awful injustices, crimes, and misery that we have seen throughout history, from every person—gathered it into himself, and brought it to an end by dying. The good news is that by faith in him, we are involved in that death.

In Romans 6:6, Paul says,

> *For we know that our old self was crucified with him so that the body of sin might be rendered powerless, that we should no longer be slaves to sin—*

This is the way the Lord did it. As described in chapter 7, he (*Christ-made-sin*) was the first husband to whom we were married; and he died. When the first husband died we were free to be married to the second husband, who is *Christ-risen-from-the-dead*. Thus he has tied us to himself as a risen, ascended Lord, and we are his from now on.

This is true not only for a few Christians who have gone beyond all the rest and have some special experience; *all* Christians are one with Christ. If you are a Christian at all, this is who you are. It is always who you are. To let yourself believe anything else is to delude yourself. To believe your feelings about yourself at any moment of evil or sin is to fool yourself. This is who you really are. By the gift of God, without earning it or without ever deserving it, you are righteous in his sight, just like Jesus; you are righteous with the righteousness of God. The very righteousness which the law demands is fulfilled in us the minute we believe what God has done about our evil. That righteousness becomes ours continually, as a gift.

Believe the Change

The last thing the apostle says is that this becomes real to us when we choose to live according to the Spirit and not according to our sinful nature. When we believe what God says about us and see ourselves in a new way, then we will change the way we act. This is always God's way of deliverance. We think we have to change the way we act in order to be different; God says, "No, I have made you different, and when you believe it, you will automatically change the way you act." Do you see the difference?

I once heard a beautiful story about the daughter of one of the royal families of Europe. She had a big, bulbous nose that destroyed her beauty in the eyes of others—and especially in her own eyes. She grew up with a terrible image of herself as an ugly person. So her family hired a plastic surgeon to change the contour of her nose. He did the work, and there came the moment when they took off the bandages and the girl could see the results.

When the doctor removed the bandages, he saw that the operation had been a total success. All the ugly contours were gone. Her nose was different. When the incisions healed and the redness disappeared, she would be a beautiful girl. He held a mirror up for the girl to see. But so deeply embedded was this girl's ugly image of herself that when she saw herself in the mirror, she couldn't see any change. She broke into tears and cried out, "Oh, I knew it wouldn't work!" The doctor labored with that girl for six months before she would finally accept the fact that she was indeed different. And the moment she accepted that fact, her whole behavior began to change.

We, too, act from what we know we are. If the evil in us deceives us into thinking we are not what God says we are, then we are going to keep on acting evilly. The way to break the power of the most vicious and evil habit is to see yourself as God sees you. Then you begin to act that way. You can't help it. As this verse makes clear, you are one with Jesus and you share his life; and he himself, with all the beauty of his character, is one with you. He is married to you and you to him, and there is no distinction. If you can see this when you have temporarily believed something false about yourself and are struggling, then you will be set free.

Many of us can testify that this works. God sets us free in this way. This is what Paul has been saying all along. Sin shall not have dominion over you, for you are not under the law, with its nagging demand that you be different before you can be accepted. You are under grace, with its affirmation that God has already made you different.

Now believe it!

19
WHY NOT LIVE?

(Romans 8:3-13)

In Romans the phrase *gift of righteousness* is used in two ways. We have already seen righteousness as the worth instantly imparted to us when we believe in Jesus, and continually available to us by faith. We can turn to it any time we feel pressure or insecurity or need. Up to this point, this is the only way the word *righteousness* has been used in Romans.

Now a new form of righteousness comes before us. It is what we might call "righteousness displayed." It is righteousness which has worked its way out to visibility. That is, it is righteousness actually visible in actions, deeds, words, and thoughts. We begin acting like Christ. As well as being like him in the spirit, we now begin to act like him.

This is the righteousness referred to in Romans 8:3-4.

> *For what the law was powerless to do {that is, pro-duce righteousness} in that it was weakened by the sinful nature, God did by sending his own Son in the likeness of sinful man to be a sin offering. And so he condemned sin in sinful man, in order that the righteous requirements of the law {the right be-havior which the law insisted on} might be fully met in us, who do not live according to the sinful nature but according to the Spirit.*

This is what the Bible calls "sanctification," that is, righteousness displayed. This is our new behavior. And it is ours, the apostle says, when live not accord-ing to our sinful nature, but according to the Spirit.

Verses 5 through 13 explain that just being a Christian does not mean you automatically look, act, talk, think, and react like Jesus Christ. You do not become Christlike simply by becoming a Christian. Your human spirit becomes like Christ, for it is linked with him; but you may not act that way for quite some time. It depends on whether you are walking (behaving) "according to the flesh" or "ac-cording to the Spirit." These two choices are made clear in the passage before us.

Two Possibilities

Are we going to live according to the Spirit, or ac-cording to the flesh? Verse 5 describes these alterna-tives so that we can identify them and recognize them in our lives:

Those who live according to the sinful nature have their minds set on what that nature desires; but those who live in accordance with the Spirit have their minds set on what the Spirit desires (8:5).

There is the difference. Whether we display the righteousness demanded by the law depends on whether we walk according to the Spirit or according to the flesh. Notice that the difference lies in what we set our minds on. What are we thinking about all through the day? What is important to us? How do we view life? Do we have the viewpoint of the flesh, which governs the thinking of the world? Or do we have the Spirit's viewpoint—God's viewpoint?

What is the mindset of the person who lives according to the flesh, or (as the NIV puts it), those who have "their minds set on what that sinful nature desires"? We need only look around to see what it is. Listen to the television or radio, or read the newspapers, or observe people—even ourselves—and we will see what this is. It is the natural viewpoint on life.

What do people want in life? They want to make money, because money pays for the comforts and conveniences they would like to have. People also want to have fun—the pursuit of pleasure. There is also a passion in the human heart to be known and recognized. We're always manipulating people and circumstances to acquire some degree of fame, to be seen and known. People will give anything to gain influence, standing, prestige, and following. Finally, I think people desire to fulfill themselves. They want to use every capability within them. They want, somehow, to feel useful and needed. These are what the world lives for, aren't they? And the world wants them all *now*, not later. This is the natural point of view.

You ask, "Well, what's wrong with that?" There is really nothing wrong with it—unless it is all you want. And if it is all you want, then it is terribly wrong. This is what the Scriptures help us see—that there is another point of view on life, one that is according to the Spirit.

"Ah," you say, "I know what that means!" That means you have to forget about making money, having fun, and fulfilling yourself. All you do is go around memorizing Scripture and thinking about God all day long. Whenever anyone asks you to do something, you're too busy thinking about God and too involved in spiritual things to get your hands dirty. So you become a religious recluse. You go about reciting Scripture verses and telling people what is wrong with their lives—and that is being spiritual!

Unfortunately, many think this is what we are talking about when we say we are to set our minds on the things of the Spirit. But, of course, as many who try it discover, this kind of life does not produce the results this passage requires. It is really nothing but another way of being run by the flesh—it is a religious form of it, but it is actually the same thing.

What does it mean, then, to have your mind set on the Spirit? It means that in the midst of making money, having fun, gaining fame, and fulfilling yourself, you are primarily concerned with showing love, helping others, speaking truth, and, above all, loving God and seeking his glory. The only trouble with the world is that it is content with *just* making money, having fun, and fulfilling itself—that is all it wants. The end is man. But the mind set on the Spirit desires that God be glorified in all these things.

When your mind is set on the Spirit you look at the events of life from God's point of view, not from the world's. Your value system is changed and it touches everything you do. You no longer believe the most important thing is to make a lot of money. The important thing is that, in seeking to fulfill your needs, God is glorified. It is to live on the basis of a new identity and a new power. This is what makes the difference. This is the mind set on the Spirit. It does not remove you from life—it puts you right back into it. But it does so with a different point of view.

Existential Death

In verse 6 the apostle describes the results you can expect from either of the two courses outlined in verse 5. He says,

> *The mind of sinful man is death, but the mind controlled by the Spirit is life and peace. . . .*

We could also translate this verse, "The thinking of the flesh is death, but the thinking of the Spirit is life and peace."

What happens when you, as a Christian, let yourself live as the world does and never bring the perspective of God into what you do? Then you are living according to the flesh. And the thinking of the flesh is death, while that of the Spirit is life and peace. This describes the results that come *right now*. Death, in our present experience, always consists of four basic things: fear, guilt, hostility, and emptiness. These are the forms of death which come when you have your mind set on those things—and only those things—that the flesh desires: making money, having fun, fulfilling yourself, and gaining fame. If that is all you want out of life, then you will also have with

it fear, guilt, hostility, and emptiness, in all their
various forms.

Fear can appear as worry, anxiety, dread, or timidity. Guilt can show up as shame, self-hatred, self-
righteousness, or perfectionism. Hostility will mani-
fest itself as hate, resentment, bitterness, revenge, or
cruelty. Emptiness can show up as loneliness, depression, discouragement, despair, meaninglessness.
They are all symptoms of death.

As if that were not enough, these symptoms of
death not only have an immediate effect on our feelings, but they actually go on to settle into the body
and affect our health. We can develop nervous
twitches, tics, rashes, eczema, ulcers, stuttering,
heart attacks, cancer, and many other diseases. This,
literally, is death. We are killing ourselves if, as
Christians, we continue to live, think, and act as the
world lives, thinks and acts.

What, then, is living with the mind set on the
Spirit? It is facing all these things—making money,
enjoying pleasure, fulfilling yourself, even achieving
a degree of fame—but at the same time realizing that
God is at work in you. He supplies the power to do
these things. Expect him to be at work and to be
glorified in all these things, and the result will be life
and peace.

What, then, is life? To summarize all that the
Scriptures say on this, life includes four basic things
that are opposites of death. If death is fear, then life is
trust, hope, and confidence. If death is guilt, then
life is a feeling of acceptance, security, and assurance.
If death is hostility, then life is love, friendliness,
kindness, and reaching out to others. If death is emptiness, then life is a sense of well-being, fulfillment,
excitement, vitality, and fullness. With life comes
peace, which, of course, is an inner calm, a quiet

spirit, a remarkable sense of being able to cope with and to handle life. This is what comes when the mind is set on the Spirit.

But the apostle does not stop with this; he tells why this is true. In verse 7 he explains why the mind set on the flesh produces death:

> . . . *the sinful mind is hostile to God. It does not submit to God's law, nor can it do so.*

The mind set on the flesh brings death because it is hostile to God and cannot obey the law of God. It actually opposes it. Anyone who thinks life consists only of gaining money, pleasure, enjoyment, and a degree of notoriety, is hostile to God. That thinking is against God. James 4:6 says, "God opposes the proud, but gives grace to the humble." It scares me to think that whenever I am trying to further my own advancement, God is lined up against me; he resists this kind of thinking. That is why James 3:16 can say, "Where you have envy and selfish ambition, there you find disorder and every evil practice." God resists the proud who live for themselves and gives grace to the humble.

Though not stated here, the implication is clear. The mind set on the Spirit pleases God. This is what God wants, and he gives grace to that end; he advances it and helps it. He works on behalf of one whose outlook on life is not proud self-confidence, but humble trust in the living God—the God who is ready to work with him and through him to do whatever needs to be done. This is the difference between life and death, between heaven and hell.

Who Belongs to Christ?

A parenthesis appears in verses 8 and 9 which the apostle uses to show us the difference between a

Christian who lives "according to the flesh" and a
non-Christian, who is "in the flesh." These terms are
entirely different and need to be carefully recognized
as such.

> *Those controlled by the sinful nature {literally,
> "those who are in the flesh"} cannot please God.
> You, however, are controlled not by the sinful na-
> ture but by the Spirit, if the Spirit of God lives in
> you. And if anyone does not have the Spirit of
> Christ, he does not belong to Christ (8:8-9).*

This is as plain as you can make it. If anyone does
not have the Spirit of Christ, he does not belong to
Christ. Such a person is said to be "in the flesh" as
contrasted with a Christian who, though he is not "in
the flesh," may be living "according to the flesh."
You cannot tell if a person is a Christian by what he
does at any given moment. He may act exactly as a
non-Christian. Both of them may be cruel, vindic-
tive, hateful, lustful, and sinful in every way. At that
moment, you cannot see any difference between
them. But there is a difference, Paul says. One has
the Spirit of Christ within him—the Holy Spirit—
and eventually the Spirit will make a fantastic difference in his behavior. The other does not, and he will
continue in sin and even become worse.

In fact, the apostle suggests that a non-Christian's
actions may sometimes be much better than those of
a Christian. There are non-Christians who are kinder,
more thoughtful, and more gracious than many
Christians. People say, "Look at them! If their lives
are so nice and pleasant, surely they must be Christians." But it is not necessarily so. He who does not
have the Spirit of Christ does not belong to Christ.
The difference will show up in the ultimate tests of
life. When the crunch comes, one will collapse and

fall, and the other will rise and eventually conquer.

Verses 10 and 11 are the apostle's conclusion in this matter. This is what he is aiming at:

> *But if Christ is in you, your body is dead because of sin, yet your spirit is alive because of righteousness. And if the Spirit of him who raised Jesus from the dead is living in you, he who raised Christ from the dead will also give life to your mortal bodies through his Spirit, who lives in you.*

This is a great statement. Notice first of all the helpful teaching about the Spirit here. He is called the Spirit of God and the Spirit of Christ. Then it is made clear that the Spirit actually is the means by which Jesus Christ himself is in us. All this refers to the work of the Holy Spirit. These terms refer to the same thing. Through the Spirit, Christ is in you. And if Christ is in you, your body is dead because of sin. You may not realize it, but it is true.

The problem is, our bodies are yet unredeemed. As a consequence, they are the source of the sin that troubles us so. And the sin that is in us—still there in our bodies—affects the body. That is why the body lusts, the body loves comfort, and the body seeks after pleasure; that is why our minds and attitudes react with hate, bitterness, resentment, hostility. Sin finds its seat in the body. Our bodies keep growing old. They are dying because of sin.

I have been watching some of my friends through the years. Although I haven't noticed much change in myself, I have noticed they seem to be deteriorating. They are growing older and getting weaker. Their hair is turning gray (if they still have some); they groan and creak where once they leaped and ran. Their bodies are dying because of sin.

For one who is not a Christian, that is the whole

story. The body is dead, and so is the spirit. It is falling apart, and will continue to do so. But that is not the final answer for the Christian. The human spirit of the Christian is alive because of the gift of righteousness. Christ has come in and we are linked with him. As Paul puts it in 2 Corinthians 4:16— "Though outwardly we are wasting away, yet inwardly we are being renewed day by day." This is the joy of being a Christian. Though the body, with the sin that is within it, is giving us trouble and difficulty, tempting us, confounding us at times, nevertheless, the spirit is alive because of righteousness.

Sin has its seat in the actual physical body, and it rises up (as Paul describes in Romans 7) like a powerful beast. Stimulated by the law, it can rise up and attack us, overwhelm us, and conquer us. But we have an answer, an answer put so clearly in 1 John 4:4—"The one who is in you is greater than the one who is in the world." In other words, the Spirit of God within us is stronger than the sin that is in our bodies. We have strength to control the body. That is what Paul is saying in verse 11: "And if the Spirit of him who raised Jesus from the dead is living in you, he who raised Jesus from the dead will also give life to your mortal bodies through his Spirit, who lives in you."

Strength to Say No

Unfortunately, many commentators say this verse refers to the promise of resurrection at the end of life, when God is going to make our bodies alive. But that is not what Paul is saying. He is talking about the Spirit in us, giving life to our *mortal* bodies. Now, a mortal body is not yet dead. A mortal body is one that is subject to death. It is dying, but it is not yet dead. Therefore, this does not refer to the resurrection. Later Paul will come to that, but in this chapter he is talking about what the Spirit does in us now.

He says that though sin in our mortal bodies is going to tempt us severely, and at times rise up with great power (we have all felt the power of temptation in our lives . . . this urgent, almost irresistible desire to do something that we know is wrong), we must never forget that because our human spirit has been made alive in Jesus Christ, and the Spirit of God himself dwells in us, we have the strength to say no to that expression of evil.

We cannot reverse the processes of physical death—no one can. Our bodies are going to die. But we can refuse to let the members of our bodies become the instruments of sin. By the power of the Spirit within, we can refuse to give in or to let our members be used for evil purpose. We don't have to let our eyes look at wrong things. Nor do we have to let our tongues say evil, hurtful, sarcastic, and vicious things; we don't have to let them lie. We don't have to let our ears hear things that are hurtful or let our minds give way to thinking about things in a wrong and vicious fashion. Nor do we have to let our hands be used for wrong purposes. We don't have to let our legs and feet lead us into places where we ought not to be, nor do we have to let our sexual organs be used for wrong purposes. We don't have to let the members of our bodies be used wrongly. This is what Paul said back in 6:12-13.

> Therefore do not let sin reign in your mortal body so that you obey its evil desires. Do not offer the parts of your body to sin, as instruments of wickedness, but rather offer yourselves to God, as those who have been brought from death to life; and offer the parts of your body to him as instruments of righteousness.

This is as plain as can be. We don't have to sin. By resurrection power, by the power of the one who raised Jesus from the dead, and who lives in us, we can say *no* to these temptations and desires for evil. This is why, in chapter 12 of this letter, Paul says, "Therefore, I urge you, brothers, in view of God's mercy, to offer your bodies as living sacrifices, holy and pleasing to God—which is your spiritual worship." And we can do that.

In 8:12-13, Paul gives his conclusion. He tells us we have only one obligation:

> *Therefore, brothers, we have an obligation—but it is not to the sinful nature, to live according to it. For if you live according to the sinful nature, you will die {death becomes your experience in your present existence}; but if by the Spirit you put to death the misdeeds of the body, you will live.*

You will live, with all that true life means in terms of security, trust, fulfillment, vitality, joy, and peace. Notice that Paul stresses this must be done *by the Spirit*, that is, simply by believing what the Spirit of God has said. This is the way you act by the Spirit—by faith. When you believe God has said these sins of your body do not need to be yielded to— they can be controlled, they have been crucified with Christ, they are worthless, they cannot help you, nothing worthwhile can come from them—then you can say no to sin and you can live by the Spirit. Then you can serve others, make money, enjoy work and pleasure, gain fame, and fulfill yourself. And through it all, God will be glorified. You will display, in your present experience, love, joy, peace, and the grace of Jesus Christ. The very righteousness which the law demands is fulfilled in those who walk not after the flesh but after the Spirit. All this is beautiful, isn't it?

I vividly recall seeing a series of illustrations published in a magazine at the close of World War II. The first showed a huge army tank bearing down on the tiny figure of a soldier, about to crush him. How frightened he was, as this massive tank was about to overwhelm him! The picture made clear the odds involved when a foot soldier with only a rifle faced a tank. The second illustration showed the same soldier, but this time with a bazooka in his hands. The third picture showed the tank again, but this time shrunken in size until it was no bigger than the soldier.

This is what Paul is saying to us. Without the power of God released in our lives, we are like an infantry soldier facing a tank. We cannot do a thing. It is too much for us. But by trust in the power of the living God, we can rise up in the face of temptation and, armed with the bazooka of the Spirit, we can say no and make it stick. We can turn and begin to live as God intended us to live.

The question this raises, then, is this: Why not live? Why spend most of your Christian life in weakness, constantly feeling guilt, fear, loneliness, depression, and discouragement? Why not live?

Jesus said, "I am come that they might have life and that they might have it more abundantly." Paul is simply describing how we might, indeed, find that life.

20
THE SONS
OF GOD
AMONG MEN

(Romans 8:14-17)

In the second half of Romans 8, Paul explains further what being in Christ and in the Spirit actually means. The apostle has been leading us step by step to understand more fully our new identity in Jesus Christ. The more we understand that identity, and the more we believe it, the more quickly we will begin to experience life in Christ. In verses 14 and 15, Paul uses a term he has never used before in this letter. He says,

Those who are led by the Spirit of God are sons of God. For you did not receive a spirit that makes you a slave again to fear, but you received the Spirit of sonship. And by him we cry, "Abba, Father."

For the first time in this letter Paul uses the phrase "the sons of God." Now, I want to make something clear. This is a generic term that includes both sexes. All believers in Christ who have received the gift of righteousness by faith are sons of God—regardless of whether they are male or female. There is no need for any differentiation of the sexes here. This is why the Scriptures speak freely of us—all of us—as the sons of the living God. This speaks of something that is true of our spirit, and the spirit is sexless. Spirit is not male or female, so what is true of the human spirit is quite apart from what is true of the body.

Offspring and Sons

It is important to recognize right away that not everyone is a son of God. According to Galatians 5, we are sons of God *by faith in Jesus Christ*. Faith—and nothing else—makes you a son of God. It is true that we are all creatures of God by natural birth. When Paul preached in Athens, that great intellectual center, he mentioned that even the Athenians' own poets recognized that men owed their existence to God. We are the offspring of God, and in him "we live and move and have our being," he said. This is true of all human beings everywhere in the world at all times. They are all creatures of God. They are the offspring of God.

But Paul is careful to use a quite different term in Romans: "sons of God." We are in the family of God, and this is a distinctive term. I want to underscore how important this is, because God wants us to return to it when we are in trouble. If you are having trouble handling your behavior—whether you are not doing what you want to do, or doing what you don't want to do—the way to handle it is to remind

yourself of what God has made you to be. This ter-
minology helps tremendously.

In your struggle with sin within you, you are not a
slave, helplessly struggling against a cruel and powerful master; you are a son, a son of the living God,
with power to overcome the evil—even though it *is* a
struggle. And though you may be temporarily overcome, you are never ultimately defeated. You cannot
be, because you are already children of God. This is
why Paul could say in Romans 6, "Sin shall not be
your master, because you are not under law but under
grace." In this gracious relationship we are made and
constituted sons of the living God. No matter what
happens to us, that is what we are. Nothing can
change it. This is the place from which we start.

It is important also for us to see *how* we become
sons of God. Paul says, "You did not receive a spirit
that makes you a slave again to fear." When the Spirit
of God came into your heart, he did not make you a
slave to fear. Remember how Paul puts this in 2
Timothy 1:7—"For God did not give us a spirit of
timidity, but a spirit of power, of love and of self-
discipline." This is the nature of the Holy Spirit.
What did the Spirit do? Paul says, "You received the
Spirit of sonship," or, literally, "the Spirit of adoption, who adopted you as sons." How did you become
a son of God? Well, the Spirit of God found you, and
he found me, and he adopted us into God's family.

One night I was with a family where there were
two adopted or "chosen" children and two children
born to the parents. I watched all evening to see if I
could tell the difference between them. I finally had
to ask the parents because I could not tell any difference—even from their looks. Two were adopted into
the family and two were born into it, but they were

all treated so beautifully and so naturally that I could not tell the difference.

Some of you may be saying at this point, "Look, you are confusing me. What do you mean when you say we are adopted into the family of God? I have been taught from the Scriptures that I was born into the family of God. I have been born again." That is the term much bandied about these days. Even politicians are boasting, "I've been born again." Thank God, some of them are. So you say, "I thought we were born, not adopted. What do you mean by 'adopted'?"

Aspects of Belonging

I am glad you asked. You see, both of these are true. We are both adopted *and* born into the family of God. As Jesus said on another occasion, "With men it is impossible, but with God, all things are possible." We can't be both adopted and born into a human family, but we can in God's family. God uses both these terms because he wants to highlight two different aspects of our belonging to the family of God.

We are said to be adopted because God wants us to remember always that we are not naturally part of the family of God. We have been seeing all along in this letter that we are born into Adam's family, and we are all children of Adam by natural birth. We belong to the human family, and we inherit Adam's nature. All his defects, all his problems, all the evil that came into his life by his act of disobedience—all these were passed along to us by natural birth. So by nature we are not part of God's family. In the same way, some people were born into one family, and then, by a legal process, were taken out of that family and were adopted into another family. From then on they became part of the family that adopted them.

This is what has happened to us. God has taken us out of our natural state in Adam, and by the process of the Spirit has made us legally sons of God. We are now part of his family. But he reminds us that we are in his family by adoption so that we might never take it for granted, or forget that if we were left in our natural state we would not have a part in the family of God. It is only by the grace of God that we come into his family.

But it is also true that we are born into God's family. Once we have been adopted, it is also true that, because God is God, he not only makes us legally his sons, but he makes us actually share his nature. It is astonishing! This tie with Jesus is so real that we are actually one with him, and as Peter puts it, "We have been made partakers of the divine nature." So we are as much a part of God's family as if we had originally been born into it, and we are born into it by the grace of God.

So both these statements are true. There is nothing more wonderful than to remind yourself, morning by morning and day by day, of this great fact: If you are a Christian, you are a son of the living God, adopted and born into his family. Because you are his son, God loves you, God protects you, God provides for you, God plans for you, God hears you, God claims you and openly acknowledges you. He chastens and corrects you, and he honors you. All of this is true because you are his son.

We know how we treat our natural children. There is a difference between them and the neighbors' children. Our children are considerably superior, of course. We may love the neighbors' children—they may be delightful, but they are not our children. We have a special relationship with our own children.

We care for them, hurt for them, love and protect them, plan for them, and watch out for them. There are special ties with them. In this same way, God has a special relationship to us. We are the sons of God turned loose among the sons of men.

It would be helpful, I know, if God would put a little mark on us that would indicate we are his sons. If we had a little red star on our foreheads, then we could recognize all the other sons of God. Or, perhaps if we had a special glow that never dimmed in the slightest.

But there is no such mark. Outwardly, there is no distinction; but inwardly, there is a tremendous distinction, and we need to understand this. We can't tell by looking at anyone whether he or she is a child of God, though often there is an underlying sensitivity that allows brothers and sisters in Christ to identify one another. But there is a vast difference within, and because of this difference, God has a special relationship with us.

Now, the great question in all this is, "If everything depends on my being a son of God, how can I be sure that I am a son?" Paul has been leading up to this question all through his letter. Whether or not you are a son of God will make the essential difference in your life—not only now, in the way you behave, but for all eternity. So the greatest question in life is, "Am I or am I not a son of God?" You can't ask a more important question than that. Your whole behavior, your happiness as an individual, your ultimate destiny, your whole relationship to the greatness and the glory of God, all depends on the answer to this question.

So the apostle in this passage gives us three very practical tests—three levels of assurance—by which we can know whether we are God's sons.

Proof by Observation

First, Paul says, we are sons of God if we are led by the Spirit of God. Now, to be led by the Spirit means that one is controlled by someone other than himself. This, therefore, is a proof which arises from our circumstances, from our experiences, from the events and reactions that happen to us, over which we have no deliberate control. Paul is saying that we can learn the answer to this question by observing. This is proof addressed to the mind. We can reason it; we can observe it. We can look around in our lives and see if we are being led by the Spirit of God. If there is proof that we are, then we are sons of God.

What are some of these signs? The Scriptures tells us the Spirit of God will do certain things when he comes into our lives. If he has done them, and we can see that he has, we have immediate assurance that we are sons of God. "Those who are led by the Spirit of God are the sons of God." So let's look at the signs of being led by the Spirit.

The most evident and important sign to me—and one that obviously doesn't come from a human source—is that when I read the Scriptures I am taught by the Spirit. He opens my mind to understand the Word of God. He is called the Spirit of truth. So when he comes into my life, the first thing he will do is to make the Bible a living Word to me. I will see it as truth, and know it as truth. My eyes are opened to understand that here at least is reality. This understanding is the work of the Spirit of God.

Have you ever been reading a passage of Scripture when suddenly something leaped out at you? The passage takes on a new, fresh, and glowing meaning. If this has happened, you are being led by the Spirit of God. He is doing his work of opening the truth to your mind and heart. This, of course, is what Paul refers to in verse 13: "If *by the Spirit* you put to death the misdeeds of the body, you will live." He is talking about our understanding of what the Spirit of God has already done with the flesh within us, how it was crucified with Christ, and how, therefore, we can be freed from it. We can rise up and refuse to obey that flesh because its connection with us has been broken. If you understand this, you are being led by the Spirit of God, and therefore you are a son of God.

Some years ago when I was in a city some distance from home, I was feeling discouraged. I opened the Scriptures and read one of Paul's letters, and was so impressed by these words: "Remember that you are chosen of God, and precious in his sight." Suddenly the realization came home to me that this applied to *me*. I was chosen of God and precious in his sight! This kind of experience is given by the Spirit of God within us, teaching us the truth.

The Spirit also arouses us to pray. Have you ever felt you just had to pray, that you had to get away somewhere and have a few quiet moments in God's presence? You may not have prayed for several days, but suddenly you are compelled to. You have to open up and talk to your Father. Now this is being led of the Spirit of God. It is he who arouses in us the desire to pray. Those who have had these experiences can know by them that we are children of God.

Another thing the Spirit does is awaken a love for the brethren. When you meet someone and learn he is a Christian, do you ever feel a special bond with him right away? Have you ever longed to be with Christians? Do you sometimes get tired of even the closest of friends who are not Christians? Do you long to be with brothers and sisters in the family? The

Spirit awakens within us a love for the brethren. John says in his first letter that if you have a love for the brethren it is a sign that you are in Christ.

Another sign is that the Spirit makes the world empty, and he makes God real. The Spirit directs us and checks us. Do you ever feel this? These are signs that we are being led by the Spirit of God.

Of course, ultimately, the Spirit produces the fruit of the Spirit in us. If we have evidence at all that we are truly loving—especially when it is hard to be loving—if we feel love, joy, peace, gentleness, compassion, goodness, and faith, then we know these have all been awakened by the Spirit of God. "Those who are led by the Spirit of God are sons of God." This is one test by which we can know if we are sons of God.

An Emotional Response

There is another level of assurance of our sonship mentioned in the closing part of verse 15: "And by him we cry, 'Abba, Father.'" *Abba* is the Aramaic word for father. Of course, the Greek word is translated "father" here, also. So, by means of the Spirit, we are given an emotional response to God in which we are aware of his fatherhood, and our soul cries out within us, "Abba, Father." "Abba" is a baby's word.

I remember years ago hearing a story about Dr. Alan McRae, the great Bible student and Hebrew scholar. Some time after the McRaes' baby boy was born, Dr. McRae had to go away for three or four weeks. When he came back, his wife was showing him how the baby had learned to say a few words. When this eminent Hebrew scholar came in, his little son stretched out his arms and said, "Ab-Abba, abba!" Dr. McRae said, "Look, he's speaking Aramaic already!" The closest and most intimate relationship you can have is the awareness that you belong to a father, with a father's arms around you, a father's heart concerned for you, a father's wisdom planning for you, and a father's love protecting and guarding you. If you have ever sensed the fatherhood of God and the brotherhood of Jesus, it is because God's Spirit has awakened your heart to sense that you belong to the family of God.

I have seen tears come to people's eyes when something from the Scriptures reminds them of their relationship to God the Father. It can happen when you are driving your car, or sitting with your family, or going through a time of sorrow. Suddenly and unexpectedly, that wonderful sense that you belong to the Father comes, and you cherish that relationship. Your soul cries, "Abba, my Father!" This, by the way, is the word Jesus himself used in the agony of Gethsemane. As he knelt to pray in his hour of anguish, he cried out, "Oh Abba—my Father!" Even in his anguish he was aware of this relationship.

Verse 16 tells us of still another level of assurance that the Spirit is in us:

> *The Spirit himself testifies with our spirit that we are God's children.*

This is the deepest level of assurance. Beyond the emotions, beyond the feelings, is a deep conviction born of the Spirit of God himself, an underlying awareness that we cannot deny we are part of God's family. We are the children of God. I think this is the basic thing to which our emotions respond with the cry, "Abba, Father." That is our love to him, but this is his love to us. It is what Paul refers to in Romans 5 when he says, "God has poured out his love into our hearts by the Holy Spirit, whom he has given us."

As I look back on my own life, I can understand how this is true. I think I became a Christian when I was about eleven years old, in a Methodist brush arbor meeting. I responded to the invitation and, with tears, came and knelt in front and received the Lord. I had a wonderful time of fellowship with the Lord that summer and the next winter, and there were occasions when I would be overwhelmed with the sense of nearness and dearness of God. I used to sing hymns until tears would flow as the meaning of those old words reflected on the relationship that I had with God. I used to preach to the cows as I brought them home. Those cows were a very good audience, too, by the way; they never went to sleep on me.

Seven-Year Prodigal

But the next fall we moved to a town that did not even have a church. Gradually, because of that lack of Christian fellowship, I drifted away from a warm relationship with God into many ugly and shameful things—habits and thought patterns that I am now ashamed of. I developed some liberal attitudes toward the Scriptures. I did not believe in the inspiration of the Bible. I argued against it, and during high school and college I was known as a skeptic.

But all through those years there was a relationship with God I could not deny. Somehow I knew, deep down inside, that I still belonged to him; and there were things I could not do, even though I was tempted. I could not do them because I felt I had a tie with God. This is the witness of the Spirit—Calvin called it "the testimonium"—which we cannot deny and which is especially discernible in times of gross sin and despair. In 1 John 3:19-20 we read,

This then is how we know that we belong to the
truth, and how we set our hearts at rest in his pres-
ence whenever our hearts condemn us. For God is
greater than our hearts, and he knows everything.

God knows everything. There is a witness born of the
Spirit which you cannot shake, which is there with
the ultimate testimony that we belong with the children of God.

This is where to begin when you get into trouble.
Go back to this relationship. Remind yourself of who
you are. You can see it in your life as you look around.
You are led by the Spirit of God. You can feel it in
your heart. There are times when your emotions are
stirred by the Spirit, and you sense at the level of your
spirit that you belong to God.

In verse 17 the apostle mentions an even greater
and deeper relationship. This verse introduces the
next section in the passage, but I want to set it before
you now:

Now if we are children, then we are heirs—heirs
of God and co-heirs with Christ, if indeed we
share in his sufferings in order that we may also
share in his glory.

This introduces the very climax of this epistle. We
learn of the glory that awaits us and its tie with the
sufferings that we go through now. We started in
Adam; we are now, by faith, in Christ, and in the
Spirit; if we are in the Spirit, we can walk according
to the Spirit; if we walk according to the Spirit, we
are therefore led by the Spirit; if we are led by the
Spirit, we are the sons of God; and if we are the sons
of God, we are heirs of God. All that God owns is to
be committed to us.

These are staggering, mind-stretching things; but
they are what the apostle writes, and they run all

throughout the Scriptures. The thread is found from Genesis right through Revelation. In variously subtle and open ways the Old Testament constantly hints that something fantastic is coming. What God has in mind for this beguiled and driven race of men who are now redeemed by faith in Christ is beyond description! This is what Paul is going to bring before us now, as we consider the heritage waiting for us in Jesus Christ.

And all this is for us to remember when we get into trouble. This is not just hope for the future; it is deliverance for the present. If we remember who we are, by an absolute psychological certainty we will start acting like who we are. When we do, we will find there is power available to say *no* to the flesh, to say *yes* to the Spirit, and to walk in a way that glorifies God.

21
THE AGONY
AND THE
ECSTASY

(Romans 8:17-28)

The apostle John writes, "Dear friends, now we are children of God, and what we will be has not yet been made known" (1 John 3:2). This is the theme Paul brings into focus as we continue in Romans 8. He actually deals with two themes: the sufferings of believers, and their ultimate glorification.

As a pastor I have always found comfort in 1 John 3:2. Sometimes when I am beset by saints who come to me and criticize various things that are going on, I have a difficult time relating to them. Then I remind myself, "Well, they are still children of God even though it does not yet appear what they shall be." I also see the increasing decrepitude in many deteriorating bodies as they grow older. I have to say again, "It does not yet appear what we shall be." Things are moving toward a great day, but it is not here yet; and until that day, we have to put up with the difficulties, the hardships, and the sufferings to which our current situations bring us. These are the themes Paul links together in this great section of Romans 8.

Earlier he stated this plainly in verse 17:

> Now if we are children, then we are heirs—heirs of God and co-heirs with Christ, if indeed we share in his sufferings in order that we may also share in his glory.

This verse links two things that we would probably not put together: sufferings and glory—hurts and hallelujahs. They belong together, and you find them together in almost every passage of Scripture that deals with the suffering of the Christian. In fact, in 2 Corinthians 4:17 the apostle links them directly: "For our light and momentary troubles are achieving for us an eternal glory that outweighs them all." So, our sufferings as believers—physical, emotional, whatever they may be—are directly linked with the glory that is coming. The important thing we need to see is that both the sufferings and the glory are privileges given to us.

It is easy for Christians reading these passages to get the idea that we earn our glory by the sufferings we go through. Those who go through the greatest suffering will earn the greatest glory. But it is wrong to see it that way. We never earn glory. As this passage makes clear, glory is given to us as part of our inheritance in Christ. And suffering, too, is our inheritance in Christ. Suffering is a privilege committed to us. Paul says this plainly in Philippians 1:29—

> *For it has been granted to you on behalf of Christ*
> *{or, for his name's sake} not only to believe on him,*
> *but also to suffer for him.*

The early part of Acts records that the first Christians actually rejoiced in their sufferings. They rejoiced because they were counted worthy to suffer for the sake of the Lord. And though they were beaten and mistreated, they went away rejoicing because God had counted them worthy to bear suffering for his name's sake. This is the transforming view that makes it possible for us to endure suffering and, more than that, to actually rise above it with triumphant rejoicing. We can do this when we see that our sufferings are privileges committed to us. Our Lord Jesus said this himself: "Blessed are you when people insult you, persecute you and falsely say all kinds of evil against you because of me. Rejoice and be glad, because great is your reward in heaven, for in the same way they persecuted the prophets who were before you" (Matthew 5:11-12).

Nothing will help us more to endure suffering than a clear view of the glory linked to it. This is the theme we begin to encounter in Romans 8:18.

> *I consider that our present sufferings are not worth*
> *comparing with the glory that will be revealed in*
> *us.*

The theme of this verse and the next nine is that incomparable glory lies ahead—glory beyond description, greater than anything you can compare it with on earth. A magnificent and fantastic prospect awaits us. All through the Scriptures there has been a rumor of hope running through the Old Testament, through the prophetic writings, and into the New Testament. This rumor speaks of a day when all the hurt, heartache, injustice, weakness, and suffering of today will be explained and justified, and will result in a time of incredible blessing upon the earth. The whisper of this in the Old Testament increases in intensity as it approaches the New Testament, where you come to proclamations like this that speak of the incomparable glory ahead.

We tend to make careful note of our suffering. I once received a mimeographed letter from a man who had written out in extreme detail (even though rather humorously) a report of his recent operation. He said he'd had to listen to all the reports of other people's operations for years, and now it was his turn! We make detailed reports of what we go through in our sufferings. But here the apostle says, "Don't even mention them! They are not worthy to be mentioned in comparison with the glory that is to follow."

This statement would be just so much hot air if it did not come from a man like Paul. Here is a man who suffered intensely. None of us has gone through even a fraction of the suffering Paul endured. He was beaten, stoned (with rocks!), chained, imprisoned, shipwrecked, starved, often hungry, naked, and cold. He himself tells us this. And yet he takes pen in hand and says, "Our present sufferings are not worth comparing with the glory that will be revealed in us." The glory that is coming is incomparable.

Our sufferings hurt us, I know. I am not trying to make light of them or diminish the terrible physical and emotional pain that suffering can bring. It can be awful, almost unendurable. Its intensity can increase to such a degree that we scream with terror and pain. We think we can no longer endure. But the apostle says that the intensity of our suffering is not even a drop in the bucket compared with the intensity of coming glory. Paul strains language in trying to describe this fantastic thing about to happen.

United with Beauty

This glory is not only incomparable in its intensity, but incomparable in its locality. It is not going to be revealed *to* us, but *in* us. The word literally means "into us." This glory is not going to be like a spectator sport, where we will sit up in some cosmic grandstand and watch an amusing or beautiful performance in which we actually have no part. We are to be on stage. We are going to be involved in it. It is a glory that will be "revealed into us," and we are part of it.

The incomparable C. S. Lewis has explained this more accurately than anyone else, I think, in *The Weight of Glory*:

> *We are to shine as the sun. We are to be given the morning star. I think I begin to see what it means. In one way, of course, God has given us the morning star already. You can go and enjoy the gift on many fine mornings, if you get up early enough. "What more," you may ask, "do we want?" Ah, but we want so much more. Something the books on aesthetics take little notice of. But the poets and mythologies know all about it. We do not want merely to see beauty, though God knows even that is bounty enough—we want something else which can hardly be put into words—to be united with the beauty we see, to pass into it, to receive it into ourselves, to bathe in it, to become part of it. That is why the poets tell us such lovely falsehoods. They talk as if the west wind could really sweep into a human soul. But it can't. They tell us that beauty, born of murmuring sound, will pass into a human face. But it won't—or not yet, at least.*

Lewis sums it up in this way:

*The door on which we have been knocking all our
lives will open at last.*

This is what Paul says is about to happen. This is
the incredible glory God has prepared for those who
love him, for us—not because we have been faithful,
not because we earn it, but because we are heirs of
God, and co-heirs with Christ.

Thus we are called and entrusted with the
privilege of suffering. All Christians suffer. There are
no exceptions. If you are a true and genuine believer
in Jesus Christ, you will suffer. But we are not only
given the privilege of suffering with him now, but
also sharing in his glory yet to come. We can endure
the suffering, and even triumph in it, because we see
the glory that will follow.

In the next paragraph the apostle shows us two
proofs that confirm this hope of glory, bearing witness of this day to come. The first is from nature, and
the second from our own experience.

Verses 19 through 22 explain the testimony found
in nature. First, nature is waiting for something:

*The creation waits in eager expectation for the
sons of God to be revealed (8:19).*

The Greek word translated here as "eager expectation" is an interesting picture of a man standing and
waiting for something to happen, craning his neck,
visibly displaying anticipation for what is coming. J.
B. Phillips correctly captures the sense: "The whole
creation is standing on tiptoe, eagerly awaiting the
revelation of the sons of God." This is what Paul says
the world of nature is doing. It is eagerly awaiting
this remarkable event toward which the world is hastening, and has been hastening since the beginning
of time.

Paul goes on to explain why he makes such a statement:

> *For the creation was subjected to frustration, not by its own choice, but by the will of the one who subjected it, in hope that the creation itself will be liberated from its bondage to decay and brought into the glorious freedom of the children of God (8:20-21).*

Creation not only is waiting for something, but it is doing so because it is linked with man. Creation fell with man, the apostle declares. Not only did our whole race fall into the bondage of sin and death, but the entire physical universe fell as well. It was man's sin that put thorns on roses. It was man's sin that made the animals hate and fear each other and brought predators and carnivores into being. With the fall of man came the spread of fear, hostility, and hatred in the animal world, and the whole of nature testifies to it. It is, as Paul describes it here, subjected to frustration.

Futility Prevails

Sometimes we hear about plants that are sensitive to people, that they even understand something of our words and and attitudes. Can you imagine how frustrated a plant can get when it wants to produce and grow, and yet it is treated so that it cannot? Some of us have to live with these frustrated plants in our home! Think of the beauty of nature—and yet every area is spoiled by thorns and thistles and other marks of decay. Futility prevails in the natural world.

The phrase "bondage to decay" is an accurate description of what scientists call the second law of thermodynamics. This is the law of increasing entropy. Everything is decaying; everything, without exception, is running down. Though for a while something may seem to grow, eventually it dies. Even human life dies, and so does all that is with it. All of this is because of the fall of man.

I sometimes spend a few days in the beautiful High Sierra where the great sequoia trees grow. As I walk about, I am saddened to see how the crush of man is spoiling what is left of the beauty of creation. There once had been a great forest—the world's greatest forest of sequoia trees, those majestic redwoods. But man came in, and in less than a decade there was nothing but thousands of blackened stumps and rotting logs. It is ironic that although the forest was razed in the name of profit, no one made a dime on the whole operation. At least half of the felled timber was never removed and was left to rot. This is how man despoils creation wherever he goes. He pollutes the air and ruins the environment. This is all a part of the bondage to decay that we see all around us.

But if this is true, the apostle argues, it is also true that when man is delivered from this decay, nature will be delivered too. When the hour strikes and the sons of God are revealed as they truly are, when what we have become in our spirits—sons of the living God—shall become obvious to all; in that hour, nature will be freed from its bondage. It will burst into a glorious, unimaginable bloom. The desert will blossom like the rose, the prophet says, and the lions will lie down with the lambs. None shall hurt and destroy in all of God's holy mountain. Rivers will run free, clear, and sweet again.

All that God intended in nature will come to pass in that day. Nature will be delivered into "the glorious freedom of the children of God"—literally, "the freedom and the glory," meaning that the glory has a great deal of freedom about it. We will step into such liberty as we have never dreamed, such as has never come into our imaginations. It is incomparable glory.

Now, in anticipation of that day, nature groans, though it groans in hope:

> *We know that the whole creation has been groaning as in the pains of childbirth right up to the present time (8:22).*

As Paul has said earlier, nature groans in the hope that the creation itself will be liberated from its bondage to decay and brought into the glorious freedom of the children of God. Someone has pointed out that all the sounds of nature are in a minor key. Listen to the sighing of the wind. Listen to the roaring of the tide. Even most bird sounds are in a minor key. All nature is singing, but it is singing a song of bondage. Yet it sings in hope, looking forward to the day when it will step into the freedom of the children of God.

The Groan and the Glory

Not only does nature testify to this bondage, bearing witness to the hope that is waiting, but we ourselves have this testimony. Our present experience confirms that glory is coming. Paul sets this before us in verse 23:

> *Not only so, but we ourselves, who have the firstfruits of the Spirit, groan inwardly as we wait eagerly for our adoption as sons, the redemption of our bodies.*

In some ways, this is the most remarkable statement in this whole remarkable paragraph. Paul says that though we are redeemed in spirit, our bodies are not yet redeemed; therefore we, too, are groaning. All through this paragraph there is a constant contrast between the groan and the glory; yet there is a link between the two. Nature groans; we groan. And yet the groan produces the glory. I remind you again of what Paul said in 2 Corinthians 4:17—

> *For our light and momentary troubles are achieving for us an eternal glory that far outweighs them all.*

Have you ever thought of afflictions in that way? Our afflictions are working for us. Every time we groan, it is a reminder to us of the promise of glory. I do not think anything will transform our sufferings more than remembering that.

Our lives consist of groans. We groan because of the ravages of sin in our lives and in the lives of those we love. We groan in disappointment because we see possibilities that are not captured and employed, and gifted people whose lives are being wasted. We groan in breavement and sorrow, just as Jesus groaned when he drew near the tomb of Lazarus, burdened by the ravages sin had made in a believing family.

But the apostle immediately adds that this groaning is in hope:

> *For in this hope we were saved. But hope that is seen is no hope at all. Who hopes for what he already has? But if we hope for what we do not yet have, we wait for it patiently (8:24-25).*

As nature groans in hope, so do we. For in this hope we were saved, in the anticipation that God has a plan for our bodies.

Among the Greeks it was taught that the body was evil, that the best thing was to get out of it, to escape into whatever glory awaited the human spirit. The body was seen as a prison. I am afraid this pagan concept is more prevalent among Christians than we like to think. Many Christians have an ejection-seat mentality. As soon as they get into difficulty, they want to pull the cord and zip off into glory. They want to get away from it all. We are all tempted to feel this way, but it is not the true Christian point of view.

The Christian viewpoint is that, though the body is in pain and suffering and is limited now, it is an important aspect of our lives. It is part of the whole program and plan of God, part of the privilege committed to us as Christians. We suffer with Christ. As he suffered, so do we, that we might be glorified as he is. Therefore, what is happening to us now is never meaningless. It holds great meaning. Boredom—seeing nothing meaningful in what you're going through now as you wait for something better—is the most unchristian attitude we can have.

We are saved in hope, Paul says, and by that hope we live. It is true that hope, by its very nature, is something yet in the future ("Hope that is seen is no hope at all. . . . But if we hope for what we do not yet have, we wait for it patiently"). What makes it possible to wait is that we already have the firstfruits of the Spirit. We know that the Spirit of God is able to give joy in the midst of heartache. He is able to make us feel at peace even when there is turmoil all around. This happens to even the weakest and newest among us. This is what Paul calls the firstfruits of the Spirit—the power of God to make a heart calm and restful and peaceful in the midst of turbulent, trying, and difficult circumstances. Because we have these firstfruits we can wait patiently for the hour when, at last, even our bodies will be set free, and we will step into an incomparable glory, such as we have never imagined. No one, in all the wildest dreams of science fiction, has ever imagined or conceived of something as vast and magnificent as the glory God has waiting for us.

More Groans

But there is more involved in this program of patient waiting, as the apostle goes on to explain in verse 26 and 27:

In the same way, the Spirit helps us in our weakness. We do not know what we ought to pray, but the Spirit himself intercedes for us with groans that words cannot express. And he who searches our hearts knows the mind of the Spirit, because the Spirit intercedes for the saints in accordance with God's will.

Now it is the Spirit groaning. There are three groans in this passage. Nature is groaning, we are groaning, and now the Spirit is groaning, with words which cannot be uttered. This passage helps us to understand prayer. The apostle says that we do not know what to pray for. We lack wisdom. I want to point out immediately that this is not an encouragement to cease praying. Some people think this means that if we don't know how to pray as we ought, and if the Spirit is going to pray for us anyway, then we don't need to pray. But that would contradict many other Scripture passages, especially James 4:2, which says, "You have not because you ask not." God does want us to pray, and we are constantly encouraged to pray. Jesus taught us to pray. In Philippians 4:6, Paul tells us that we are never to be troubled or anxious, but in everything, with prayer and supplication, we are to let our requests be made known to God.

Many times we know something is wrong, but do not know how to analyze it, or how to explain it, or how to ask God to do something about it. We are without wisdom. In those times, the apostle tells us, the Spirit of God voices, without words, his requests to the Father.

I have always been amazed at those who emphasize the gift of tongues and who take this verse as proof that the Spirit prays in tongues through us. This verse could not mean that. Paul tells us that this praying of the Spirit is done with groans which words cannot express. Now, tongues are words, words of other languages. If this referred to the gift of tongues, it would merely be putting into other languages the feelings of our heart. But this passage has nothing to do with that. This describes the groans of the Spirit within, so deep and so impossible to verbalize that we cannot say anything at all. We just feel deeply. The apostle says that when that happens, it is the Spirit of God who is praying. The Spirit is putting our prayer into a form which God the Father, who searches the heart, understands. The Spirit is asking for something concerning the situation that we are trying to pray about.

What is the Spirit asking for? That is explained in verse 28:

> And we know that in all things God works for the good of those who love him, who have been called according to his purpose.

Never separate this verse from the previous two. The apostle says that what the Spirit prays for is what happens. The Spirit prays according to the mind of God, and the Father answers by bringing into our lives whatever we need. He sends into our lives the experiences that we need, no matter what they may be.

This means that even the trials and tragedies that happen to us are an answer from the Father to the praying of the Spirit. What we need to understand is that these things do not happen by accident. They happen because the Spirit who is in you prayed and asked that the Father allow them to happen—because you or someone close to you needs it. These are the results of praying in the Spirit.

The joys, the unexpected blessings, and the unusual things that happen to you are also the result of the Spirit's praying. The Spirit is praying these things will happen, he is voicing the deep concern of God himself for your needs and mine. Out of this grows the assurance that no matter what happens, it will work together for good. This verse does not tell us that everything that happens to us is good. It does say that whether the situation is bad or good, it will work together for good if you are loved and called by God. What a difference that makes as we wait for the coming of the glory! God is working out his purposes within us.

Paul tells us here that we can wait with patience because nature testifies to his glorious coming. Our own experience confirms it. We are being prepared for something—we can't really tell what it is, specifically, but we are getting ready for something. And one of these days, at the end of our lives, if not before, we will step out of time into an incredible experience of glory, something that surpasses description—a glory that Christ himself shares, and that we will all share with him.

That is what God is preparing us for. No wonder the apostle closes this passage with one of the greatest paeans of praise in the Scriptures. As we face our sufferings, what a blessing, and what a help it is to remember the glory granted to us. We have been counted worthy to suffer for his name, that we may also share in the glory that is to come.

22
IF GOD BE
FOR US

(Romans 8:28-39)

The glory of Christianity is that, whether our hearts are aching or rejoicing, there is no incident or circumstance—no matter how trivial—that is without purpose or meaning. God has declared that "in all things God works for the good of those who love him, who have been called according to his purpose" (8:28).

That great statement introduces to us the crowning concept of Romans. We are called "according to his purpose." God has a purpose for us. There is purpose in life. What seems to be a meaningless jumble of events in history is not meaningless at all; there is a purpose to every event. Everything is moving to accomplish a desired end, and that end is the subject of this whole letter. God's purpose, in effect, is to have many sons, all of whom will love him with all their hearts, just as Jesus said: "You shall love the Lord your God with all your heart and all your mind and all your soul and all your strength. This is the first and greatest commandment."

To accomplish this, God called the world into being, set up the whole universe, populated the earth with a race of men, permitted them to fall, sent into this sin-ridden world his own beloved Son, accomplished his people's redemption through the Cross and the Resurrection, and now—as Paul so clearly says— "works for the good of those who love him, who have been called according to that great purpose."

In this we have a tremendous statement of what life is all about. We see that God wills to have a race of people, his own children, who will love him. Love is the end and aim of life. Now Paul looks back through his letter and sums up in five brief steps the process God follows to accomplish that end:

> *For those God foreknew he also predestined to be conformed to the likeness of his Son, that he might be the firstborn among many brothers. And those he predestined, he also called; those he called, he also justified; those he justified, he also glorified (8:29-30).*

These are the five steps God takes, stretching from eternity to eternity—far beyond the scope of any of our lives. I want to make clear that in this passage Paul is not explaining why some people believe and some do not. That is the problem of election. All that man is told about that subject is stated in the ninth chapter. But Paul does not face the mystery of election here. He is simply describing what has already happened when, as Christians, we look back to see how God brought us to belief.

A Question of Existence

The first step is that God foreknew us. Many people imagine this means God foreknew what we were going to do, he foreknew that we would believe in Christ. There is a certain line of teaching that says God looked down the corridor of time and saw that we would believe in Christ, and therefore he chose us to be part of his elect because of what we were going to do. But this verse, as I have already suggested, is not dealing with that question. This verse says, "*those whom* he foreknew," not "*that which* he foreknew." It is concerned, therefore, with the question of existence. It tells us that from among the tremendous number of people who have been born on this earth since the creation of man, God foreknew that you and I would be there—as well as all the believers who have preceded us or who will follow us in the course of history.

This is a remarkable statement, when you consider the infinitesimal chances of knowing at the moment of human conception all the future characteristics of that person. Because of the abundance of sperm to one ovum, doctors tell us that the possibility that any one particular person could be foretold and foreknown is fantastic—the odds are in the range of one in two hundred million for every single birth. So when you consider that out of all those possibilities God has foreknown us—and not only us, but all believers of all time—you begin to get some faint understanding of the mind and wisdom of God.

We are impressed by great computers that amass huge numbers of facts and put together amounts of information that none of us, alone, could ever handle. But these computers are nothing! They are children's toys compared with the greatness of the mind of God, who saw all the fantastic possibilities and knew that we would be there. Not only that, but he knew it long before the world was ever called into being! That is the amazing statement of the Scriptures. Before the foundation of the earth, God foreknew that we would be here. I cannot go any further than this. It baffles and bewilders me; nevertheless, it is fact. This is where Paul begins.

The next step is that God predestined. "Ah," you say, "I know what that means! That means God looked over the whole group and said, 'Now these will go to hell, and those will go to heaven.'" But predestination has absolutely nothing to do with going to hell. In the Word of God, predestination is never related to that. To think of predestination in those terms is completely unbiblical. Predestination has to do only with believers. It simply tells us that God has selected beforehand the goal toward which he is going to move every one of us who believes in Christ. That goal is conformity to the character of Christ. Everything that happens to us focuses on that one supreme purpose.

If we understand that, it will help to explain some of the conundrums of our lives. We think that God's primary objective is our happiness, but the Scriptures never say that. God is interested in our happiness, and eventually our happiness is involved in all that God does, but that is not his primary concern. His primary concern is for our character. God knows we can never develop the character he wants without times of difficulty and trial and suffering. That is why suffering is an inevitable part of the picture. It helps us to remember that God's primary objective is not that we be happy all the time. He is not that kind of father. Rather, his primary objective is that we be holy, which means "whole," "complete," all that we were intended to be, functioning as God intended us to function, like Jesus.

We have all noticed that God forms a lot of characters! In fact, he is going to end up with a heaven full of them. But one distinctive thing about those characters is that they are all like Jesus. They all have different personalities, but they will all have the same basic, fundamental character: loving, gracious, gentle, wholesome, helpful, compassionate—all the things that marked the magnificent life of Jesus interpreted in a thousand and one different ways. That is the wonder and the glory of God. That is what he has predestined: There shall be many brethren, and Jesus is the firstborn among many just like him.

The Holy Spirit Gets into the Act

The third step is that God called us. "Those whom God foreknew he also predestined; and those he predestined, he also called." This is where we get into the act. Up to this point, the passage has been concerned with God's mind and purpose, but now we suddenly become involved. Those whom God foreknew and predestined, he now calls. I could not begin to describe the mystery and wonder involved in this. This means the Holy Spirit somehow begins to work in our lives. We may be far removed from God, we may have grown up in a non-Christian family, we may be from a Christian home. It does not make any difference. God begins to work and he draws us to himself.

Jesus said, "All that my Father has given me shall come unto me." Not one shall be lost. The Holy Spirit begins to draw us and woo us and open our minds and create interest in our hearts. We think we are getting religious, but we are only responding to the drawing of the Spirit of God. We are not aware of this—we think it is our choice. In a sense, we do have to make a choice, and in chapter 9 Paul explains more fully this mystery of our free will and God's sovereign choice. Nevertheless, we are being drawn in ways we do not understand.

The apostle Paul was converted on the Damascus road when he saw the glory of the Lord shining about him with a brilliance greater than the sun. He heard a voice that said to him, "Saul, Saul, why do you persecute me? Is it not hard for you to kick against the goad?" By that last phrase the Lord Jesus declared Paul was fighting, struggling, kicking, trying to hold on to his independence—but he was being goaded relentlessly to a fate he could not escape. This is what happens to all of us. We do not understand it, but it is true.

Dr. Harry Ironside used to tell about a man who gave his testimony, telling how God had sought and found him, how God had loved him, called him, saved him, delivered him, cleansed him, and healed him—a tremendous testimony to the glory of God. After the meeting, one rather legalistic brother took him aside and said, "You know, I appreciate all that you said about what God did for you, but you didn't mention anything about your part in it. Salvation is really part us and part God, and you should have mentioned something about your part." "Oh," the man said, "I apologize. I'm sorry; I really should have mentioned that. My part was running away, and his part was running after me until he found me." That is what Paul is saying here. God called us. Those whom he predestined, he also called.

Fourth, those God called, he justified. All along in this letter we have been looking at what justification means. It is God's gift of worth. Those who are justified are rendered valuable in his sight. They are forgiven, cleansed, loved, accepted, and wanted. This is justification—being given the gift of worth without any merit at all on your part. By the cross God was freed to give the gift of righteousness. Had he given it apart from the cross he could have been properly accused of condoning sin—but the cross freed him. It established his righteous justice on other grounds, so that he is now free to give to us the gift of worth without any merit on our part.

Then, finally, those God justified, he also glorified. Paul writes as though this had already happened—and it is true that it has already begun. Glorification is what Paul calls "the revelation of the sons of God." It is the exciting day which the whole creation anticipates, when God is suddenly going to pull back the curtains on what he has been doing with the human race. Suddenly, the sons of God will stand out in glory.

But in a sense, this has already begun. It is what we call *sanctification*. Sanctification is the process by which the inner worth which God imparts to our human spirit by faith in Christ begins to work itself out into our conduct. We actually begin to change. We begin to be like what we actually are. Our attitudes change, and our actions change. As our habits begin to change, we stop certain things and begin others. Our whole demeanor is different; we become much more gracious, happy, and wholesome. This is called sanctification and glorification; it has already started. It is the process Paul says is inevitable. God has started it, he is continuing it, and he is going to complete it. So Paul writes here as though it were already done: "Those whom God justified, he also glorified."

None are lost in the process. Those whom he foreknew, before the foundation of the world, he also predestined to conform to the likeness of his Son. The same number of people he also called; and the ones he called, he also justified. The very ones he justified, he also glorified. No one is lost, because God is responsible for the entire process. It will involve pain and toil, death and tears, disappointment, bereavement, sorrow, sin, stumbling, failure, falling, forgiveness—all these things. But it is going to happen, because what God sets out to do, he does—no matter what it takes.

At this point Paul asks the final question:

What, then, shall we say in response to this? (8:31)

What can you say? All you can say is, "Thank you. How great thou art!" The response of the heart is, "Father, I love you." And that is what God is after. He is after the love of men—the uncoerced, unforced love of men, despite their pressures, their problems, their heartaches, whatever they go through. The rest of this chapter is a beautiful description of how to love God. The process of loving God is outlined for us in three questions which the apostle asks in this last section. The first one is found in verses 31 and 32:

If God is for us, who can be against us? He who did not spare his own Son, but gave him up for us all—how will he not also, along with him, graciously give us all things?

If you have understood all that God has done for you, your first response of love is to say to yourself,

"If God is for me, who can be against me?" You love God when you reflect on the implications of his saving commitment to you. The moment you think this through and say to yourself, "If God has done this, and God is for me, then this and this and this must be true." As you rejoice in that truth, you are loving God. You are responding as he intended you to respond to his love for you.

In the Shadow of Mike

Now, what is the effect of this? It is clear from this passage that it is the removal of fear. If God is for us, who can be against us? All fear of successful opposition is removed. It is not that there is no opposition. The devil is still there, his legions are still there, the communists are still there— there is still going to be opposition. But Paul is saying, "If God is for us, what difference does it make?" If God is for us, who can be against us?

One of our elders told us of the plight of his grandson, a thirteen-year-old who strongly resembled his Chicano father. In his school in Missouri, the boy ran into a nest of white racists who gave him torment and persecution. He came home weeping one day after having been beaten. His mother, not knowing what to do, wrote to us and asked us to pray for him, and we did.

A week or so later we received another letter from her. She described how one night the biggest kid in school appeared at their door and said he was a Christian, and that he had told the other kids in school that if they ever did anything to that boy again they would answer to him. I don't know what that big boy's name was, but let's call him Mike. I can imagine the grandson going back to school, walking in Mike's shadow as all his tormentors looked on, and saying to himself, "If Mike is for me, who can be against me?"

This is what Paul is saying here, and what David said in the twenty-seventh Psalm:

> *The Lord is my light and my salvation—*
> *whom shall I fear?*
> *The Lord is the stronghold of my life—*
> *of whom shall I be afraid?*

This is what we ought to be saying when trouble strikes, when difficulty comes, when opposition appears. We ought to think it through and say, "If God is for me, who can be against me?" This is the way we love God.

Not only does our belief in God's love for us remove our fear of opposition, but, as verse 32 indicates, it also removes our fear of want:

> *He who did not spare his own Son, but gave him*
> *up for us all—how will he not also, along with*
> *him, graciously give us all things?*

He who has already given us the best, the greatest, the dearest, the most precious thing he has, and who did so while we were sinners—while we were enemies, while we were helpless—will he not also give us some of these trivial, piddling little things that we need? That is Paul's next argument.

If someone thinks enough of you to give you a costly, brilliant, beautiful, flawless diamond, do you think he will object when you ask him for the box that goes with it? If a mother will give up a baby, do you think she will object if they ask to take his clothes, too? And if God has given us his own Son already, do you really think he will withhold anything else that we need? Paul's argument is unanswerable. Of course he won't. We can say with David in the twenty-third Psalm, "The Lord is my shepherd, I shall not want." The first sign that we love God, then, is that all fear is removed. We begin to face our lack, to face our enemies, and to say, "If God is for us, who can be against us?"

The second question Paul asks of those who know God's love is found in verses 33 and 34:

> *Who will bring any charge against those whom God has chosen? It is God who justifies. Who is he that condemns? Christ Jesus, who died—more than that, who was raised to life—is at the right hand of God and is also interceding for us (8:33-34).*

This is a reminder of the work God has done. We love God when we trust in the full effect of his work on our behalf. Paul is looking back over the letter, and sees two great works that God has done. The first is justification. "Who will bring any charge against those whom God has chosen?" Who can? It is God who justifies.

Justification means that nothing and no one anywhere can successfully accuse us before God. Now, the devil is the accuser of the brethren. He will constantly accuse us. This verse tells us we must not listen to his voice. We must not listen to these thoughts that condemn us, that put us down, that make us feel there is no hope for us. These thoughts will come—they cannot be stopped—but we do not have to listen to them, just as we know God is not listening to them. So who can condemn us when God justifies us?

Therefore we refuse to be condemned. We do this not by ignoring our sin or trying to cover it up, but by admitting that although we fully deserve to be condemned, God, through Christ, has already borne our guilt. This is the only way out. This is why Christians should not hesitate to admit their failure and

their sin. We will never be justified until we admit
our need of it. But when we admit it, then we also
can face the full glory of the fact that God justifies the
ungodly, and therefore there is no condemnation.

In Touch with a Living Person

Then Paul raises the question, "Who is he that
condemns?" Who is going to do this? The only one
who has the right is Jesus—and Jesus died for us.
More than that, he was raised to life for us, he is now
at the right hand of God in power for us, and he is
also interceding for us. So there is no chance that he
is going to condemn us. This refers to the power we
have to take hold afresh of the life of Jesus. Not only
is our guilt set aside, but power is imparted to us—
his life in us, his risen life made available to us now.
So we can rise up and say no to the temptations that
surround us and the habits that drag us down; we can
be a victor over them. This is not a mere dogma; we
are in touch with a living person. That is the glory of
Christianity. The unique distinction of Christians is
that we have Jesus.

I know that every cult, every new faith, every false
faith around, old and new, offers some kind of experience—perhaps a mystical experience, or some sense
of peace or freedom. We must not discount these, for
they can deliver some of these things. But the difference is they have no grounding in history. There is
no assurance that these experiences are real. But we
Christians have a grounding in the history of Jesus.
He came, he died, he rose again. These are unmistak-
able facts. Therefore, when we come to Jesus, we
come to someone we know exists. We know he is
there. Our experience is real. Dr. A. W. Tozer, that
grand old prophet, states this truth in *Man, the
Dwelling Place of God:*

The teaching of the New Testament is that now, at this very moment, there is a Man in heaven appearing in the presence of God for us. He is as certainly a man as was Adam or Moses or Paul; he is a man glorified, but his glorification did not dehumanize him. Today he is a real man, of the race of mankind, bearing our lineaments and dimensions, a visible and audible man, whom any other man would recognize instantly as one of us. But more than this, he is the heir of all things, Lord of all lords, head of the church, firstborn of the new creation. He is the way to God, the life of the believer, the hope of Israel, and the high priest of every true worshiper. He holds the keys of death and hell, and stands as advocate and surety for everyone who believes on him in truth. Salvation comes not by accepting the finished work, or deciding for Christ; it comes by believing on the Lord Jesus Christ, the whole, living, victorious Lord who, as God and man, fought our fight and won it, accepted our debt as his own and paid it, took our sins and died under them, and rose again to set us free. This is the true Christ; nothing less will do.

Our whole relationship rests upon that magnificent person. We are freed from the condemnation of guilt because of him.

That brings us to the third and last question relating to how we love God. We love him by reminding ourselves of the implications of his continual, unchanging commitment to us. We love him by remembering and trusting the full effect of his work for us. And finally, we love God by answering this question:

Who shall separate us from the love of Christ? (8:35)

Is there any force, anywhere, that can come between you and Jesus? Here the apostle faces a question many people ask. Is there any way to lose your salvation? Who can remove us from Christ, once we fully come to him? Paul's answer is, "Let's take a look at the possibilities." First, can all the troubles and dangers of life separate us from his love?

> *Shall trouble or hardship or persecution or famine or nakedness or danger or sword? As it is written: "For your sake we face death all day long; we are considered as sheep to be slaughtered" (8:35-36).*

This is life at its worst. Will that do it?

> *No, in all these things we are more than conquerors through him who loved us (8:37).*

"Trouble" means catastrophe and disasters. "Hardship" refers to the tight, narrow places we sometimes have to go through. Will persecution do it? That is hurt deliberately inflicted on us because we are Christians. Will famine—will lack of food and money do it? Will nakedness, or lack of clothes? Will danger, or threat to our lives? Will the sword (war, riot, uprising) do it?

"No," Paul says. In these we are super conquerors. Why? Because rather than dividing us from Christ, they draw us closer to him. They make us cling harder. They scare us and make us run to him. When we are independent and think we can make it on our own, these things strike, and we start whimpering and running for home, and we cling all the closer. We can never be defeated then, so we are more than conquerors.

What about supernatural forces? What about people and powers and demons and strange beings?

> *For I am convinced that neither death nor life,*
> *neither angels nor demons, neither the present nor*
> *the future, nor any powers, neither height nor*
> *depth, nor anything else in all creation {literally,*
> *anything even in a different creation}, will be able*
> *to separate us from the love of God that is in Christ*
> *Jesus our Lord (8:38-39).*

Nothing is left out of that list, is there? Everything is there—demons and dark powers, black magic and angels, truth and error, death and life—whether in this creation or any other creation. Paul takes in everything and says that nothing, no being or force, is capable of separating us from the love of Jesus Christ our Lord.

So we love God when we say, "If God be for us, who can be against us?" We love God because of what he himself has done on our behalf, and the nature of that commitment is that he loves us. Nothing can separate us from that.

This is the highest point of the letter. Obviously, Paul cannot go beyond this, and neither can we. What can you say? What can you do but love when you are confronted by a God like this?

I want to bring this study to an end by giving you a modern paraphrase of these final verses of Romans 8, expressed in personal terms by Ruth Harms Calkin:

> *God, I may fall flat on my face; I may fail until I*
> *feel old and beaten and done in. Yet Your love for*
> *me is changeless. All the music may go out of my*
> *life, my private world may shatter to dust. Even*
> *so, You will hold me in the palm of Your steady*
> *hand. No turn in the affairs of my fractured life*
> *can baffle You. Satan with all his braggadocio*

cannot distract You. Nothing can separate me from Your measureless love—pain can't, disappointment can't, anguish can't. Yesterday, today, tomorrow can't. The loss of my dearest love can't. Death can't. Life can't. Riots, war, insanity, unidentity, hunger, neurosis, disease—none of these nor all of them heaped together can budge the fact that I am dearly loved, completely forgiven, and forever free through Jesus Christ Your beloved Son.

How can you add anything to that? The only thing you can do is—believe it!